REENGINEERING PERFORMANCE MEASUREMENT

How to Align Systems to Improve Processes, Products, and Profits

REENGINEERING PERFORMANCE MEASUREMENT
How to Align Systems to Improve Processes, Products, and Profits

Archie Lockamy III

James F Cox III

IRWIN
Professional Publishing

Burr Ridge, Illinois
New York, New York

Sponsoring editor: Jean Marie Geracie
Project editor: Amy E. Lund
Production manager: Laurie Kersch
Designer: Larry J. Cope
Art coordinator: Heather Burbridge
Compositor: Precision Typographers
Typeface: 10/13 Times Roman
Printer: Book Press, Inc.

Library of Congress Cataloging-in-Publication Data

Lockamy, Archie.
    Reengineering performance measurement: how to align systems to
improve processes, products, and profits / by Archie Lockamy III,
James F. Cox III.
        p.   cm.
    Includes bibliographical references and index.
    ISBN 1-55623-916-5
    1. Efficiency, Industrial.   2. Production management.   I. Cox,
James F., Ph.D.   II. Title.
    T58.8.L63   1994
    658.5—dc20

                                                        93–30788

Printed in the United States of America
1   2   3   4   5   6   7   8   9   0   BP   0   9   8   7   6   5   4   3

To our wives, Vicki and Mary Ann

Thank you for your patience, support, and love during our completion of this project.

Acknowledgments

Thanks to the APICS Educational & Research Foundation Inc. for providing the financial support for this research project. Special thanks go to Mr. Charles Mertens and Mr. Mike Spencer for recognizing the value of this research and recommending its funding by the foundation.

Thanks to the companies that participated in this study. A special thanks goes to the following individuals who were instrumental in making access into their organizations possible: Mr. Marion Kosem and Mr. Mike Offik of Reliance Electric; Mr. Nick Yanagi and Ms. Christy Copeland of Yamaha Motor Manufacturing Corporation; Mr. Harry Standinger and Mr. Ray Mendenhall of Clark Material Handling Company; Mr. Mike O'Neil and Mr. Cris Moore of Northern Telecom; Mr. Joe Douglas and Mr. Mike Zitterman of Hill's® Pet Products; and Mr. Bruce Achenbach of Trane Corporation. Thanks to the academic and practitioner experts who provided the names of world-class manufacturing firms as potential study participants. Additionally, we appreciate the detailed manuscript reviews provided by Mr. Tom Brown, Mr. Larry Shoemaker, and Mr. Greg Stanley. Their hard work helped improve this book significantly.

It would have been impossible for us to have envisioned the complete paradigm shift in organization strategy, performance measurement systems, and actions required to achieve world-class organizational status without continuously reviewing the works of Dr. Eliyahu M. Goldratt. Dr. Goldratt is a modern-day educator and philosopher and is a catalyst in creating change. His views on logistics, the cost world versus the throughput world, and the logical thinking process shaped our thoughts in the first six chapters. We are deeply indebted to him. Like Dr. Goldratt, we feel common intuition is far more powerful than common practice in striving for world-class organizational status.

Preface

"Tell me how you measure me and I'll tell you how I will perform. If you measure me in an illogical way . . . Do not complain about illogical behavior."

Goldratt, *Theory of Constraints*

This statement is true of the performance measurement systems and subsequent behaviors of most US manufacturers and, more generally, US organizations today. Three primary functions (customer, resource, and finance) and their supporting performance measurement systems exist in most organizations. Each function and its measurements are viewed as separate and distinct, and each operates somewhat independent of the others. In most US manufacturing organizations, each of these functions attempts to optimize its measurements without regard to either of the other two functions.

In a world-class firm, performance measurement is quite different. To respond to the customers' expectations, the customer function (marketing, sales, and field service) must provide top management information from its performance measurement system, assessing the financial impact of falling short, meeting, or exceeding customers' needs. The actual and potential use of resources is measured by the resource performance measurement system. The resource function (design, purchasing, production, warehousing, and transportation) then translates this information into the increased investment and the incremental expenses associated with the change in resource use. The finance function (accounting and finance) takes accounting data and, through its performance measurement system, translates the data into organizational performance. In this manner, before a decision is made, the impact of the decision on each function and on the organization's goal can be measured.

Some organizations have three well-defined performance measurement systems. Fewer organizations have their measurement systems synchronized to reflect the impact of actions in one function on the resources and measures of the other functions. And still fewer have the appropriate measures in place to ascertain the impact of local decisions on the organization's bottom line.

So what is this book about? What makes this book different from other books on performance measurement? This book is about the paradigm shift required to achieve world-class organizational competitiveness. It is about a different way of viewing an organization—a view that recognizes, by definition, that an organization is a system of dependent resources whose strategies, actions, and performance measurement systems must be linked together and performance measures must be totally aligned to achieve the organization's goal. Prior to a decision being made, linkages among the three functions are used to ascertain the impact of any action on the other functions and on the organization's goal. Local actions impact not only its function but also can significantly impact other functions and certainly the movement of the organization toward its goal.

This book is about changing the direction of US manufacturing. This book provides the framework for focusing local decisions and actions, so that global results can be achieved. It is about catching and surpassing the Japanese—it is about becoming a world-class organization.

In order for the manufacturing function to become a competitive weapon, decision making within operations must be consistent with the organization's strategic objectives. This book illustrates how a few world-class manufacturers have linked plant and division performance measures to focus on customers' needs.

This book also shows how firms can achieve competitive advantages by integrating their strategic direction and operational activities via performance measurement systems. We provide case studies of firms who are integrating strategic and operational activities, and we describe conceptual models for developing cost, quality, lead time, and delivery performance measurement systems.

In summary, this book is focused on changing manufacturers into world-class organizations—top management, the customer function, the resource function, and the finance function having the singular focus of working together to attain the organization's goal.

Archie Lockamy III
James F Cox III

Contents

Chapter One

Why Are You Losing the Battle with Global Competition?

"In all affairs, it's a healthy thing now and then to hang a question mark on the things you have long taken for granted."

Bertrand Russell (1872–1970)

THE BUSINESS ENVIRONMENT

Today, US industry is facing intense pressure to continuously improve. Global competition has intensified. The Japanese have captured large market shares in industry after industry. Other Pacific Rim nations are improving as are Western European countries.[1] US companies have merged to gain economies of scale, diversified to reduced financial risks, vertically integrated to reduce lead times and ensure material availability, and sold off whole business segments in an attempt to remain profitable and competitive. Most of these actions have failed.

Business is more complex today than it was at the turn of the century. Business decision making was once based on sound management theory. Has the business environment gotten so complex that traditional management theory no longer applies? Certainly traditional theory needs a reexamination.[2] Let's explore several simple examples of business processes and measures to understand the traditional decision-making logic, desired results, actions taken, and actual results. In this manner, we might identify some areas for redesigning business processes and measures. We will briefly examine thirteen different typical problems from the vast array

1

faced by today's business managers. The problems will be selected from three broad functions of business: the resource function, the customer function, and the finance function.

The Resource Function

The following areas comprise the resource function: design, purchasing, production, warehousing and transportation. We will provide you a scenario of business processes and measures from each of these areas.

As the product engineering manager for a company, you decide that minimizing product cost is the key to strategic success. To monitor progress toward this objective, target costs are developed for each product. This strategy leads to engineering designs that attempt to minimize the cost of purchasing or manufacturing each component of a given product.

Does this strategy sound like a good idea? Perhaps it does on the surface, but, although the desired result is a low-cost product, the actual results are frequent field failures, high warranty costs, customer dissatisfaction, and eventual loss of market share. To save money in one area creates a loss of revenues and additional expenses in other areas. The end result is a loss of profits.[3]

As the company's purchasing agent, you desire to save the company money on several parts currently manufactured internally. You compare the cost of making these parts internally to the cost of purchasing them from a local vendor. The manufacturing (make) cost is higher in several instances than the purchase (buy) cost. You decide to purchase the items.

Is this a good decision? Perhaps not. The assumption of the make versus buy decision is this: If a product is purchased instead of made internally, then all of the product cost of making the item is eliminated. Is this really the case? Do you eliminate some of your direct labor and so-called "overhead" costs? Or, if you purchase externally, do you end up paying the vendor, the direct labor, and a large portion of the overhead costs also?[4]

Suppose you are a manufacturing manager, and your strategy is to minimize direct-labor costs. The measure you might use to assist you is direct-labor efficiency [(standard hours/actual hours) $\times$ 100%]. Your desired results are to realize an efficiency of 100 percent or greater, thus fully utilizing your workers and reducing the direct-labor cost per unit. To achieve this result, you would strive to always keep every worker busy.

Does this process sound logical for achieving the desired results? Yes! Does this process achieve the desired results? No! What are the actual results achieved by always keeping every worker busy? The actual results include excessive work-in-process and finished goods inventory, high costs, poor quality, long manufacturing lead times, and poor due date performance.[5]

Suppose you are the warehouse manager. Because of recent incidents of missed sales, late shipments, and stockouts, customer service is adopted as the primary objective. To measure performance, an inventory stock service level percentage of 95 percent is selected and closely watched for each stock-keeping unit (SKU). What process will this lead to? In an effort to maintain the 95 percent level, you will order and hold large amounts of each SKU.

Does this necessarily lead to high levels of customer service? No. The results are a high inventory investment level, large amounts of surplus and obsolete inventory, long manufacturing lead times, and recurrent stockouts caused by production constraints. Because of production's inability to manufacture large quantities of each product in a timely manner, customer service will actually be reduced.[6]

Suppose you are the traffic manager and your strategy is to minimize transportation cost. The measure you might use to assist you is shipping cost per unit. To economize on shipping, you hold customer orders going to the same geographical area until a full truckload is achieved.

Does this action sound logical for minimizing transportation cost? Yes! Does this action achieve the desired result? No! Although this process seems to achieve a cost advantage in the marketplace, what is the actual result? The actual result is poor customer service based on poor due date performance and excessive lead times.[7]

The Customer Function

The customer function includes marketing, sales, and field service. Scenarios of business processes and measures for each element of the customer function will be provided. As division product manager, your goal is to increase market share. To achieve this goal, your strategy is to provide a wide variety of products and product lines to the marketplace. Although your desire is to gain market share, what really happens? The actual results are increased product proliferation, increased levels of inventory to support current and future sales, and increased operating expenses to support product variety. Because of your inability to provide logistical support to the wide product line economically, market share actually declines.[8]

Promotional strategies are often used to increase market share or sales revenue for a given item. Processes used to promote the product may include advertising the item at a discount. Sales dollars and advertising expenditures for the product are observed intently, but something unexpected happens. Although advertising dollars are increasing, sales revenues have begun to decline. Why? One reason might be the inability of production to support the increase in demand. Another reason might be poor communication between production and marketing in defining the proper product mix. Having the wrong product mix available has led to stockouts, expediting, and excessive transportation costs.[9]

Your performance as sales manager is measured based on total sales. However, your sales force is rewarded via sales commissions. To maximize total sales, you maintain a standard stock level for each item in anticipation of future sales. To maximize sales commissions, the sales personnel sell what makes them the highest commission. The result? Neither the sales manager nor the sales force achieves its objective.[10]

To minimize the cost of after-sale service, you, as the field service manager, constantly monitor warranty and repair costs. So what process do you use to efficiently manage this cost center? Do as little warranty repair work as possible. The results are predictable—high levels of customer dissatisfaction along with little future business. What about managing field service as a separate profit center? Repair work would be encouraged, because the desired result is to now make high profits from repairs. How would these high profits be accomplished? Charge the customer an excessive amount for each repair job. What happens next? The actual result is high customer dissatisfaction along with little return business for repairs or for buying a replacement product. As a separate profit center, you end up with the same result as in the cost center scenario—less profit for the business.[11]

The Finance Function

Let's examine business processes and measures associated with the finance function. Your firm has decided to adopt a strategy that calls for maximizing profits on each product sold. As the accounting manager, you decide to track product cost so that product prices can be set to reflect the full production cost of an item and provide a good profit margin. The desired result is clearly high company profits. However, what actually happens? The firm experiences excess capacity and inventory on some items but not enough on others. Because of these imbalances, some orders are missed, perhaps not even accepted. The firm experiences an overall decline in profitability.[12]

In an effort to control departmental costs, you, the accounting manager, scrutinize monthly budget variances. The desired result is to reduce budget variances, particularly negative variances, which would imply better control of departmental cost. What process will department managers use? Most managers will limit their activities based upon budgetary constraints, often at the expense of actual departmental needs. The actual result is a lack of organizational flexibility. In some departments, you spend money—money currently allocated to these departments in the budget—on unnecessary items, while, in other departments, you forgo much-needed items because there is no money allocated in the departmental budget.[13]

Your firm is in an industry that has been under intense pressure from tough global competition for a number of years. Its profitability has been on the decline, and it is currently losing money. The company decides to focus its processes on maximizing quarterly profits. As the financial manager, you insist on quarterly profit and loss statements from each operating division. The desired result is straightforward. By maximizing quarterly profits, long-term profitability is inevitable. Makes sense? Think again. How will division managers increase short-term profits under these conditions? By forgoing long-term capital investment. The actual result? Long-term profitability is severely damaged. Market share erodes. Future survival of the business is questionable.[14]

It is evident that your company desperately needs to increase capital investment to remain competitive. The finance department develops targets for all capital projects using the following measures: return on investment (ROI), internal rate of return, and net present value. The expected result is an increase in capital investments that yields high returns and leads to competitive advantages. But what actually happens? Capital projects that are strategically desired for survival but whose benefits are difficult to quantify are not funded. Thus, projects that are easily justified but have little long-term effect on competitiveness get approved at the expense of projects with major strategic implications. The company continues to lose its competitive position.[15]

THE UNDERLYING PROBLEM OF THE TRADITIONAL MANAGEMENT PHILOSOPHY

These examples of simple business processes and measures suggest that principles and approaches of traditional management theory can lead to actual results that are totally opposite from the desired result. Why does this occur? Is there something fundamentally wrong with the theory? The answer is yes. Let's examine the theory.

Traditional management theory suggests that each functional area (for example, R&D, operations, marketing, finance, and distribution) must strive to achieve a *local optimum*. If these local optima are achieved, then their sum should result in a *global optimum*.[16] Therefore, the firm should become a world-class competitor using this approach. Is there a fundamental problem with this assumption? Unfortunately, the answer is again yes. The problem lies in the fact that each function will develop performance measurement systems relative to local objectives rather than to the global objectives of the firm. These measurement systems encourage management actions and decisions that may improve local performance but that create dysfunctional and noncompetitive organizations.

Let's summarize our diverse examples. Marketing, sales, and field service are responsible for identifying and satisfying the customers' needs. The criteria (characteristics being measured) of the traditional performance measurement system for the customer function are sales, market share, sales commissions, sales quotas, sales generated, and so forth. The elements of a performance measurement system are defined and discussed in Chapter 2, Defining the New Philosophy: Resource Management. The primary focus of the customer function performance measurement system is on increasing revenues.

On the other hand, engineering, purchasing, production, warehousing, and transportation are responsible for making effective use of the organization's resources. The criteria of the traditional performance measurement system for the resource function are efficiencies of labor and staff, utilization of equipment, volume discounts for purchasing and transportation, and so on. The primary focus of this performance measurement system is on reducing costs.

Finally, top management is responsible for setting the organization's direction by identifying and implementing strategic objectives and for ensuring that the firm is financially stable and profitable. The criteria of the traditional performance measurement system for the finance function are the myriad performance measures related to the financial statements. The primary focus of the finance function performance measurement system is on making money *now*—net profit. Can you see the organizational problems and conflicts created by assuming that improvement in a local performance criterion translates into global improvement?

Our traditional management philosophy has resulted in the use of three separate, disjoined, and competing functional performance measurement systems in most organizations. The elements of the traditional management philosophy are illustrated in Table 1-1.

The basic assumption of these traditional performance measurement systems is that, when marketing, sales, and field service focus their actions on maximizing revenues; when engineering, purchasing, production, warehousing, and transportation focus their actions on minimizing costs; and when finance makes decisions concerning the organization's actions based on these unrelated short-term revenue and cost streams, long-term net profit is maximized. The underlying problem with the traditional management philosophy is illustrated in Table 1-2.

As shown in Table 1-2, the underlying assumption of the traditional management philosophy—that optimizing local measures is equivalent to optimizing global measures—is false. It is doubtful that this assumption was ever true. In the past, however, managing based on this assumption was not a problem. Your competitors used the

TABLE 1–1
Traditional Management Philosophy

Category	Function Components	Primary Focus
Customer Function	Marketing Sales Field service	Increasing revenues
Resource Function	Design engineering Purchasing Production Warehousing Transportation	Reducing costs
Finance Function	Finance Accounting	Increasing short-term profits

TABLE 1–2
The Underlying Problem with the Traditional Management Philosophy

Category	Primary Objective
Customer function	+ Maximize Revenues
Resource function	+ Minimize costs
Finance function	+ Maximize short-term profits
Total company	Maximize long-term profits

Assumption: Optimizing local measures equals a global optimization

same traditional management philosophy and similar performance measurement systems and, therefore, made similar local decisions with the same mediocre global results. These results are totally unacceptable today.

Let's start by answering some basic questions. What is the goal of your organization? How does your organization achieve this goal? How should you design your business processes to achieve the organization's goal? Is your organization stuck in the traditional approach to structuring and measuring business processes?

The world has changed dramatically with the emergence of Japanese manufacturers as world-class competitors. The Japanese don't focus on generating revenues in dealing with customers; the Japanese don't focus on reducing costs in using resources; the Japanese don't manage by maximizing today's net profits.

How does your organization make decisions? Does it make decisions by using the traditional management philosophy? Japanese managerial decision making is by group consensus—via the verbalization of the group's intuition. Before making a decision, Japanese managers collectively discuss all aspects of the problem. Intuition is powerful. Group intuition is more powerful and certainly superior to managing by outdated performance criteria that have outlived their usefulness.

THE NEW PHILOSOPHY: MEASURES AND LINKAGES

How can your organization regain its competitive advantage? First, let's examine several aspects of the three functions: objectives, information requirements, performance measurement systems, and required linkages. The customer function via market information recognizes the potential for increasing revenues by changing the current product offering to match the customers' needs and expectations. These *customers' needs* must be linked to the **resource function** used to produce the new and existing product offering and also linked to the **finance function** to provide an estimate of the revenues generated from the new product offering. Any additional investment in resources required to produce the new product offering in support of the customers' needs must be identified by the resource function and communicated to the finance function. Supplementary expenses in such areas as labor and utilities must also be estimated and communicated to the finance function. The assessment and its communication are the customer-finance-resource linkages of the organization's performance measurement system. An overview of the functions and linkages for the new management philosophy is presented in Figure 1–1.

The concept of linkage is critical to the understanding of the new philosophy, so let's clearly define it. According to *Webster's Dictionary*, a linkage is simply a "bond."[17] We further refine this definition of linkage as a bond providing information on the goal and strategy of the organization; the synchronized actions of each function in achieving the organization's goal and strategies; and the supporting performance measurement system.

How can your organization effectively compete today? The answer is becoming more apparent. Companies must link functional areas to synchronize their efforts in achieving the organization's goal. However, synchronizing the actions of each function with the other functions is not sufficient. Changing the organization's performance measurement system is vitally important. The critical linkages needed to synchronize actions and align performance measures are currently evolving in some leading businesses. This alignment process is the subject of this book.

You must reengineer your organization's actions to create logical business pro-

FIGURE 1-1

*An Overview of the Functions and Linkages for the New Management
Philosophy*

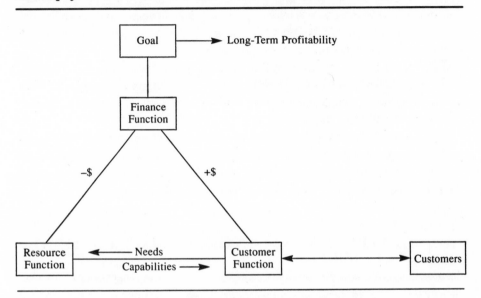

cesses. There are dozens of business processes and measures in any organization.
You cannot change all of them. But what business processes and measures are
candidates for reengineering? Where should you focus your attention?

How is this new philosophy different from the traditional management philosophy? Several differences exist between the proposed management philosophy and its
supporting performance measurement systems and traditional thought—a paradigm
shift.

First, few traditional managers understand that an organization, by definition,
consists of a series of *dependent resources* joined together for a common purpose.[18]
Actions taken to achieve the common purpose by one resource may negatively affect
the other resources.

Second, the missing elements of most traditional performance measurement systems are the linkages among the functional performance measurement systems.
These linkages provide information to top management on the significance of a local
decision to the other functions of the organization and more importantly to achieving
the goal of the organization. Only by linking performance measurement systems
between organizational levels and across functions can your company ensure that its
resources are being used *effectively*.

Third, few managers recognize that constraints dictate the capabilities of an organization, and an organization has only a few constraints. A *constraint* is defined as anything that inhibits the organization's ability to achieve its goal. Conversely, nonconstraint resources do not inhibit the organization's ability to achieve its goal. This characteristic translates into one set of measures for constraint resources and another set of measures for nonconstraint resources.

Fourth, most US firms use a traditional cost accounting system to cost-justify resource decisions related to improving quality, reducing lead time, and so forth. Cost justification of quality improvements and lead time reductions inhibits organizations from making true improvements.

These four differences provide the basis for our conceptual models on aligning performance measurement systems for competitive advantages. A philosophy for regaining competitiveness is provided in Chapter 2, Defining the New Philosophy: Resource Management.

THE PROCESS OF CONTINUOUS IMPROVEMENT

Because the business environment is dynamic, the new management philosophy must also include a process of continuous improvement. The improvement process is shown in Table 1–3. You must first identify the goal of your organization. In most for-profit organizations, the goal is to make more money now and in the future.[19]

Second, you must design a performance measurement system that tells you when your organization is moving toward its goal. Throughput, inventory, and operating expense measures[20] are discussed in Chapter 3, The Primary Functions and the Organization's Performance Measurement System Model, and provide an accurate assessment of goal attainment.

Third, the five focusing steps (also known as the current reality tree) of the theory of constraints should be used to identify what is preventing the organization from achieving its goal. Of all the many actions a manager can take in any function of an organization, what action will significantly move the organization toward its goal? Use the performance measures to answer this question.

Fourth, what product or service characteristic (price/cost, quality, lead time, and other factors) do your customers deem important? The role of marketing, sales, and field service must include identifying how the organization can meet or exceed customers' needs. Is there a new product, a new market, or a product or service characteristic so important that improving it would increase demand or allow you to increase product price without reducing demand? Is price, quality, or lead time the product characteristic limiting your organization's ability to achieve its goal?

TABLE 1–3
Process of Continuous Improvement for World-Class Organizations

---

Stage One

---

1. Identify the *goal (or goals)* of the organization.
2. Design a *comprehensive performance measurement system* that tells you when you're moving toward the goal.
3. Implement theory of constraints to *identify the current constraints* to moving toward the goal, implement appropriate actions, and measure constraint and goal results.

Stage Two

---

4. Identify the *competitive edge* for each product and market (price/cost, quality, lead time, and so on) that constrains your organization from reaching its goal through market growth.
5. Design a *comprehensive performance measurement system* that tells you when you are improving on the constraining competitive edge and its effect on profit.
6. Identify and implement *appropriate actions* at the competitive edge constraint and measure the impact of the actions on both the competitive edge and on the organization's goal. In this step if the constraint is broken, go to step 3.

Stage Three

---

7. Identify functional *savings opportunities* that do not impede attaining the organization's goal.
8. Design a *functional cost measurement system* to determine the effect of local actions on the function and on the organization's goal and its competitive edge.
9. Identify and implement the *actions needed to reduce functional costs and measure the action*, its effects on local measures, and its impact on the competitive edge and on the organization's goal. In this step if the constraint is broken, go to step 3.

Fifth, design a measurement system to ascertain the effect of your actions on both the competitive edge, as viewed from the customers' perspective, and the organization's movement toward its goal.

Sixth, decide which actions are appropriate, implement them, and measure the results on both the goal and the competitive edge. Almost an infinite number of different actions can be taken. Which actions are most effective in meeting the customers' needs and moving the organization toward its goal?

Seventh, search for cost reduction activities that do not reduce the organization's ability to attain its goal.

Eighth, design a functional cost measurement system that measures the cost and impact of local actions on achieving the organization's goal.

Ninth, identify actions to reduce functional costs without affecting movement toward the organization's goal. Implement these actions and measure results of the actions and their impact on the organization's goal. Management emphasis should be placed on stage 1 first, then on stage 2, and finally on stage 3. Remember, the primary goal of a business is to *make* money (stages 1 and 2), not to save money (stage 3). Each of these steps will be developed in more detail in Chapter 3, The Primary Functions and the Organization's Performance Measurement System Model, and Chapter 4, Linking the Primary Functions through Performance Measurement Systems.

ORGANIZATION OF THE BOOK

The book is organized into 13 chapters. This chapter discussed how the problems of poor management are created by using detached local area performance measurement systems. Resource management is defined, and its components are developed in Chapter 2, Defining the New Philosophy: Resource Management. Chapter 3, The Primary Functions and the Organization's Performance Measurement System Model provides performance measurement system models for integrative resource management. Actions required for linking together functional areas and performance measurement systems are presented in Chapter 4, Linking the Primary Functions through Performance Measurement Systems. These first four chapters provide the conceptual framework for aligning functional actions and performance measures to the firm's strategy and goals.

In Chapter 5, The Process of Continuous Improvement for World-Class Organizations, the continuous improvement process introduced in this chapter is discussed in detail and demonstrated through exercises. Actions required for achieving world-class organization status are presented in Chapter 6, Actions To Achieve Bottom Line Results. Illustrations of world-class performance measurement systems by the participating firms are provided in Chapter 7, Illustrations of Integrative Performance Measurement Systems.

Case studies summarizing division- and plant-level strategic objectives, their performance measurement systems, and their performance measurement system linkages are presented in Chapters 8 through 13. The case studies are presented in the following sequence: Reliance Electric: Industrial Controls Division; Yamaha Motor Manufacturing Corporation of America; Northern Telecom, Inc.: Transmission Access Division; Clark Equipment Company: Clark Material Handling Business Unit; the Trane Corporation: Self-Contained Systems Business Unit; and the Colgate-Palmolive Company: Hill's® Pet Products Division.

Each case study begins with an introduction describing which linkages will be illustrated. The case study information is then presented in the following order: company background; division or strategic business unit organization; the strategic objectives of the firm; business unit or division departments or functions; plant departments or functions; performance measurement system; and performance measurement system linkages. The lessons learned on the development of performance measurement system linkages between systems and functions are at the end of each case study. The companies described in Chapters 8 through 13 illustrate many of the linkages from the conceptual framework.

Chapter Two

Defining the New Philosophy: Resource Management

In this chapter, we first discuss the general areas of the organization's goal, planning and strategic objectives, competitive edges, customer satisfaction, product or service, and organizational resources. Second, we define resource management and a describe the operational details of effective scheduling and control. Third, we define a world-class organization and describe how resource management is fundamental to achieving world-class organizational status.

ELEMENTS OF THE NEW PHILOSOPHY

The Organization's Goal: More Money Now and in the Future

The relationships of the organization's goal, plans, and performance measurement systems to the planning horizon are illustrated in Table 2–1.

Goldratt states that the goal of a company is to make more money now and in the future. Profitability in the short to long run is the primary goal of for-profit companies.[1] Not-for-profit organizations have goals different from making money. For example, the goal of the military is to reach and maintain some level of combat readiness. Money is necessary to achieve this goal. In contrast, the goal of the American Production and Inventory Control Society (APICS), a nonprofit educational organization, is to develop and provide education through presentations, written materials, and other media for its members and for nonmembers. Money is necessary for APICS to achieve this goal, but money should not be the measure of success for a nonprofit organization.

Is your organization achieving its goal? Are your business processes moving

TABLE 2–1
The Relationship of the Organizational Goals, Plans and Performance Measurement Systems to Time

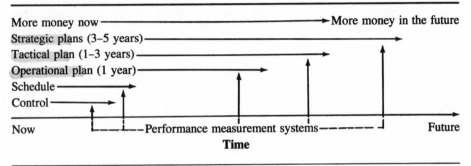

More money now ————————————————————→ More money in the future
Strategic plans (3–5 years) ————————————————————→
Tactical plan (1–3 years) ————————————————→
Operational plan (1 year) ————————————→
Schedule ————————→
Control ————→

Now   └———┴——Performance measurement systems———————┘   Future

Time

it closer to its goal? Or are your business processes only exceeding a necessary condition?

Many companies confuse goals and necessary conditions. Goals such as having the highest customer satisfaction or happy employees are prime examples of misdirected goals of for-profit organizations. Customers, employees, suppliers, and government agencies set necessary conditions on the operation of an organization. For example, as a customer, you would like the highest-quality product right now in as many colors as possible for free. Can a company meet this goal *and* stay in business? No. This, therefore, cannot be the goal of the for-profit organization. If the goal of an organization is to have happy employees, what might you as an employee desire from the organization to achieve happiness? Guaranteed employment, flexible hours, shorter hours, higher pay, increased benefits, and so forth? Can a company afford to meet this goal? No. This, therefore, also cannot be the goal of a for-profit organization. In both instances, necessary conditions for product characteristics and employee benefits are set in the marketplace by competitors. Being a little above the level set by these necessary conditions provides the organization some amount of protection against market shifts. Being a lot above the level set by a necessary condition can be quite expensive and unnecessary in achieving the primary goal of for-profit organizations—to make money now and in the future.

Providing customer satisfaction and achieving market share growth can be the means of achieving the primary goal associated with both for-profit and not-for-profit organizations. Regardless of the goal of the firm, it needs a performance measurement system that measures achievement in relation to the organization's primary goal and provides timely information to support a process of continual improvement toward that goal. The goals of the organization should reflect the legitimate desires of owners; be initiated through organizational strategies, tactics, policies, and procedures; be realized through the development of competitive edges and performance measurement systems to support customer expectations; and be reinforced by the performance measurement system for resources, employees, suppliers, and so on.

Planning and Strategic Objectives

For your organization to achieve its goals, you need a long-range strategy or plan that considers current and future areas for achieving strategic advantages. Thus, your organization must develop a strategy. The word **strategy** is derived from the Greek military term *strategos,* meaning literally "the general's art." Hofer and Schendel have defined the roles of corporate, division, and functional strategies, along with their interrelationships:[2]

- *Corporate strategy:* a plan that specifies two areas of overall interest to the firm: (1) the definition of the businesses of the corporation and (2) the acquisition and allocation of corporate resources to support each of these businesses.

- *Business strategy:* a plan specifying the scope of a given business and its link to the corporation's strategy. Business strategy also specifies how the business unit will achieve and maintain a competitive advantage.

- *Functional strategy:* Functional strategies are plans created for marketing, manufacturing, research and development, finance, distribution, field services, and so forth. Each functional strategy reinforces and supports the business strategy.

Christensen et al. have defined five important characteristics of strategy:[3]

1. *Time horizon:* an extended period of time.
2. *Impact:* the result of pursuing a given strategy.
3. *Concentration of effort:* a focus on a narrow range of activities.
4. *Pattern of decisions:* decisions made over time that must be supportive of and consistent with one another.
5. *Pervasiveness:* the extent to which all levels and functions of an organization reinforce and support the strategy.

Each level of strategy links the organization's goal, its competitive edges, and its various functional policies and operational plans used to guide daily activities.

Organizations also develop strategic objectives for each level of strategy. The

TABLE 2–2
The Relationship among Various Levels of Strategy

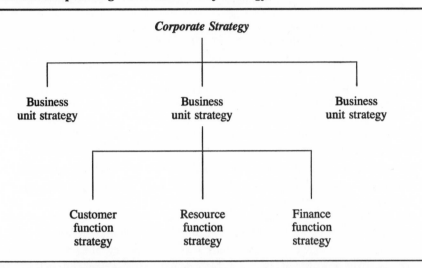

relationships among the levels of strategy are shown in Table 2–2. **Strategic objectives** are initiatives directed to affect the long-term health of the firm. For example, corporate- and business-level strategic objectives might include greater market share, increased revenues, and higher profits. Functional-level strategic objectives may include a more flexible work force and shorter new product development cycles for the resource function, and more responsive field service for the customer function. In addition, **competitive edges** are product or service characteristics for which the firm strives to achieve advantages in a given market (this definition is explained later in this chapter). Thus, effective business planning consists of the development of corporate-, business-, and functional-level strategies and objectives. These objectives must then be translated into competitive edges that support achievement of the organization's goal.

An organization's corporate, business, and supporting functional strategies must be consistent and supportive between organizational levels and across functions within a business unit. These long-range plans must be translated into tactical and operational plans. Operational plans provide the basis for effective scheduling, execution, and control of key resources.

Performance Measurement Systems

Performance measurement systems provide a mechanism for assessing progress toward the organizational goal. This progress is tracked by the performance measurement system in the form of increasing productivity levels. We define productivity as any progress made toward goal achievement.[4] Let's define a performance measurement system and its components.[5]

- *Performance measurement system:* a systematic way of evaluating the inputs, outputs, transformation, and productivity in a manufacturing or non-manufacturing operation. The system includes performance criteria, standards, and measures.
- *Performance criterion:* the relative element (such as parts per million defects and manufacturing lead time) used to evaluate macro- and micro-performance, long-term and short-term performance, functional performance (accounting, marketing, manufacturing, and so on), and overall performance.
- *Performance standard:* the accepted satisfactory level of performance.
- *Performance measure:* the actual value of the performance criterion.

A performance measurement system is composed of performance criteria, standards, and measures that allow for the planning, scheduling, monitoring, and control of resources to satisfy customers' needs to achieve the organization's goal. McNair et al. stated that the ultimate goal of a performance measurement system is to integrate the organization's actions across various managerial levels and functions to achieve its goal.[6] Such focus results in the firm's concentration of effort on a narrow range of pursuits, a consistent pattern of decision making, and strategic objectives that are embraced by the entire company.

A comprehensive performance measurement system is essential to monitoring and controlling improvement on the firm's goal, its strategic objectives, and competitive edges for its products and services.

Competitive Edges

Competitive edges are product or service characteristics for which the firm strives to achieve advantages in a given market. World-class firms focus resources on such areas for continuous improvement. Firms must establish performance criteria, standards, and measures for each competitive edge to ensure their continual improvement.

The *APICS Dictionary* (1992) defines nine "competitive edges" on which world-class companies can compete:

1. Price.
2. Quality.
3. Lead time.
4. Due date performance (delivery).

5. Product flexibility.
6. Process flexibility.
7. Field service.
8. Innovation.
9. Product introduction responsiveness.

How does a firm determine the competitive edges on which to focus? Although many competitive edges may be important to a world-class organization, continual improvements in any or all competitive edges may not lead to more profit. Hill argues that, in a given market, **order-qualifying criteria** of a product allow firms to be considered as a potential supplier of the product, whereas **order-winning criteria** can be exploited for competitive advantage.[7] Goldratt uses the term **necessary condition** to describe order qualifiers.[8] Improvements above a threshold or necessary condition level in qualifying criteria will not win orders. Such improvements merely prevent a company from losing orders to its competitors.

Is there much difference in your eyes in the quality of two cars if manufacturer A advertises a 5 parts per million defects level and manufacturer B advertises an 8 parts per million defects level? These manufacturers are in the same quality paradigm. You might be indifferent with respect to product quality as to whether you buy your car from manufacturer A or manufacturer B.

Both A and B have reached the order-qualifying criteria, or necessary condition level, on product quality. Any additional improvement in product quality is seen as unnecessary to customers, particularly if customers are dissatisfied with other aspects of the product or services provided.

What if manufacturer C is producing cars with defects at the 1 to 2 percent level? Has C reached the order qualifying level yet? Is C considered to be in the same quality paradigm as A and B? Do customers disregard C's car based on its inability to meet their necessary condition level for quality?

Manufacturing firms must, therefore, develop strategic objectives of continual improvement on order-winning criteria to maintain competitiveness. However, order-qualifying criteria must also be met and maintained because they are necessary conditions for competition. If necessary conditions are not met, then market share will erode. This concept explains the decline of the American automotive industry. Thus, competitive edges should be developed within the framework of the firm's selected area or areas of competition. This competitive framework should evolve from the development of corporate, business unit, and functional-level strategies that reflect current and future opportunities and threats in the marketplace.

For an area to be considered a true competitive edge, the firm must eventually realize an increase in profitability as a direct result of focusing organizational resources on continually improving the area. The performance measurement system must be capable of assessing the impact of competitive edge improvement on changes in profitability.

Customer Satisfaction

Customer satisfaction occurs when the product or service meets or exceeds customers' expectations on the competitive edges defined by the market. World-class firms aim to "delight" the customer with their product offering. Thus, market information is required to determine whether the products or services provided by the company are satisfying the customer. How can this be determined? Market information is required on the dimensions that define customer satisfaction for specific products and services—that is, the competitive edges. Customer satisfaction is achieved by eliminating sources of dissatisfaction. These sources must be traceable to the specific resource that caused the dissatisfaction with the product or service.

For example, let's suppose that you are the manager of an engineer-to-order firm whose primary competitive edge is fast delivery. You design each product to the specifications of each customer order, so you must ensure that every step in the product delivery system is conducted in a timely manner. Therefore, the synchronization of functional resources, such as design engineering, procurement, manufacturing, and distribution, is critical to continually meet or exceed the customers' delivery expectations.

To maintain your competitive edge, you must constantly collect and use market information on expected and actual delivery performance to improve your management of the product delivery process. If this market information is not integrated into the resource management process through a performance measurement system, the creation of a *sustainable* competitive advantage or edge (in this case, on-time delivery) is impossible.

Product or Service

Resource management focuses on improving your firm's ability to deliver a product or service to customers. How you manage your organizational resources directly affects the manner in which the product or service is delivered. For example, if organizational resources are managed in a reactionary mode, then products are constantly expedited through the production system to meet customer delivery requirements. This reactive management results in product or service quality problems; excess capacity to support expediting and the loss of effective constraint capacity caused by expediting; myopic actions that ignore organizational performance; and a dysfunctional organization incapable of developing competitive edges. Only through the proactive management of organizational resources can customer satisfaction be achieved.

Organizational Resources

Resources include the physical and intellectual assets that provide value to a product or service and move the firm toward its goal. Resources include raw materials, direct and indirect labor, facilities, patents, staff, and management. The challenge facing management today is to synchronize the activities of its resources to achieve the organizational goal.

Why is this so difficult? One needs only to examine traditional organizational structures so prevalent in businesses today. These structures are designed to classify resources by **function** (production, transportation, or sales) and **level** (department, plant, division, business unit, and so on). Each function focuses on achieving local objectives by using its resources to support these objectives at specific organizational levels. However, in order to achieve the organization's goal, local objectives must be consistent with and supportive of this goal. By linking functions and performance measurement systems across the organization (horizontally) and up the organization (vertically), resources can be synchronized to support the organization's goal.

RESOURCE MANAGEMENT

Definition of Resource Management

According to APICS, "Resource management is the **planning,** *effective scheduling,* and *control* of **organization resources** to produce a **product or service** that provides **customer satisfaction** and supports the organization's **competitive edges** and ultimately the organization's **goals**."[9] To fully understand the implications of resource management on how you should manage in your organizations, let's define and examine the remaining elements of the definition (in italics).

Effective scheduling.   What is meant by effective scheduling? **Effective scheduling** occurs when all organizational resources are focused on supporting external customers' needs. **Internal customers** exist within the organization and are simply the recipients of output from a previous activity. **External customers** are the users of the product or service provided by the firm. All efforts to satisfy internal customers are subordinated to supporting external customers' needs. In world-class firms, this external customer concept is extended to suppliers and distributors.

To effectively schedule resources, managers must recognize the difference between constraint and nonconstraint resources. We previously defined a **constraint** as anything that limits a system's achievement of its goal. A **constraint resource** represents a physical limitation, such as a piece of equipment in a manufacturing process that reduces the organization's ability to achieve its goal.[10] **Non-constraint resources,** also previously defined, do not limit the capacity of the organization to achieve its goal. Although nonconstraint resources do not have inherent physical limitations, mismanagement of such resources often leads to the creation of "temporary constraints," which limit performance. Therefore, although resources in general must be scheduled to effectively support external customer needs, constraint and nonconstraint resources must be scheduled differently based on their support of the organization's goal.

Control.   In referring to Table 2–1, we see the control function depicted in the present time frame—the execution stage of each plan. The schedule represents the near-term portion of each plan—the operational plan, the tactical plan, and the strategic plans. Each of these plans must be internally consistent with the capabilities of the customer, resource, and finance functions and externally linked to each of the other plans across time. The schedule being executed today is a step toward executing the organization's strategic plans.

Control is vital to fulfilling the schedule, the operational plan, the tactical plan, and the strategic plans. In order to effectively control, performance measurement systems must be **valid** (providing true progress), **reliable** (providing consistent results), **responsive** (identifying changes quickly), and **timely** (providing information quickly).

Local performance measurement systems have been in place for decades, but most fail to provide valid results with respect to progress toward the organization's goal. Progress in the local area is not equivalent to progress toward the organization's goal. Valid local performance measurement systems are vital to the control function in moving the organization toward its goal.

Other Uses for Resource Management

Resource management is also appropriate for governmental and not-for-profit organizations. The goals of government and its agencies are significantly different from for-profit organizations. A clear definition of the goal of each agency and program, effective performance measurement systems, and the determination of appropriate resource actions to satisfy customers' needs is critical today at the local, state, and federal levels of government. The principles of resource management would ensure that the resources of these governing bodies are linked to the citizens' needs of the community, state, and nation.

Not-for-profit firms can expand services through more effective resource management. Resource management can play a key role in restoring confidence in government and in allowing not-for-profit firms to improve the quality and quantity of goods and services provided.

ACHIEVING WORLD-CLASS STATUS

In 1986 Schonberger defined world-class manufacturing as "continuous and rapid improvement in such areas as quality, cost, lead time and customer service."[11] What has happened to the world-class manufacturing organizations of the 1980s? Many of these firms have laid off tens of thousands of manufacturing and other workers.[12]

What has happened to these world-class manufacturing firms? The underlying problem—the use of the traditional management philosophy—was discussed previously. The result of its use was that the constraint moved to the customer function— the resource function could manufacture more than what was demanded at the current price by customers.

For many reasons, including accounting's use of product cost for pricing decisions, and sales' and marketing's focus on the current product line instead of the customers' needs and market potential, excess resources had to be eliminated to reduce operating expenses.

The only avenue to a process of continuous improvement is increasing throughput—through marketing and selling the *capabilities of the firm* and not just the current product line. The customer function is critical to ensuring continuous improvement by identifying existing and potential customers' needs and expectations and providing this information to the resource function.

In addition, the finance function must provide an assessment of organizational productivity—movement toward the goal based on meeting the customers' needs through the effective use of the resource function.

We therefore define a **world-class organization** as an organization whose customer, resource, and finance functions synchronize their activities to achieve the organization's goal by meeting customers' current and potential needs and expectations. A first step in becoming a world-class organization is understanding the relationships between the three primary functions and their performance measurement systems. This is the subject of the next chapter.

World-class status can be achieved by properly linking the elements of resource management through performance measurement. Now that we understand the elements of resource management, how is effective resource management achieved? The key to achieving effective resource management is to understand how the basic performance measurement systems of a business are interrelated. Once it understands this relationship, the firm must develop methods for linking the systems. The links facilitate the correct measurement of actions across resources to achieve the firm's goal. But what is the model for accomplishing this feat?

Chapter Three

The Primary Functions and the Organization's Performance Measurement System Model

"Daring as it is to investigate the unknown, even more so is it to question the known."

Kaspar

COMMON SENSE VERSUS COMMON PRACTICE

For firms to gain a competitive advantage, new management approaches and performance measurement systems are needed. Organizations can no longer be run as a collection of functional "silos" whose primary goal is to achieve a local optimum, often at the expense of other functional areas.[1]

In achieving the organization's goal, the new management philosophy must link local activities and performance measures across the three primary functions. Effective business processes must link engineering design to purchasing, production resources, and customers' needs. Which traditional business processes and performance measures must be changed to align activities with the goal? How can business processes and measures be structured to be more effective?

Let's examine the operations of an organization. Traditional management practice utilizes local optimum thinking—common practices instead of common sense. Economic order quantities, lowest unit cost of products, and labor efficiency are prime examples of traditional management thinking that focuses on local optima. Using these traditional tools has become common practice. In contrast, common sense tells us that we must distinguish between the use of performance measures at constraints and at nonconstraints, and develop policies and procedures to achieve the effective use of constraint and nonconstraint resources.* We would like to be very efficient and have high utilization at the constraint. In contrast, we would like for nonconstraints to work at a utilization level necessary to support the constraint. Utilization and efficiency measures should not be optimized at the nonconstraint resources. Measures that reduce lead time are more appropriate. Is this approach no more than common sense?

What is required to achieve organizational improvement? We must reengineer the functional performance measurement systems to align with one another. Additionally, improvement in the measurement system must cause improvement in the organizational goal. This causal linkage requires that we know what business process is constraining the organization and then focus our improvement efforts on this constraint. Attempting to improve elsewhere has little to no impact on improving on the organization's goal.

In this chapter, we describe the performance measurement system model and its link to the organization's goal, its strategic objectives, and competitive edges. Next, we discuss each type of function (finance, customer, and resource functions) and its performance measurement system. We also discuss the purpose of each performance measurement system and the performance measures.

MODEL DESCRIPTION

To ensure an integrative approach in using resources and to monitor resource effectiveness in supporting the organization's goal, an improvement process and a comprehensive performance measurement system are required. The improvement process will focus on attaining the organization's goal. The measurement system will allow the assessment of progress toward developing and maintaining competitive edges to support customers' needs and the assessment of various resources' effect on the organization's ability to achieve its goal. Such a performance measurement system is presented in Figure 3–1. The model is a modified version of the performance measurement system being developed by Cox and Blackstone.[2] In the preceding chapter, we describe the relationship of the organization's goal to planning and

---

* Goldratt's five focusing steps provide a methodology for managing physical constraints and nonconstraints. This methodology is discussed in more detail in Chapter 4, Linking the Primary Functions through Performance Measurement Systems.

FIGURE 3–1

Generalized Organizational Performance Measurement System Model

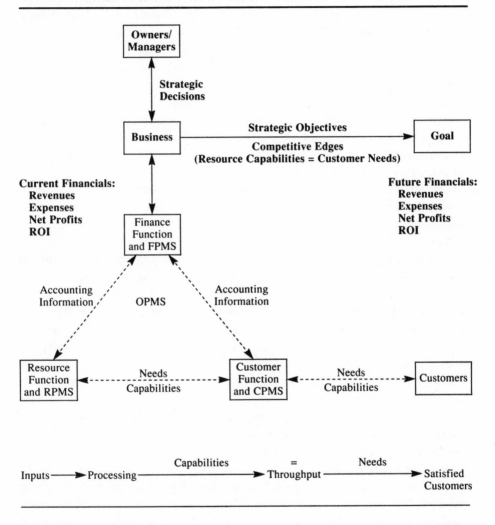

strategy, strategic objectives, competitive edges, resource capability, and customer needs. This description is represented by the top portion of Figure 3–1.

Before diving into the details of each function and its performance measurement system and the various linkages, several terms are again defined and a brief description of the decision-making linkage between the owner or manager, the business, and its goal is provided. This is represented at the top of Figure 3–1. A **goal** is an end someone strives to achieve. For example, more money now and in the future is the goal of a for-profit organization. In contrast, a **necessary condition** represents an acceptable level of an item. More (less) of an item is not necessarily considered better but less (more) of the item may have a devastating impact.

A **strategic objective** is an initiative directed to maintaining the long-term health of the firm. The firm believes that achieving the strategic objective is the means to achieving its goal.

A **competitive edge** is a product or service characteristic that is recognized in the market as superior to competitors and that fits the customers' needs. Over time, a competitive edge can become a necessary condition for remaining in the market. For example, quality was considered a competitive edge of the Japanese automobile industry 10 years ago. Today, quality is a necessary condition for survival for US car manufacturers. However, until American cars are perceived by consumers as having the same quality level as Japanese cars, the US automotive manufacturers' market share (and profits) will continue to shrink. When you violate a necessary condition, nothing else matters—your survival is threatened.

In small, privately held firms, owners define the goals of the business. A for-profit business generally has the goal of making more money now and in the future.[3] This is the primary goal of the organization and is a necessary condition for its long-run survival. Any other goals are subordinated to this goal. Necessary conditions have to be met for the firm to remain viable. For example, a positive cash flow is a necessary condition for remaining in business. A safe workplace is another necessary condition. Strategic objectives and necessary conditions must also be established in relation to achieving customers' needs. The model shows the strategic decision-making link between the owners or managers and the business in moving the business toward its goals. The decisions concern the organization's resource capabilities for producing goods and services to meet customers' needs via the competitive edges.

In a larger, publicly held business, managers act on behalf of the owners (that is, stockholders) and determine the goals of the firm. Top management must develop measures that will ensure the long-term viability of the business via profitability, return on assets, and market share growth (a surrogate measure for more money in the future). Market share as a measure must be carefully used. It does not in itself translate into more money now and in the future. Current profitability can be measured, but future profitability can only be estimated. Market share provides valuable information on the customer base, but it does not have a direct cause-and-effect relationship with long-term profitability. These measures must be supported by strategic decisions and actions that translate into competitive edges in each market served. Therefore, top management or owners need performance information regarding the desired and actual financial impact of its decisions on these measures.

THE THREE FUNCTIONS AND THE LINKED PERFORMANCE MEASUREMENT SYSTEMS

A major objective of the finance function is to provide estimates of the impact of decisions in the resource and customer functions on the organization's financial status. This information is provided by the performance measurement systems (illustrated in Figure 3-1) concerning the proposed and actual use of organizational resources and the level of customer satisfaction. This information provides projections based on the production and sale of goods and services.

Although this description might sound like some performance measurement systems used in industry today, it is a radical departure from common practice. Not only are we recommending linking performance across functions to achieve the organization's goal, but we also maintain that traditional management techniques will no longer provide competitiveness.

Notice the three separate but linked performance measurement systems in Figure 3-1. The performance measurement systems support the different orientations of each of the major functions, and each function must translate its actions into the financial impact on the organization. This translation can be completed only by ascertaining one function's impact on the other functions through their performance measurement systems. In this manner many win-win opportunities are possible.

Win-win and focused actions are the only means of regaining competitiveness. Management actions are the topic of a later chapter. Let's now discuss each of the functions—finance, resource, and customers—and their supporting performance measurement systems.

The Finance Function and Performance Measurement System

Most companies possess well-defined financial functions and finance performance measurement systems. This performance measurement system uses accounting data to track financial performance in terms of revenue, cost, profit, assets, and liabilities. The accounting system provides the means of planning and controlling the firm; it provides the firm with the ability to track actual against budgeted expenses.

The accounting system is top management's link between the primary functions—

finance, resources and customers—and the finance (FPMS), resource (RPMS), and customer (CPMS) performance measurement systems. A cost accounting system serves as the primary vehicle for collecting expense data and monitoring revenue streams. Information contained in the finance system, such as product, plant, division, or corporate profitability, is used to make short- and long-term decisions that affect the firm's fiscal conditions.

Investment decisions based on ROI, net present value, internal rates of return, and payback period are driven primarily by the finance performance measurement system. Budgetary allocations to departments are also based on information held within this system. In many cases, long-term capital investment decisions along with short-term budgetary decisions are made solely on the information provided by the internal cost accounting system. Capital investments in production equipment, support equipment, furniture, buildings, and so forth are accumulated in the accounting system. Operating expenses for direct labor, indirect labor, and salaries of staff specialists and line management are collected in addition to expenses for utilities, raw materials, indirect and support materials, transportation, sales commissions, advertising, sales, and other needs.

The accounting system collects the financial details associated with the investments and expenses of the resource system (engineering, purchasing, production, warehousing, and distribution) and the investment, revenues, and expenses of the customer system (marketing, sales, and field service). Many cost-accounting systems contain over 100 different T-account classifications for accumulating financial data. Some have more.

The Resource Function and Performance Measurement System

The resource function includes R&D, design engineering, procurement, production, warehousing, and distribution. RPMSs are designed to regulate the effective use of organizational resources engaged in the development, creation, and delivery of goods and services. Three broad performance criteria—price/cost, quality, and lead time—are tracked to various degrees by the RPMS.

Price/cost. Cost information collected by the resource function relates to the firm's transformation processes. Thousands of cost transactions are recorded. Of all the various recorded costs, which ones are really important? Which are not important? Costs must be relevant to the decision being made. Costs should be categorized as variable (in strict economic terms, this is a cost that varies directly with an increase or decrease by one unit of output) or fixed. In addition, at each level of decision making, costs must be classified as controllable or uncontrollable. Notice that as decisions move up the various decision-making levels, fixed costs become more variable and uncontrollable costs become more controllable. The collection of irrelevant cost information leads to illogical managerial decisions, resulting in poor resource utilization.

The use of some traditional measures are meaningless in certain environments and quite important in other environments. For example, the use of individual labor efficiency and machine utilization as performance criteria in a cellular manufacturing environment results in the improper **activation** (use of resources to optimize local measures) of people and equipment to produce excessive work-in-process and finished goods inventories. These measures are certainly incorrect for such an environment. Performance criteria should promote reduction of manufacturing **cycle time** (the time required to produce the part or product) and encourage better **utilization** (use of resources to achieve a competitive edge) of the cell. The manager must ensure that items scheduled through the cell represent sales to customers and are not parts scheduled just to keep the cell busy. In contrast, labor efficiency and machine utilization are important performance criteria if used at the constraint. Improvement on these local measures has a direct and significant effect on the organization's goal.

The structure of the firm's cost accounting system directly affects the types of cost information collected on organizational resources. Under traditional cost accounting thinking, product costs can be computed with great precision (to six decimal places). But what are the true costs associated with making a product? Raw materials, direct labor, and variable factory overhead are usually assigned directly to a product, and fixed factory overhead is usually allocated based on direct labor costs or hours, machine hours, and so on. This is the traditional cost accounting practice.

Is this classification and allocation correct? Is it correct for your firm? Does your direct labor cost vary when one additional unit of product is produced? Do you pay a piece or incentive pay rate based on quantity of products produced? The answer is probably no. Most industries do not pay workers based on the quantity of items produced, but on a fixed salary or hourly wage rate. So why do we still consider labor costs and most of the costs in variable overhead allocable on a quantity-produced basis? How many of your organization's costs vary if you produce just one more unit of output?

Costs that vary directly with output are raw materials, sales commissions, subcontracting, and possibly transportation. Most of the remaining costs are fixed across an extremely wide range of output. Do you hire and fire your direct laborers daily? Your staff? Your managers? Can you eliminate a part of your equipment depreciation, your building depreciation, and your interest expenses just because you have reduced production by 1 unit, 10 units, or even 100 units? Is it even possible?

If not, then why do you run your accounting system and make product decisions as though you can? What does product cost mean today? Should your sales and investment decisions be based on traditional product costs? Are product cost and product profit meaningful concepts in your organization today?

Quality.   In the area of quality, many firms have begun to institute a philosophy of total quality management (TQM). Quality information is collected by the firm's resource function and relates to the design, procurement, and production areas. Too many firms assume that TQM is an internal quality improvement program focusing on eliminating scrap and quality inspectors. The objective of TQM should not be to *save* money but to *make* money. Most firms focus only on the savings opportunities of TQM, using the traditional management philosophy to justify resource investments.[4]

Suppose you can buy a machine for $100,000 to improve the quality of a part. The current defect rate is 10 percent. Cost accounting data related to quality indicate that a 1 percent reduction in defects saves $10,000 per year. The new equipment can cut defects by 90 percent—that is, from a 10 percent to a 1 percent defect rate. This equipment investment translates into a $90,000 annual savings—a payback period of 1.1 years. You decide to buy the equipment to support your TQM program.

Six months later new equipment is introduced to the market costing $100,000, and again it will cut your current defect rate by 90 percent. Your cost accounting data still indicate a 1 percent reduction in defects will save $10,000 per year. Your current defect rate is 1 percent. This equipment investment saves $9,000 per year— a payback period of over 11 years. After much bloodshed and debate, you convince management that the investment must be made in the name of TQM. After all, you are committed to quality (if it doesn't cost too much).

You guessed it—six months later a new machine costing $100,000 is introduced into the market, and it will cut the defect rate by 90 percent. Again, cost accounting data indicate that a 1 percent reduction in defects saves $10,000. Your current defect rate is 0.1 percent. Your annual savings is $900—a payback of 111.1 years! You refuse to consider the investment—0.1 percent defects is good enough, considering the investment.

If a 0.1 percent defect rate is good enough, why are the Japanese striving for 0.0001 percent, or a parts per million defect rate? Don't Japanese managers use traditional management techniques for decision making? Could it be that they are intuitively looking at the profit potential of the investment—the money the investment can make and not the cost savings opportunity? Is the defect a flaw that prevents our product from meeting customers' needs? Or is it a flaw that has little to no impact on revenue? Quality data related to customers' needs and expectations must be collected by the customer function, translated into opportunities for revenue generation, and translated into equipment requirements and costs on the resource function. Only by comparing the revenue opportunities with the incremental costs can valid business decisions be made.

Enlightened managers now understand the relationship between quality and cost. Quality improvements can lead to true cost reductions, although some level of initial investment is often required. More importantly, quality improvements can lead to additional sales if the improvements are based on the "voice of the customer." Quality function deployment (QFD) provides a means for incorporating the customer's voice into the initial phase of product development. This is where TQM must focus on continuous improvement. The resource performance measurement system must be able to track true cost reductions (and possibly throughput improvement) directly attributable to improvements in the quality of material inputs, processing, and finished products. The system must also monitor true costs associated with two additional areas: people and equipment.

Manufacturing firms traditionally have used individual labor efficiency and machine utilization as the primary performance criteria for direct workers and equipment, respectively. Firms that have adopted JIT techniques such as group technology, focused manufacturing cells, cross-trained workers, and employee involvement are aware of the problems associated with these traditional measurement criteria. The resource performance system must be consistent with the operating environment of the company's resources.

Lead time.   Stalk and Hout argue that time is an essential competitive edge in the marketplace.[5] Numerous industry examples support this position. Shorter product development and production cycles are considered key competitive weapons for Japanese car manufacturers. The advent of overnight package delivery by Federal Express and others has led to the creation of an entire industry based on time. In fact, the US Postal Service had no choice but to develop its own brand of overnight service. Organizational resources must contribute to a firm's ability to deliver products and services **effectively** (here meaning with a minimal passage of time). Resource performance measurement systems must include time-based performance criteria, measures, and standards that assess how well the firm's resources strengthen its ability to compete.

A reduction in lead time can affect the bottom line in several ways. First, reducing lead time by improving engineering and manufacturing work flow can lead to significant reductions of work-in-process (WIP) and finished goods inventories. You will have to carry less finished goods inventory, because you have the ability to replenish inventory stocks and respond to customers' needs more quickly. In fact, some firms have been able to reduce lead times enough to virtually eliminate finished goods inventory and move to a make-to-order environment.

A second way to affect the bottom line considers the relationship of lead time reduction and quality improvement. As WIP inventory is reduced, quality should improve significantly. The source of quality problems can more easily be identified in a low-inventory environment.

The most important way reducing lead time can impact the bottom line is through increased sales. Is time a competitive advantage that your customers desire? If you reduce your lead time, will customers buy more product from you? Will they pay a premium for prompt service?

Our first question related to true organizational improvement should be "What is the impact of the change on a competitive edge on revenue?" Focus on what the customers want. "What is the true cost of the improvements?" should be our second question. Does the purchase of the equipment move us toward the firm's goal? That is improvement—moving toward the goal of making more money.

Focusing on local savings is a mirage, particularly when most operating expenses are fixed. For example, a manufacturer believed that it could improve the appearance of its products by investing $2 million in a new paint machine. After the investment, little change in profits resulted. By contacting two major customers, the manufacturer discovered that it didn't have a quality problem with paint. However, if the manufacturer could reduce its lead time by three weeks it could double its sales from the two clients. Identifying what the customers really want translates into bottom-line results.

Quality function deployment (QFD) facilitates reductions in the new product development cycle. The RPMS must track the time reductions realized in the QFD process. The system must collect information used to determine resource constraints in the design process. Continual improvement efforts can then be focused on the lead time constraints, resulting in shorter product development cycles.

Using JIT.   JIT concepts are used to shorten procurement, manufacturing, and delivery lead times. Strategic alliances with suppliers provide for more frequent deliveries of materials directly to their point of use. Point-of-use material delivery eliminates incoming inspection and excess material handling steps and reduces lead time. The reduction of WIP inventory shortens manufacturing lead times. Less WIP also improves quality, which also reduces lead time. The JIT concept of small-lot shipments also reduces delivery time. The RPMS must contain time metrics designed to monitor the effectiveness of both external (suppliers and external distributors) and internal (design, production, warehousing, and transportation) resources within the product delivery system.

Using business process reengineering.   Business process reengineering involves the fundamental redesign of business processes to facilitate goal achievement. The organization must identify and eliminate all non-value-added activities discovered in each process. Also, value-added process activities are improved to provide greater customer satisfaction. Successful business process reengineering results in an organization that is market driven, flexibly responsive, and focused on continually improving business processes. The hierarchical management structure becomes obsolete. A team-based management approach centered around business processes is adopted. The RPMS must contain process-based metrics that relate local process performance to the organizations goal. The RPMS must monitor the effectiveness of organizational resources used in value-added process activities. It must also provide information on processes that use resources ineffectively and are possible candidates for reengineering.

Using information.   Information collected by the RPMS is used in making short-, medium-, and long-term managerial decisions. In the short term, managers must make resource decisions such as the stocking levels of materials, the appropriate number of employees, and the required amount of short-term capacity to support current orders. The RPMS must provide managers information for **resource control** in the short term to make decisions concerning the effective scheduling, monitoring, and controlling of organizational resources. Similar decisions must also be made for the medium and long terms, but different information is required. In the medium and long term, managers need information for **resource planning**. Managers must assess the use of organizational resources to support strategic objectives that contribute to the overall goal of the firm. Therefore, an effective RPMS must contain the appropriate information need for short-, medium-, and long-term managerial decision making.

The Customer Function and Performance Measurement System

Marketing, sales, and field service comprise the customer function. The customer performance measurement system (CPMS) links the firm and the market. Marketing is responsible for determining the proper product mix for a given market segment, establishing pricing strategies, promoting the product mix for customer awareness, and identifying the strategic location of product outlets within a given market area. The CPMS must provide marketing and management with the necessary information for decision making. But what is the correct information to support this decision making? What product or service characteristics are really important to your customers? What are your necessary condition levels for quality and lead time? What do your customers say they want? What do they really need? What is the fair price (a win-win price) your customers will pay for your product? What are your competitors charging? What problems is each of your customers having with your product? Are field service problems solved to retain your customers? Why do your customers change brands?

Sales personnel provide their organization a direct link to customers. Sales staff help customers define specific product or service requirements, solve customers' problems, collect field information on competitors, and serve as the firm's primary representative to customers. The CPMS must effectively translate information obtained through field contacts with customers into its impact on the finance and resource functions.

Criteria used to evaluate the performance of sales personnel must be consistent with the behaviors and actions the organization expects from these personnel. As seen in Chapter 1, Why Are You Losing the Battle with Global Competition?, using a sales commission structure based on product price or contribution margin promotes the sale of only a few items within the product offering. To effectively use the sales personnel, management must pay attention to the compatibility of performance criteria, measures, and standards established for the marketing and sales organizations, as well as the compatibility of sales managers, field sales personnel, and the goals of the firm.

You must avoid the use of inconsistent metrics that drive marketing staffs, sales personnel, and the organization toward the optimization of personal and functional objectives and the suboptimization of customers' needs and the firm's goals. Sales commissions and the functional objectives of marketing and sales must be aligned with the resource capabilities to support the organization's goals; thus, when employees strive to meet these local criteria, resources can be effectively utilized to satisfy the customers' needs, and, of primary importance, the firm will move closer to its goal.

Field service organizations provide customers with repair, replacement, and troubleshooting assistance. These activities not only provide an opportunity to develop increased customer loyalty but also provide a unique opportunity to collect vital information for product and service improvement. For example, product warranty and field failure information can be used to pinpoint exactly where product and process improvements are needed. Comparative information from customers on the performance of your company's offering against that of competitors can be used in developing next-generation products or enhancing current products.

CPMS must capture field service information to continually improve products and processes. The information must be linked to the resource and finance functions and their performance measurement systems. The integration and alignment of these functions through their performance measurement systems will ensure that resources are effectively and efficiently used toward accomplishing the company goal. But how is this integration achieved? The linkages required to support decision making are discussed in the next chapter.

Chapter Four

Linking the Primary Functions through Performance Measurement Systems

This chapter builds on the last one. Previously, we discussed the three primary functions, their information requirements, and their supporting performance measurement systems. We also defined linkage (in Chapter 1, Why Are You Losing the Battle with Global Competition?) as a bond providing information on the strategy of the organization; the synchronized actions of each function to achieve the organization's goal; and the supporting performance measurement system. In this chapter, we provide details related to this linkage.

LINKAGES BETWEEN SYSTEMS

As shown in Figure 4–1, three linkages tie the finance, resource, and customer performance measurement systems together. These linkages are *finance and resource, finance and customer,* and *customer and resource.* Information must flow through each link to assess the impact of any action on all functions so that managers can make valid decisions. Next, we will define the finance and resource link, the finance and customer link, and the customer and resource link, and then provide an example of the information flow through each of the linkages in making a business decision.

Finance and Resource Linkage

This section is considerably longer than the other linkage sections for several reasons. First, the cost and managerial accounting systems link the functions of a business together for decision-making purposes. Accounting data link all three

FIGURE 4-1
Generalized Organizational Performance Measurement System Model

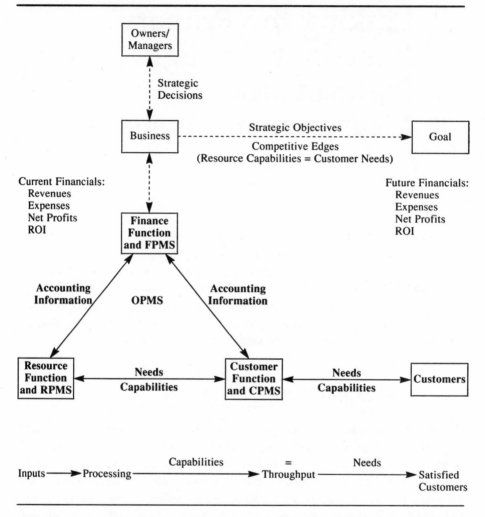

performance measurement systems and are the common language for all business decision making. Second, accounting systems have evolved slowly in stark contrast to the revolutionary changes in manufacturing thought. The end result is that traditional accounting no longer provides a valid decision-making framework.[1] We will discuss several of the problems with traditional accounting and two alternative accounting systems: activity-based costing (ABC) and theory of constraints (TOC) accounting.

Management accounting systems evolved during the late nineteenth and early twentieth centuries to support the growing industrial activities in Europe and the United States. Most of the features seen in today's traditional cost and managerial accounting systems were established by the 1930s. Whereas the US manufacturing environment has undergone dramatic changes since the 1970s, the fundamental principles used in the supporting accounting systems have changed very little.

Most firms have separate financial and management accounting systems. Financial accounting systems are designed to translate company activities into dollar values, which are reported to various external entities. The methods and procedures must conform to generally accepted accounting principles (GAAP). This system acts on behalf of shareholders and other concerned parties, such as the government and other stakeholders, to reflect the current and future realities of the business in financial terms. Through the analysis of financial reports, stakeholders are provided *information* for making short- and long-term investment decisions, judgments concerning acquisitions or joint ventures, and so forth. In theory, cost and managerial accounting systems are designed to furnish information for internal decision making. These systems should provide the firm with revenue and cost information that realistically reflects the current and future state of the business in relation to goals, customers, finances, and resources.

Real conflicts exist between these financial and management accounting systems. Let's briefly examine one conflict. Financial accounting views inventory as an asset. Banks even lend money using inventory as collateral. In the new business environment, however, most inventory is a liability—it hides quality problems, extends new product introduction lead times, extends lead times for customer orders, and ties up capital unnecessarily. What is the answer to the inventory conflict? Common sense suggests there should be a given level of inventory viewed as an asset, and amounts beyond this level should be considered a liability.[2]

Traditional accounting systems. In most manufacturing firms, traditional financial and management accounting systems are incapable of realistically reflecting the current or future state of the business. The reason is quite straightforward: these systems fail to recognize changes in the business and its environment. The result is that such systems reflect a business fantasy that provides irrelevant data for managerial decision making. Managers then make illogical decisions, encourage detrimental actions, and indulge in behaviors that may ultimately destroy the firm.

For resources to be adequately allocated, resource requirements must be converted into financial needs. This conversion is achieved through established linkages between resource and finance performance measurement systems. In most companies, this linkage is accomplished through the cost accounting system.

Recent research on performance measurement problems focuses on the use of traditional accounting systems in firms that are in transition to world-class manufacturing principles and techniques. We want to emphasize this research so that you may examine this literature for yourself to understand the full ramifications of relying on traditional accounting for business decision making. Kaplan was among the first to identify the shortcomings of traditional cost accounting in today's manufacturing environment.[3] Others such as Miller et al., Goldratt and Fox, Howell, Johnson and Kaplan, Foster and Horngren, Plossl, Worthy, and Burns and Kaplan have continued to reveal the fallacies of traditional cost accounting practices and the misrepresentation and distortion of true operational and division performance.[4-13]

Finch and Cox challenged the assumption that inventory was an asset and illustrated how this assumption misrepresented plant and business performance.[14] Fry and Cox examined the ways in which traditional cost accounting systems promote local optimization of resources within a manufacturing facility, and they called for the adoption of global measures that optimize the performance of the entire business.[15] Plossl states that advances in the technology of manufacturing planning, control, and operation have made conventional cost accounting practices not only obsolete but dangerous.[16] According to Plossl, as a percentage of manufacturing costs, direct labor and variable overhead costs have declined dramatically, owing to higher-quality materials, fewer interruptions, automation, and robotics. Conversely, fixed overhead costs have increased greatly and now predominate. Thus, revisions of conventional cost accounting systems are needed.

Why are traditional accounting systems out of step with current business realities? Maskell defined five problem areas associated with traditional accounting systems in today's business environments: lack of relevance; cost distortion; inflexibility; impediment to progress of world-class manufacturing; and subordination to the needs of financial accounting.[17]

Traditional accounting systems fail to monitor the firm's success on competitive edges that are nonfinancial in nature: quality, lead time, due date performance (delivery), product flexibility, process flexibility, field service, innovation, and product introduction responsiveness. Therefore, discontinuities exist between traditional accounting systems and the goal of the firm. Traditional accounting systems are not synchronized with the requirements of the market, because a low price may not be sufficient for continued customer satisfaction. Many customers may pay a premium price for higher quality and lower lead times.

The relevance of traditional accounting information is also questionable for operational control and product pricing. Financial metrics are inadequate for daily operational control. Measures are needed for monitoring resource activities including scheduling jobs, manufacturing products, ensuring quality standards, shipping orders, and so on. Many firms are now using market-driven pricing to establish product price versus the traditional cost-driven approach. The new business reality is that firms must formulate prices based on market demand versus detailed product cost analysis. Manufacturing costs should be analyzed to determine organizational resource investments for process improvements, not for computing the cost and eventual price of a given product. Company profit is a reality—a goal. Product profit is a mirage.

Dramatic changes have occurred in the composition of product costs since the emergence of traditional accounting systems. During the formation of current accounting practices, direct labor constituted 50 to 70 percent of the total product cost. Today, direct labor amounts to 5 to 10 percent of the cost of many products. However, traditional accounting systems are designed to focus organizational energies on tracking direct labor. Overhead, the fastest-growing aspect of product cost, is not directly tracked and tied to products within the traditional systems.

In the new business reality, distinctions between direct and indirect costs and fixed and variable costs are becoming increasingly obscure. World-class manufacturers use workers conventionally viewed as direct labor to perform many indirect activities: preventive maintenance, changeovers, in-process inspections, training, and so on. Traditional accounting systems show "nonproductive time" of direct laborers as a negative variance, although the workers may have been adding value to the organization.

As overhead costs increase, elements that may be treated as fixed or variable costs are more difficult to determine. To compound the problem, overhead costs are often allocated based on an ever-shrinking pool of labor cost or hours. The effect is a total distortion of product costs, eventually leading to product prices that are either too high or too low. The less important direct labor becomes in the production process, the more important it becomes in the allocation process. Any allocation process, no matter what the base is, distorts true product costs.

An additional point is that product price should be determined by the basic economic laws of supply and demand. What is the customer willing to pay for the product? What are competitors selling similar products for? This is product price. Product cost should cover variable cost across the planning process for the company's decision. That is the strongest statement we can make related to product cost. Our goal is to increase organizational profits in the short and long term. We must make an organizational profit to stay in business. The same products can take on several different prices for the organization to cover its costs and make a profit.

The new business reality dictates the need for performance measurement systems tailored to the needs of the organization. Traditional accounting systems require uniformity across the business entities. Firms composed of multiplant or distribution networks are often constrained by the information collected and required by the accounting system. This lack of flexibility can lead to poor managerial decisions. To accentuate the problem, by the time managers receive these inadequate data (usually monthly), they are of no value. Traditional accounting systems often do not provide timely information for proactive decision making.

A major impediment to progress toward becoming a world-class organization is the accounting system. While firms engage in activities to promote the new reality, traditional accounting information systems monitor progress based on outdated measures. Capital investment decisions based solely on discounted cash flows, net present values, payback periods, and internal rates of return discourage long-term strategic investments that improve resource- and customer-oriented performance areas. For example, a $10 million investment that would improve product introduction responsiveness 20-fold over the next 10 years is impossible to justify if the firm's short-term financial performance goal (hurdle rate return on investment) is not met. The new business reality requires that capital investment analysis decisions be made within the context of the company's goal. In addition, the investments must be viewed holistically. Traditional accounting information systems view each capital request as a stand-alone project having no relationship to either current or future ventures.

High labor efficiency and machine utilization measures are hallmarks of traditional accounting systems. These measures drive manufacturing organizations toward local optima by encouraging the unnecessary use of local resources. World-class firms attempt to synchronize organizational resources to achieve a global optimum. Labor and machines should be used only when required for the achievement of the company's goal, not to improve labor efficiencies and machine utilization.

In traditional accounting information systems, departments are penalized for negative variances on labor and machine hour variance reports. To make matters worse, for production personnel to achieve high labor and machine utilization, excess inventory is required at each work station. The inventory supports long production runs with few changeovers, leading to increased labor efficiency and machine utilization.

It is easy to see how labor efficiency and machine utilization measures lead to managerial decisions, actions, and behaviors destructive to achieving world-class manufacturing capabilities. If accounting systems are to be of any use at all, the new business reality demands that the systems be supportive of the new manufacturing environment.

Activity-based costing and theory of constraints accounting.   Activity-based costing (ABC) and theory of constraint (TOC) accounting are alternatives to traditional full-absorption cost accounting systems. **Activity-based accounting** is defined as the collection of financial and operational performance information about significant activities of the business.[18] This methodology incorporates the idea that costs are incurred through a firm's activities. Therefore, the accounting information system is designed to capture and track performance for only those few significant activities that constitute the bulk of the total work within a given organization. Under activity-based accounting, cost allocations to products are based on the activities that drive cost. A sales price is then established based on the product cost and the desired profit margin.

Activity-based cost accounting is a cost system designed to more precisely allocate expenditures to objects (parts, products, product lines, functions, departments, plants, divisions, and so on). In contrast to traditional accounting, which usually uses direct labor as the only cost driver for overhead allocation, ABC may use several cost drivers to allocate overhead. In Box 4–1, we provide a brief overview of ABC.[19]

Initially, ABC had a number of proponents.[20, 21] More recently, however, some accounting researchers are warning companies of its shortcoming.[22-24] Selection of cost pools and cost drivers is critical. Failure to recognize the types of actions managers will take based on cost allocations can create havoc with manufacturing operations.

For example, suppose that all costs related to design changes (product or process changes, drafting, and so forth) were collected in a cost pool and allocated based on the number of engineering changes. What would be your action as a product line manager if you knew your products were going to be allocated engineering overhead costs based on the number of engineering changes? You would probably save the engineering changes and batch several together on one engineering change form.

How does this affect the resource, customer, and finance functions? Workers and engineers would probably be upset and confused by a set of drawings and instructions that incorporated several changes at one time. The customers might go to a competitor for the product because you would seem unresponsive to their needs. The product line manager might be charged less overhead in the short run, but what is the long-term effect on revenues caused by not responding to engineering changes to a product? Certainly, you as a manager might want to rethink the allocation driver so that it promotes responsiveness to customers' needs.

Think about the effect of collecting production planning and control costs into a cost pool and allocating these costs based on the number of line items in the master schedule. JIT suggests moving to making a day's demand each day. Using the number of line items in the master schedule to allocate planning and control costs could move you from daily to weekly or monthly batches to reduce your product costs. The real question is whether moving to weekly or monthly batches really significantly reduces your firm's production planning and control costs. Probably not. You must carefully think through the selection of cost pools and cost drivers. Do these allocation methods move your firm toward the goal by encouraging the appropriate actions? Accountants are still debating the virtues and shortcomings of ABC accounting.

In using **theory of constraints (TOC) accounting,** fixed costs are not allocated to products. Whereas traditional cost accounting systems focus on product costs, the TOC accounting system focuses on the firm's profitability through the measures of throughput (T), inventory (I), and operating expenses (OE). **Throughput** is defined as the rate at which the system generates money through sales. The actual money generated by the system is equal to sales minus the purchased materials (that is, true variable cost per unit) used in the specific items sold. **Inventory** is defined as all the money the system invests in purchasing things the system intends to sell. This definition disregards value-added as part of the inventory valuation (inventory is valued at raw material cost only). Equipment and facility investment are considered inventory. **Operating expense** is defined as all the money the system spends in turning inventory into throughput. Direct labor and all other general expenses are considered fixed, and as such, operating expenses. Using these definitions, net profit is computed by subtracting total operating expenses from the total throughput. Return on investment is determined by dividing net profit by inventory. In this scheme, increased profitability is achieved by increasing throughput, decreasing operating expenses, or both.

Goldratt states that an increase in throughput is the primary avenue for profit improvement because throughput is inherently unlimited.[25] Inventory is next in level of importance, owing to reductions in inventory that translate into improvements in the strategic objectives, such as improved quality, delivery, and lead time, thereby affecting *future throughput*. Operating expense (cost) is ranked third in importance.

TOC accounting uses constraint pricing to establish product prices. In constraint pricing, a minimum price for products is established based on constraint capacity. If the constraint is internal to the operation, minimum product prices are established to allow for throughput increases (producing market segmentation). If excess capacity exists, minimum product prices are set based on variable costs. The key is to segment the market so that prices in one market do not affect prices in other markets. TOC accounting is similar to a direct costing methodology with one major difference. Although neither method uses an overhead allocation scheme for determining product costs, TOC accounting considers direct labor to be fixed in the short run and treats it as an operating expense. In contrast, the direct costing approach treats labor as a variable cost, and it is specifically assigned to a product. This is significantly different from both full absorption and activity-based

---

Box 4–1

What is Activity-Based Costing?

Activity-based costing is an information system that maintains and processes data on a firm's activities and cost objects, such as products. It identifies the activities performed, traces cost to these activities, and then uses various cost drivers to trace the cost of the activities to the cost objects. These cost drivers (such as the number of part numbers or the effort expended by product) reflect the consumption of activities by the cost objects. An activity-based cost system is used by management for a variety of purposes relating to both activities and cost objects.

Activity and cost driver concepts are at the heart of activity-based costing. Activities are processes or procedures that cause work and thereby consume resources. Examples of activities include tapping threads in a hole in a metal part; telephoning a vendor to place an order for materials; and preparing a new drawing for a part to reflect a change in engineering specifications.

Cost drivers reflect the demands placed on activities by products or other cost objects. The cost driver "number of receipts," for example, measures the frequency of performing various activities connected with receiving and inspecting incoming components and updating the parts database. The cost driver "effort by vendor" measures the time required by various activities to establish and maintain vendor relations.

Cost drivers measure the demands placed on activities at both the activity and cost object levels. For example, the product cost driver "number of production runs" may show that the production scheduling department schedules 4,000 batches of product over a year. It may also show that product A is run six times in a year and will therefore be scheduled six times.

Cost drivers are also used to trace cost to objects other than products. These objects include customers, markets, distribution channels, and engineering projects. The activity "maintaining customer relations" is a customer-sustaining activity and should be traced to customers via a cost driver such as "effort by customer."

Activity-based cost systems vary in the information provided on activities. Some systems use multiple cost drivers and allocate pools of cost to each cost driver. Each cost pool contains the resources consumed by several activities, but the activities are not separately defined. These cost driver systems are economical ways of reporting accurate product cost and are useful for strategic and product design purposes. In the absence of detailed activity information, they do not directly support the management of these activities.

Source: RW Hall, HT Johnson, and PBB Turney, *Measuring Up: Charting Pathways to Manufacturing Excellence* (Homewood, IL: Business One Irwin, 1991).

accounting methods, which use overhead allocation schemes to determine product cost.

TOC accounting groups all investment, cost, and revenue transactions into one of three classifications—throughput, inventory, and operating expenses. Let's briefly restate these theory of constraint definitions and the five focusing steps.[26]

Throughput: the rate at which the system generates money through sales.

Inventory: the items the system buys that it intends to sell.

Operating expenses: the rate at which the system spends money in converting inventory into throughput.

The first three steps of our continuous improvement process of attaining world-class status can now be developed. First, a company must define its goal: to make more money now and in the future (in the case of for-profit organizations). Second, a performance measurement system is needed to let you know when local actions move the organization toward its goal. The measures of throughput, inventory, and operating expense provide the foundation for this performance measurement system. Third, you should follow the five focusing steps of TOC:

1. Identify the constraint of the system.
2. Decide how to exploit the constraint.
3. Subordinate all else to the constraint.
4. Elevate the constraint.
5. If in step 4 the constraint is broken, go back to step 1. Don't let inertia become a constraint.

The five focusing steps identify the operations and resources that should be managed more effectively to attain the organizational goal. The power of using these TOC steps to identify the organization's constraint cannot be overemphasized.

TOC accounting is a simple costing system that allows you to evaluate the effect of local decisions on the goal of the organization. TOC accounting is supported by basic economic theory related to fixed, variable, and marginal costing concepts. TOC accounting represents a major departure from the value-added concept and from the traditional view of labor being treated as a variable cost. To embrace TOC accounting would require a significant change in the role and actions of traditional managers, in the policies and procedures of the organization, and in the measurement system.

Finance and Customer Linkage

If we examined current performance measurement systems, we would find a traditional cost accounting system in the resource area with overhead allocation based on direct labor. We would find a strong link to the finance function and its performance measurement system to cost-justify investment through savings. We would find a weak link to the customer function and its performance measurement system. Few companies are tying improvements in parts lead time and improvements in parts quality to what the customers deem as a competitive edge. Firms spend millions of dollars on lead time reduction and quality improvement that have *no* impact on quoted product lead time and product quality. Without a strong link between the customer and resource functions and their performance measurement systems, correct decisions are highly unlikely.

The weakest linkage in most performance measurement systems is, however, between the finance and customer functions. In most companies, this link is virtually nonexistent. The financial impact of marketing opportunities must be objectively assessed. How will increasing our supply of product by 10 percent affect sales? How will a price increase or reduction affect total revenues? Can marketing segment the market? What price can be charged for the products in each segment? What price or product modifications have to be made to retain current customers' sales? What do the customers really need? Are our customers willing to pay for a reduction in quoted lead time from three months to one month? How much? Is this pay measured in additional sales? Is this pay measured as a premium price? Or both? Which customers are having problems with our products? Why?

Today, the customer performance measurement system provides little to no objective information about changes in product or service characteristics and their financial impact on the company. Determining each customer's needs and the financial impact of meeting those needs are critical to organizations seeking world-class status. Production and engineering can continue to recommend investment in local improvements to save money, but continuous organizational improvement (more money now and in the future) is impossible unless throughput is improved.

Customer and Resource Linkage

The customer and resource linkage comprises information related to the competitive edges for each product and service provided to the market. The firm can compete on one or several of the nine competitive edges (price/cost, quality, lead time, delivery, product flexibility, process flexibility, field service, innovation, and product introduction responsiveness).

In Figures 4–2 through 4–4, the models for price/cost, quality, and lead time are depicted, respectively. This customer-resource link is used to compare customers' needs to resource capabilities. Marketing must determine customers' needs for products, prices, quality, lead time, and so on. Resource managers (from engineering, operations, and so forth) must determine resource capabilities to produce these products, along with the product's variable costs, quality levels, manufacturing and quoted lead times, and other specifications. In addition, marketing must determine the additional revenues that customers will provide either through increased volumes of sales or increased prices. The resource function must determine both the fixed and variable costs of this additional throughput. Two comparisons have to be made. First, can the resource function meet or exceed customers' needs and expectations on the competitive edge? If the answer is yes, then a financial comparison is required.

The financial comparison is quite simple. Do the additional revenues generated from this opportunity offset the variable costs and investment? If the answer is yes, then the investment is justified. If the answer is no, then further study might be required.

Price/cost as a competitive edge.   Let's examine the competitive edge of price/cost using the performance measurement model in Figure 4–2. Suppose that a firm has a product price/cost structure of 50 percent materials, 15 percent direct labor, 25 percent overhead (15 percent fixed and 10 percent variable) and a 10 percent product profit margin. The firm is currently working at only 70 percent capacity and does not want to lay off its skilled work force. A business slowdown (a recession) has lasted for the past two years, and no upturn is in sight. An offer is extended from a new foreign customer to place a one-time order for $700,000 worth of business. The normal customer order value is $1,000,000. Should the firm take the order? The firm has the capacity to make the order without disrupting current production. The variable cost of producing the order is 50 percent direct materials and 10 percent variable overhead. The 70 percent of the retail price ($700,000/ $1,000,000 × 100%) is greater than the 60 percent variable cost (50% + 10%), so the order should be accepted. Based on dollars, the firm is receiving throughput of $100,000 ($700,000 − $600,000) and no increase in operating expenses; therefore the contribution to fixed costs and profit for the organization is $100,000. The firm is $100,000 better off than not accepting the order. Recognize that this 70 percent of retail price is 10 percent below the product cost, excluding the 20 percent product profit, yet the organization still makes a profit.

Quality as a competitive edge.   Let's examine the competitive edge of quality using the model in Figure 4–3. Suppose that customers' expectations for quality are higher than current industry results. The quality *performance criterion* might be mean time between failures (MTBF). The customers' need establishes the *performance standard* at 2000 hours between failures. The resources capability currently provides products with an actual MTBF *performance measure* of 1600 hours.

FIGURE 4–2
Competitive Edge Performance Measurement System Model to Support Price/
Cost

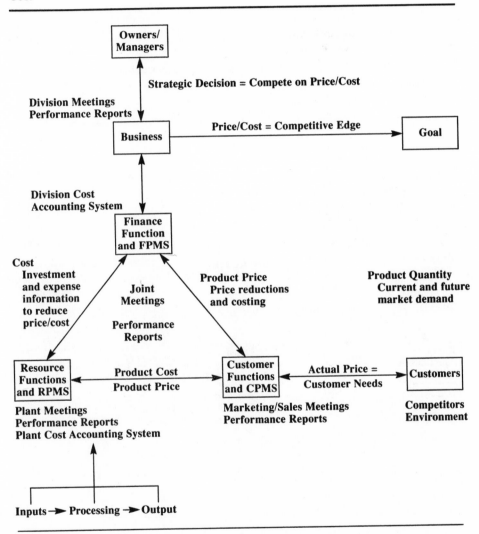

Marketing determines that if the firm can achieve the MTBF performance standard of 2000 hours, incremental revenue will increase by $600,000 per year (adjusted for the decrease in repair and replacement revenue). Engineering determines the incremental investment to be $100,000, with the addition of one worker at $30,000

FIGURE 4–3
Competitive Edge Performance Measurement System Model to Support Quality

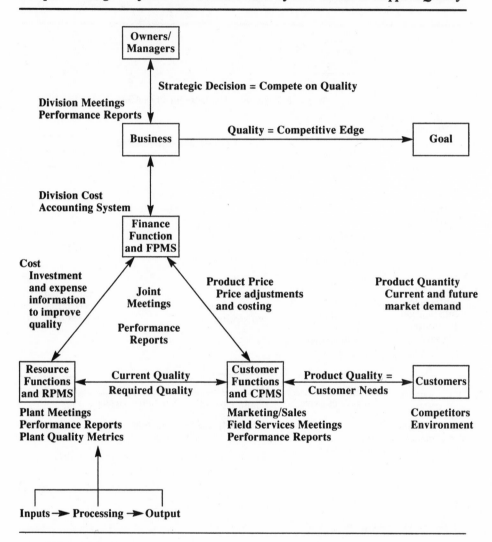

per year. Is this a good investment? Throughput increases by $600,000, investment by $100,000, and operating expenses by $30,000. By any scale, this is an attractive investment.

This investment opportunity may never have been discovered using TQM and the traditional management philosophy. Under the old philosophy, local improvement

FIGURE 4–4
*Competitive Edge Performance Measurement System Model to Support Lead
Time*

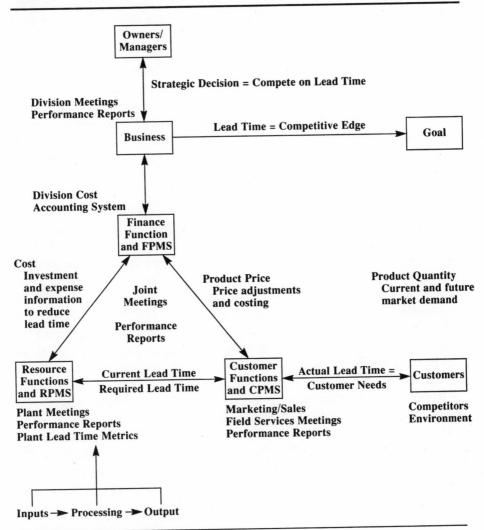

is equivalent to global improvement, and functional silos prevent resource and customer function linkages from occurring, so the organization's goal and satisfaction of
customers' needs cannot be achieved. TQM is an excellent management philosophy;
however, it lacks the performance measures and focusing power to identify true
improvement.

Remember—when you are improving on the competitive edges identified as critical by your customers, market share can increase significantly without a reduction in selling price. Conversely, you may sell your products at a premium without losing market share. This is the value of identifying what your customers really want in products or services.

Lead time as a competitive edge. Let's examine the lead time model in Figure 4–4. Suppose that you produce equipment with a quoted lead time of eight weeks, the industry average. You currently have a 15 percent market share. Your sales personnel identify lead time as a competitive edge. The competitive edge of lead time can be defined as the amount of time between customer's placing an order and customer's receiving the order. Your two biggest customers indicate that your firm would be the preferred vendor if quoted lead time was five weeks. This is the role of the *marketing function* and its customer performance measurement system. The *performance criterion* is lead time, the *performance standard* is five weeks, and your firm's current *performance measure* is eight weeks. If the standard is achieved, then annual sales to these two customers alone would increase by $1 million. What actions might be required to attain the competitive edge? To reduce the lead time competitive edge constraint, buffer management (discussed in a later chapter) must be implemented to identify constraints to lead time reductions. Once these lead time constraints are identified, appropriate JIT techniques (setup reduction, preventive maintenance, multiskilled workers, small lot production, and so on) can be applied to specific resources identified through buffer management. Throughput of $500,000 can be realized (throughput equals $1 million in sales minus $500,000 in materials). To increase throughput, the constraints must be identified and exploited. By using TOC to identify the constraint at the new production level, and by purchasing setup reduction equipment totaling $200,000 to reduce lead time, you can capture the additional market share and profit. If you used this equipment only for these two customers for these products, you would have a organizational profit of $300,000 ($500,000 − $200,000). This resource capability information is based on the resource performance measurement system, which is linked to the finance performance measurement system by valid TOC accounting information.

INFORMATION AND TECHNOLOGY

In this chapter we have detailed the linkages (information requirements) across the resource, customer, and finance functions and their performance measurement systems. Information requirements must support achievement of the organization's goal by meeting customers' needs and expectations and must support effective use of organizational resources. Supporting information and performance measurement systems must be in place in each function to schedule and control activities and monitor performance. In addition, communication across the functions is vital to the organization's survival. Functional activities must be coordinated for goal achievement. It is more important that information (not data) be shared between functions. Separate databases are favored in most environments. The *data* collected by each function are enormous in most companies today. The *information* required to make correct decisions, however, is minimal. Massive computer systems are probably not the solution to today's business problems. Selecting the right data for a decision is critical. This information is what must be shared across functions for decisions to be valid, reliable, and timely.

Computer technology between and among functions should be compatible. Remember that performance characteristics must be accumulated over time for control, for revising the schedule, and for making adjustments to the operational plan, tactical plan, and strategic plan. Aligning computer technology to support advanced information technology is a sufficient condition for achieving world-class organization and status. Determining the correct information to support organizational decision making is the necessary condition for success. Using advanced information technology to link the functions to support the information and performance measurement system requirements is a natural step in the evolution of improving organizational decision making. Determining the questions to be answered, the information required to answer these questions, the frequency of measurement and reporting of data to form information, and many other issues must be addressed in aligning linkages across the three functions for effective decision making.

Today, computer technology can effectively link the functions and control points within each function. The right information and measures must be provided first to ensure a process of continuous improvement—the subject of the next chapter.

Chapter Five

The Process of Continuous Improvement for World-Class Organizations

In the preceding two chapters, we discussed the three major functions, their supporting performance measurement systems, and the linkages among these functions that support effective decision making and goal achievement. In this chapter we will discuss our process of continuous improvement (briefly introduced in Chapter 1, Why Are You Losing the Battle with Global Competition?). It is reproduced in Table 5–1 for your convenience. In addition, we will use a simple Gedanken, which means *thinking* in German, exercise to demonstrate the synchronization of the functions, their performance measurement systems, and their linkages in achieving the organization's goal of making more money now and in the future.

THE CONTINUOUS IMPROVEMENT PROCESS

The process of continuous improvement represents a journey toward world-class organizational status. No firm will ever achieve and maintain this status without continually evaluating and reevaluating its situation for new opportunities. Our nine-step process is composed of three stages with three similar steps in each stage. At any step in any stage, you may be required to shift back to step 3 of the first stage and identify the new constraint to attaining your organization's goal and start the process again. Let's examine the complete process.

First, the goal of most businesses is to make more money now and in the future. Second, the model of the three performance measurement systems and their linkages have been discussed in the preceding two chapters. We gave definitions and examples of throughput (T), inventory (I) and operating expenses (OE), and these measures

TABLE 5–1
Process of Continuous Improvement for World-Class Organizations

---

Stage One

---

1. Identify the *goal (or goals)* of the organization.
2. Design a *comprehensive performance measurement system* that tells you when you're moving toward the goal.
3. Implement theory of constraints to *identify the current constraints* to moving toward the goal, implement appropriate actions, and measure constraint and goal results.

Stage Two

---

4. Identify the *competitive edge* for each product and market (price/cost, quality, lead time, and so on) that constrain your organization from reaching its goal through market growth.
5. Design a *comprehensive performance measurement system* that tells you when you are improving on the constraining competitive edge and its effects on profit.
6. Identify and implement *appropriate actions* at the competitive edge constraint and measure the effect of the actions on both the competitive edge and the organization's goal. In this step if the constraint is broken, go to step 3.

Stage Three

---

7. Identify functional *savings opportunities* that do not impede attainment of the goal.
8. Design a *functional cost measurement system* to determine the effect of local actions on the function and on the organization's goal and its competitive edge.
9. Identify and implement the *actions needed to reduce functional costs and measure the action,* its effects on local measures, and its impact on the competitive edge, and the organization's goal. In this step, if the constraint is broken, go to step 3.

---

provide the mechanism for measuring the effect of our decisions on the attainment of the organization's goal. All proposed local actions must be translated into their T, I, and OE components across all functions before a valid decision can be made. Third, the five focusing steps of theory of constraints discussed previously should be used to identify any physical constraint. In the case of policy constraints, other techniques such as the TOC current reality tree are quite helpful.[1] Once the constraint is identified, appropriate actions to effectively manage it have to be implemented. (These techniques are discussed in the next chapter.) The results must then be measured on the constraint and the goal.

At the second stage, the organization is in an equilibrium condition. The environment (customers, product mix, competitors actions, technology, regulations, and so forth) can change and require your response; alternatively, you might want to proactively seek your goal—to make more money. You might decide to elevate one of the marketing constraints by improving your product's price to some market segments, improving the product quality, or by reducing quoted product lead time to increase throughput.

In step 4 you have to identify what factors are important to your customers for each of your products and markets. Your focus should be on increasing market demand to increase profits. Is it price, quality, or lead time that is important in this market or to this customer? You might decide to segment a market based on this competitive edge. Can you charge different prices for the same product in different markets? Two key points are noted: (1) The price of the item in one market should not affect the price and quantity demanded in other markets; and (2) You should segment markets while trying not to segment resources. The objective is to segment markets to make more total profit for the firm by more effectively using existing resources. Remember—the customer function's new role in a world-class organization is to proactively seek new ways to satisfy customer needs to support the organization's goal. Buying additional resources and shifting resources significantly affect the existing constraint; shifting the organization's constraint should be a conscious decision. Its movement has significant consequences on all functions and performance measurement systems.

In step 5 a performance measurement system based on the selected competitive edge must be developed, tying resource capabilities to the customers' needs. The increased operating expenses and inventory (investment) in the resource function required to meet customers' needs must be compared to the increased throughput generated to determine movement toward the goal of making more money.

In step 6 the critical operations in the competitive edge constraint must be identified and appropriate actions to improve the operation must be determined. The effect of the actions must then be measured on the competitive edge and on your organization's profit.

Steps 7, 8, and 9 focus on saving the organization money, *not* on making money. Recognize that saving money is not the goal of an organization, although most managers focus almost entirely on this activity. Labor represents the primary avenue for cost reduction, yet labor (your employees) is the most valuable asset of the organization. Step 7 is to identify the functional costs that can be reduced without inhibiting progress toward the goal. This is true excess capacity within the system. This focus on cost reduction should take place only after the previous steps have been exhausted. In step 8, the design of a functional measurement system must be designed to ascertain the impact of the resource reduction, its cost saving, and its effect on the competitive edges and the organization's goal. Step 9 is the identification of the specific cost-saving actions, their implementation, measurement of the actions, and their effect on savings, competitive edges, and the organization's goal.

In the third stage, cost reduction activities are pursued. Stage one is the most important; in this stage you are identifying how to effectively organize and manage existing resources. The constraint is exploited to produce significant gains for the organization. TOC accounting is a requisite. In the second stage the competitive edges are exploited to increase market penetration with the goal of making more money. Again, TOC accounting is a requisite. Of least importance, but still representing significant potential, is the identification of cost reduction activities. Stage three seems an appropriate setting for the use of ABC accounting to determine cost drivers for potential savings. Remember—in today's environment product cost is a mirage. Do not allocate. There is a major difference between the definition of variable cost under ABC and economic theory. Stage three should be pursued only after the first two stages have been fully exploited for throughput opportunities.

EXAMPLES OF THE RPMS AND THE PROCESS OF CONTINUOUS IMPROVEMENT

Let's now use some simple Gedanken exercises to illustrate the use of our performance measurement system. These examples are similar to the P-Q exercise developed by Goldratt.[2]

Given: The NOP Company makes three products: A, B, and C. See Table 5-2 for details. NOP is a for-profit organization with the goal of making more money now and in the future. The customer function through marketing tells us the demand and selling price of each product. Product A sells for $60 per unit and has a market demand of 50 units per week; product B sells for $125 and has a market demand of 100 units per week; and product C sells for $100 per unit and has a market demand of 60 units per week. In the resource function, production, engineering, and purchasing provide operational requirements, the routing of parts to make products, the work standards, and the raw material costs.

Product A starts with raw material A', which is processed at work center (WC) Z for 10 minutes per unit, then at WC Y for 5 minutes per unit; product B starts with raw material B', which is processed at WC Z for 10 minutes per unit, at WC Y for 10 minutes, and then at WC X for 30 minutes; and product C starts with raw material C', which is processed at WC Z for 15 minutes per unit, at WC Y for 15 minutes, and at WC X for 20 minutes. Raw material A' is purchased at $40 per unit; raw material B' is purchased at $50 per unit; and raw material C' is purchased at $40

TABLE 5–2
Gedanken Exercise Information: NOP Company

Products	A	B	C
Price	$60	$125	$100
Demand (units/week)	50	100	60
		WC X 30 min./unit	WC X 20 min./unit
	WC Y 5 min./unit	WC Y 10 min./unit	WC Y 15 min./unit
	WC Z 10 min./unit	WC Z 10 min./unit	WC Z 15 min./unit
Raw material	A′	B′	C′
Cost	$40/unit	$50/unit	$40/unit

per unit. The finance performance measurement system provides the accounting data. The firm has $100,000 invested in equipment and buildings, and employs three workers (one at each WC) at $15 per hour for a 40-hour week (2400 minutes per week). Operating expenses total approximately $6,300 per week (including direct labor) based on an overhead rate of 250 percent of direct labor costs (overhead is $4,500 and direct labor is $1,800).

Exercise 1. Using traditional cost accounting, what products should the company make, how many of each product, and how much profit and return on investment will the company make?

Solution: Let's compute the profit margin of each product:

	Product		
	A	B	C
Price	$60	$125	$100
Direct labor minutes	15	50	50
Raw materials	$40.00	$ 50.00	$ 40.00
Direct labor	3.75	12.50	12.50
Overhead (250%)	9.38	31.25	31.25
Product cost	53.13	93.75	83.75
Product profit	$ 6.87	$ 31.25	$ 16.25
Rank	3	1	2

Based on product profit, the NOP company should make all of the product Bs possible, then Cs, then As. However, there is a large discrepancy in the labor content of A compared to B and C. Before we make a poor decision, let's examine our contribution per direct labor minute to determine what we should make:

	Product		
	A	B	C
Price	$60	$125	$100
Raw materials	40	50	40
contribution	$20	$ 75	$ 60
Direct labor minutes	15	50	50
Contribution per direct labor minute	$ 1.33	$ 1.50	$ 1.20
Rank	2	1	3

This analysis supports making product B first, but switches the ranking of products A and C, based on labor content. Let's check capacity to identify whether there is a priority problem based on what we can actually make:

	Product		
	A	B	C
Demand	50	100	60
WC X (min.)	0	30	20
Capacity required (min.)	0 +	3000 +	1200 = 4200
	(4200/2400 min. per week) × 100% = 175%		
WC Y (min.)	5	10	15
Capacity required (min.)	250 +	1000 +	900 = 2150
	(2150/2400 min. per week) × 100% = 90%		
WC Z (min.)	10	10	15
Capacity required (min.)	500 +	1000 +	900 = 2400
	(2400/2400 min. per week) × 100% = 100%		

We can now use our capacity calculations to conduct step one, identifying the constraint. WC X is the production system constraint. Looking back at our accounting calculations, B had the highest priority. Let's make as many Bs as we can to fully utilize WC X capacity.

Units of product B = (2400 min./week)/(30 min. of B/unit)

= 80 units/week

Demand is 100 units per week, compared to the 80 units per week we can produce. Product A does not require any of WC X; therefore, we should be able to meet the market demand for Product A in addition to the 80 units of B. There wasn't any priority conflict in reality because A didn't require any use of WC X. Let's check our capacity requirements for this product mix:

	Product	
	A	B
Make	50	80
WC X (mins)	0	2400 = 2400/2400 × 100% = 100%
WC Y (mins)	250	800 = 1050/2400 × 100% = 44%
WC Z (mins)	500	800 = 1300/2400 × 100% = 54%

This product mix is feasible. How much profit will NOP make?

	Product		
	A	B	
Price	$ 60	$ 125	
Raw materials	40	50	
Contribution	$ 20	$ 75	
Make	50	80	
Total contribution	$1000 +	$6000 =	$7000
Operating expenses			−6300
Profit per week			$ 700

Traditional cost accounting decision making based on product profit provides us with a company profit of $700 per week, or approximately $35,000 annually before taxes. ROI is 35 percent before taxes. Notice that we have identified the constraint to the production system, WC X, and are using it efficiently to 100 percent of its capacity. But are we using it effectively? We based our product mix decision on contribution per average direct labor minute in one method, and on product profit in the other method. The end result is identical. Notice that both methods assumed that all resources should be treated as equal. Are they? Or is WC X more important because it is a constraint?

Let's use our process of continuous improvement and TOC cost accounting measures (T, I, and OE) to check whether our decision is good. We have performed step one (identify the goal), step two (construct a performance measurement system), and the first element of the five focusing steps of TOC—identify the constraint. The second step in the five focusing steps is exploiting the constraint. We should examine the contribution per minute of the constraint, WC X, for making each product.

Product C's contribution is $3.00 per minute for the constraint, WC X, and product B's contribution is $2.50 per minute for using WC X. Therefore, to exploit the constraint, we should make product C, then product B. Let's check the capacity required for this ranking. WC X is the production system constraint. Let's make as many Cs as possible, and then use the remainder of WC X's capacity to make Bs. We should still be able to make our As. (Product A is a "free good" because it doesn't use the constraint resource WC X.)

| | *Product* | | |
	A	*B*	*C*
Price	$60	$125	$100
Raw materials	40	50	40
Throughput	$20	$ 75	$ 60
WC X (min.)	0	30	20
Throughput/WC X	—	$ 2.50	$ 3.00
Rank	1	2	1

Units of C = 2400 min. available/20 min. of WC X per C = 120 C's

We can make 120 Cs, but weekly demand is only 60 units.

Capacity required for Cs = 60 units × 20 min. per C = 1200 min.
2400 min. available − 1200 min. required = 1200 min.
1200 min./30 min. per B = 40 Bs.

Our desired product mix is 50 As, 40 Bs, and 60 Cs. Let's check our capacity calculations:

| | *Product* | | |
	A	*B*	*C*
Demand	50	40	60
WC X (min.)	0 +	1200 +	1200 =
	(2400/2400 × 100% = 100%		
WC Y (min.)	250 +	400 +	900 =
	(1550/2400 × 100% = 64%		
WC Z (min.)	500 +	400 +	900 =
	(1800/2400 × 100% = 75%		

This product mix is feasible. How much profit will NOP make?

		Product	
	A	B	C
Price	$ 60	$ 125	$100
Raw materials	40	50	40
Throughput	$ 20	$ 75	$ 60
Make	50	40	60
Total throughput	$1000 +	$3000 +	$3600 = $7600
Operating expenses			−6300
Profit per week			$1300

Making the decision using TOC accounting provides us with a profit of $1,300 per week, or approximately $65,000 annually before taxes (compared to $35,000 using traditional accounting) and a 65 percent rate of return (compared to 35 percent using traditional accounting). Step two, exploiting the use of the constraint, has almost doubled NOP's profit.

What if we tried to fully utilize the worker at WC Z (giving this worker 100 percent efficiency) to meet customer demand for products A, B, and C? In fact we could have WC Z perform its operations on 50, 100, and 60 units of raw materials A', B', and C', respectively. What is the effect on the organization from fully utilizing WC Z? WC Z processes 50 units of raw material A', 100 units of raw material B', and 60 units of raw material C'. WC Y can process each of the batches, and its utilization increases significantly. But what happens now? The materials will be stuck in the production system. WC Z can process only 40 units of B and 60 units of C. If we continue to overproduce at WCs X and Y, then we flood the system with excessive WIP and may reduce the responsiveness of the system to actual demand; cause the wrong product mix to be made; cause poor quality; and increase lead times for products actually demanded. So how much should WC Z be utilized? WC Z should be used only enough to support throughput. WC Z should be subordinated to the constraint's pace (step three). That is, WC Z should make 50 As, 40 Bs, and 60 Cs for a utilization of 52 percent. Less utilization reduces throughput, and more utilization increases inventory.

Let's review our example with respect to our performance measurement model before continuing. Marketing estimated weekly demand to be 50 As, 100 Bs, and 60 Cs at the current prices of $60, $125, and $100, respectively. This information is required of the CPMS. Given the market demand information, NOP can identify its constraints by comparing capacity available to capacity required for each WC. The capacity (operation, time, and routing) information and raw material and its cost requirements are part of the RPMS. Next, NOP exploits the constraint, WC X, to maximize profit. Cost accounting information is used in the FPMS to determine profit. Costs are divided into fixed and variable based on their relationship to product volume. Does the use of raw material A' increase when we make just one more unit of product A? Yes, by $40—the price of one unit of A'. This variable cost is subtracted from the selling price of product A in determining throughput. Did direct labor increase at WCs X, Y, and Z just by making one more unit of product A? No, no additional workers were hired, nor was overtime used. If the cost remains fixed over a relatively large change in output, then the cost is considered operating expense. Remember—if the cost increases or decreases with a one-unit increase or decrease in output, then the cost is considered variable and is subtracted from the selling price to determine throughput. Raw material, commissions, and sometimes transportation costs can be considered variable in many companies. If the expense is fixed for the time period considered, then it is classified as operating expense. Let's now continue to see how to use our performance measurement system model.

Exercise 2. Let's examine the most common "improvement" of saving money. This opportunity frequently occurs in the resource function. Suppose an engineer proposes that the processing times on WC Z can be cut by 40 percent if a fixture is purchased for $4,000. This 40 percent savings amounts to four minutes per unit for products A and B and six minutes per unit for product C. Using traditional cost accounting, several answers are possible based on various assumptions. By applying the 40 percent savings to the 40-hour week, the direct savings can be roughly estimated:

Direct labor savings = 40% × 40 hours × $15/hour = $240/week

Annual savings = $240/week × 50 weeks = $12,000/year

A conservative estimate might be based on actual usage:

Actual usage = (50 A's × 4 min./unit) + (80 B's × 4 min./unit)

= 200 min. + 320 min. = 520 min. or 8.67 hours

Weekly savings = 8.67 hours × $15/hour = $100/week

Annual savings = $100/week × 50 weeks = $5,000/year

What about overhead of 250 percent? The total annual savings would be $42,000 in the first case ($30,000 in overhead and $12,000 in direct labor), and $17,500 in the second case ($12,500 in overhead and $5,000 in direct labor). By any traditional measure, $5,000 annual savings in direct labor to $42,000 annual savings based on direct labor and overhead is considered an excellent investment. But is it really?

What are the true benefits and costs? Is WC Z the constraint? No. Did throughput increase by purchasing the equipment? No. Did the fixture reduce operating expense?

No, NOP company could not lay off a worker by investing in the equipment. Overhead wasn't reduced either. Was inventory reduced? No, in fact inventory increased by $4,000 (up to $104,000) with the purchase of the equipment. So what looked to be an excellent investment to save money actually cost the company money. How many equipment investments that show substantial savings using traditional accounting methods actually cost your company money? Don't answer, please; it may be quite painful.

Exercise 3. Let's again look at a local "improvement" in the resource function, but we will examine its effect on customers. Suppose another engineer proposes the purchase of a fixture that provides a 20 percent reduction in processing time for WC X. The fixture costs $50,000. This 20 percent savings amounts to no savings on product A, 6 minutes per unit on product B, and 4 minutes per unit on product C. Using traditional cost accounting, several answers are possible based on the assumptions. By applying the 20 percent direct labor savings to 40 hours per week, or by examining the actual usage, the savings can be roughly estimated:

Direct labor savings = 20% reduction × 40 hours/week × $15/hour

= $120/week

Annual savings   = $120/week × 50 weeks = $6,000/year

Applying the overhead rate of 250 percent provides an annual savings of $21,000 ($15,000 in overhead and $6,000 in direct labor). But is this a good investment— a savings of $6,000 to $21,000 annually for an investment of $50,000? Your organization would probably reject this proposal. Let me ask you this question: Can you lay off a worker in one WC for one day a week? Can you reduce your overhead based on this labor savings? The answer is probably no to both questions. If you thought about investing in this "improvement," do you still want to do so? Probably not, based on traditional cost accounting!

Let's see what TOC would provide as a solution. Is WC X the constraint? Yes. Can throughput increase if we purchase the fixture? Yes.

	Product		
	A	B	C
Time savings	0 +	40 × 6 min. +	60 × 4 min. =
	0 +	240 min. +	240 min. = 480 mins
	480 min./24 min. for B = 20 additional B's.		
Additional profit per week = 20 B's × $75		= $1,500/week	
Additional annual profit = $1500 × 50 weeks		= $75,000/year	

What an increase in throughput, $75,000 per year! Did operating expense increase?

Let's see what happened in WCs Y and Z:

	Product		
	A	*B*	*C*
Make	50	60	60
WC X (mins.)	50(0)	+ 60(24)	+ 60(16) =
	2400/2400 × 100% = 100%		
WC Y (mins.)	50(5)	+ 60(10)	+ 60(15) =
	1750/2400 × 100% = 73%		
WC Z (mins.)	50(10)	+ 60(10)	+ 60(15) =
	2000/2400 × 100% = 83%		

No additional workers or resources are needed to support the new throughput level; therefore, operating expenses remain the same—$6,300 per week. What about inventory (investment)? Inventory has increased by $50,000, and profit has increased by $75,000 per year. This investment gives us an incremental ROI of 150 percent. Is there a benefit in focusing on improving the constraint? Definitely! This example illustrates step 4, elevating the constraint.

Now let's examine the resource and customer linkage. What should production tell marketing to sell? Could the NOP company make more money by selling more B's? Maybe. It cannot currently meet the weekly demand for B. Is overtime an option? Overtime at time and a half costs $22.50 per hour, and the worker can produce 2.5 units per hour. This is an increase in throughput of $187.50 per hour of WC X for an increase in operating expenses of $22.50. Profit per hour is $165.50. If we worked an additional four hours per week, the additional profit would be $660 ($750 − $90). WCs Y and Z would not have to work any overtime to support this production level.

What can we learn from these exercises? The customer, resource, and finance functions and their performance measurement systems must be linked together to make effective local decisions that move a firm toward its goal. Market demand for products and resource capabilities for making these products must be compared to identify the constraint to goal achievement. Once in equilibrium, what should the customer and resource functions do? Look back at the TOC solution to Exercise 1. The market demand is 50 As, 100 Bs, and 60 Cs. We can make 50 As, 40 Bs, and 60 Cs. WC X is the resource constraint. By linking the customer and resource functions, we can identify options to moving toward the goal of making more money:

Can we sell more Cs at the same price of $100?

Can we segment the market for Cs and sell the 60 Cs at the current price of $100 and additional Cs for more than $90 each? (Less than the $90 price makes producing B more attractive).

We are able to manufacture only 40 Bs, but the demand is 100 units at a price of $125 per unit. Can we increase our price for B to bring demand closer to our production capabilities?

We have excess capacity at WC Y and Z. Can we sell more As at a lower price without reducing total revenue from As? Can we segment the market for As by selling the 40 for the current price of $60, and any additional units for any amount greater than $40? (Don't promise too many As without checking capacity, however, as you might create a new constraint.)

What can the resource function do to improve profitability? The primary focus should be on improving the efficiency of WC X. Analysis should be based on throughput increases for the constraint. Can marketing sell more products with the additional resource capabilities of WC X?

Any change in the resource or customer function of the firm must be evaluated using the resource, customer, and finance performance measurement systems and their linkages to ascertain the true financial impact on the organization as a whole. Too many local improvements translate into real costs to the organization, and too many opportunities are lost based on local cost analyses. Performance measurement system linkages are critical to effective decision making.

THE PERFORMANCE GAP

In Chapter 1 Why Are You Losing the Battle with Global Competition?, we say how the desired results and actual results of actions often diverge. Furthermore, throughout the Gedanken exercise on the NOP company, we encountered conflicting results between traditional accounting and TOC accounting. You should now recognize why this happened. The reason for this divergence is threefold. First, traditional business decision analysis is usually focused on cost savings instead of profitability. Second, traditional business decision analysis does not recognize the effect of constraints on a system. Third, traditional business analysis does not distinguish between true variable costs and fixed costs. The result is a performance gap. This gap represents the distance between the anticipated and actual results of a decision. In many firms, the cause of the gap is never even recognized. Because of the use of localized, disjointed performance measurement systems, companies often believe that their resources are being well managed, although no improvements in profitability, market share, or other global performance metrics have been realized. This disparity is usually explained by blaming external forces beyond the firm's control: economic downturns, competitors' actions, customers' preference changes, trade restrictions, government policies, and so forth. Although such forces do have a legitimate effect on your organization's performance, more often than not the gap between desired and actual results is caused by using traditional business analysis.

In Figure 5-1 a comparison of the savings using traditional business analysis and the income using TOC accounting is provided. Traditional analysis assumes independent resources and overestimates savings based on direct labor costs (it assumes too much variable cost). TOC accounting measures of T, I, and OE identify the true impact on the bottom line. Significant income potential exists at the system constraint, whereas other "improvement" actions have little or no effect on current income. This is the cause of the performance gap.

INSTITUTING THE NECESSARY CHANGES

After illogical decisions, actions, and behaviors are discovered, and the root causes established, what changes are required, and how can these changes be instituted? Three actions are needed for enacting the necessary changes.

1. Adopt the process of continuous improvement for achieving world-class organizational status; that is, develop an integrated view of the firm.
2. Create a cohesive performance measurement system.
3. Instill an organizational culture conducive to continual improvement.

It is extremely important for all employees to think about how their decisions, actions, and behaviors affect the entire organization. This is especially true for managers and other decision makers. The adoption of an integrated view of the organization provides the proper context for using the process of continuous improvement for making decisions, invoking actions, and reinforcing behaviors that foster effective resource management. Such an integrated view does not occur overnight and certainly involves the firm's education and investment in people. Employees must be educated in effect-cause-effect thought processes and tools. They must be given the necessary skills for understanding and assessing the effect of their decisions on not just their departments or facilities, but on the entire firm. Furthermore, companies must be willing to invest in the development of their human capital. Cross-functional assignments provide an excellent mechanism for reinforcing organizational interdependencies and supplying the necessary breadth of experience for integrative resource management. Multifunctional teams foster integrative decision-making processes within firms.

An integrated view of the firm also requires an integrated performance measurement system. As demonstrated earlier, finance, resource, and customer performance measurement systems must be synchronized to determine the effect of actions by one

FIGURE 5–1
A Comparison of Savings and Income Impact for Selected Actions

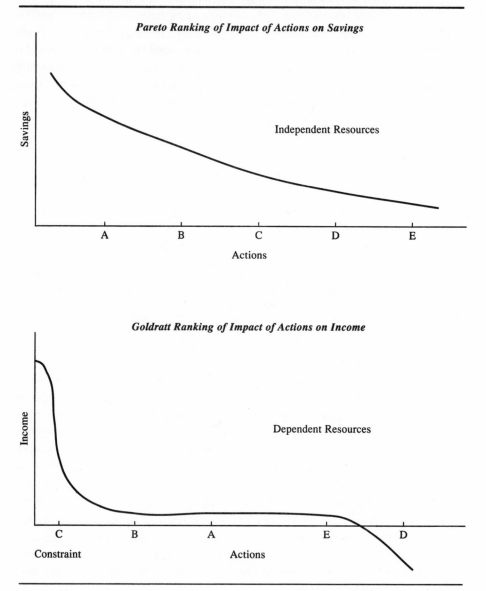

Pareto Ranking of Impact of Actions on Savings

Savings

Independent Resources

A   B   C   D   E

Actions

Goldratt Ranking of Impact of Actions on Income

Income

Dependent Resources

C   B   A   E   D

Constraint   Actions

function on the other functions and on the organization's goal. This is effective integrated resource management. It is impossible to support a holistic approach to managerial decisions, organizational actions, and employee behavior without a synchronized approach to assessing company performance. Performance metrics linked across the functions are needed for the intelligent employment of organizational resources. Integrated performance measurement systems supply decision makers with the proper information for making holistic decisions resulting in appropriate actions, positive behaviors, and effective resource utilization.

The term *corporate culture* describes the rules, norms, and expectations of an organization with regard to its employees' behavior. When organizations experience either internal or external pressures to deviate from their underlying principles, corporate culture provides a set of common values that guide decisions and actions on shared goals. Corporate culture helps to achieve focus by providing a framework for assessing a given action in relation to the firm's goal. Successful integrative resource management requires a culture that promotes global, not local, optimization; one that uses organizational resources to support company, not functional and personal goals; one that strives to continually improve resource effectiveness in attaining the company goal; and one that encourages the questioning of accepted organizational practices and procedures.

THE IMPORTANCE OF INTEGRATION

In most US manufacturing organizations, each of the three functions via its performance measurement system attempts to optimize its criteria without regard to either of the other two functions. Few organizations have their measurement systems linked together to reflect the effect of actions in one function on the other functions. Changes in resource use, product offerings, and finances are currently initiated by managers in any of the three functions without regard to the effect on the other functions and on the firm's goals. The effect of any change, however, is felt by all functions, and any change influences the measures in all functions' performance measurement systems.

Traditional performance measurement systems must be realigned to synchronize measures in a function with other measures within that function and with measures in the other functions. Once the correct measures are in place, the impact of realigning performance measurement systems is to synchronize actions in a function to support the achievement of the organization's goal.

Our system model links the proposed changes in resource use to the incremental changes in throughput, inventory, and operating expenses through the TOC accounting system. In addition, the proposed changes in resource use are passed on to the customer function to ascertain improvement on a competitive edge. The customer function must assess the impact on the customers' needs. Will the customer now pay a higher price for the product without a decrease in demand? Does the total revenue for the company increase because of the change? How much does revenue increase? This information is passed through the finance-customer linkage to top management. With the accounting information from the CPMS concerning the change in revenue created by the proposal, top management can determine whether the proposal moves the company closer to its goal of making more money.

What of marketing opportunities? These opportunities must be translated into resource and material requirements. Constraining resources must be identified and exploited. The TOC accounting and resource information must be transmitted through both the customer and finance performance measurement systems for review and analysis.

SUMMARY

In this chapter we discussed the three stages in our process of continuous improvement. We then illustrated how decisions were distorted by using traditional cost accounting methods. We also showed you how to use theory of constraints performance criteria to make valid decisions. We demonstrated the importance of knowing whether improvement was made to a constraint or a nonconstraint. We also demonstrated how changes in different functions should be linked to capabilities in other functions to increase an organization's profitability. Synchronization of resource capabilities with customers' needs is essential to achieving competitiveness. We next illustrated why most improvement projects fail to generate the projected savings and real profit. We ended the chapter with a discussion of the importance of integrated performance measurement systems to provide vital information for decision making.

In the next chapter we will examine actions useful in achieving bottom-line results. We will briefly describe the elements of the just-in-time, total quality management, and theory of constraints philosophies. Then we will discuss how to merge these philosophies to identify specific actions to support world-class organizational development.

Chapter Six

Actions to Achieve Bottom-Line Results

To achieve manufacturing excellence and improve bottom-line performance, firms increasingly need to adopt new management philosophies. Just changing your performance measurement system will not move your firm to world-class organizational status. You can attain any of the competitive edges by using the traditional management philosophy. But what is the cost? It may be astronomical. For example, to have short quoted lead times to customers, the traditional management approach suggests carrying large quantities of finished goods. Why? In traditional thought, inventory is used as a buffer between production and customer orders. The inventory investment could be quite large, in addition to the increases in operating expenses to manage the inventory. This traditional logic certainly clashes with the fundamental logic of the JIT philosophy—matching production requirements to daily demand.[1] The traditional management philosophy addresses the problem by investing in inventory, and the JIT philosophy addresses the problem by making the resource function responsive to customers' needs.

What of making quality products? The traditional philosophy assumes functional specialization, that workers make products and that inspectors weed out defective products. Many defects still get through the final inspection process to the customers. The traditional management logic certainly clashes with the logic of the TQM philosophy—that workers are responsible for quality and that they eliminate the source of defects.[2] The traditional management philosophy addresses the problem through quality inspections, and the TQM philosophy addresses the problem through the prevention of defects.

What about product costs? The traditional philosophy assumes that all workers must be kept busy and that large batches of parts and products must be made to reduce product costs. Why? In traditional thinking, product costs provide the basis for calculating product price. Many extra parts and products are therefore made to keep workers busy—to reduce costs. Finished goods inventory is considered an asset. Many of these items sit in warehouses until obsolescence, thus raising product costs.

The traditional management logic certainly clashes with the theory of constraints (TOC) philosophy—that finished goods inventory should protect the customer, but only to the extent justified to support throughput.[3]

The traditional management philosophy is based on the specialization of labor in all organizational functions and levels. The assumption is that increased efficiencies, lower costs, and so on can be gained through specialization. Plans, responsibilities, processes, and measures are viewed functionally. Actions taken in one function are assumed to be independent of other functions. Processes are designed to make the function efficient without regard to its relationship to the processes of other functions. We have found, based on global competition, that locally determining each function's processes so that it is functionally efficient does not translate into an effective business process.[4] In addition, performance measures must also be changed in accordance to the reengineered processes. Redesigning processes without considering the effect on performance measurement will not result in business improvements. In most cases, it will have a negative effect on the business.[5]

We do not want to waste your time by again discussing the shortcomings of traditional management, or by providing a lengthy discussion on how to structure business processes. A first step in improving organizations is provided by our process of continuous improvement in Tables 1-3 and 5-1. Recognize that traditional management focuses on level 3, saving money at the expense of levels 1 and 2. Business processes must be designed to support making money through a clear understanding of the organization's goal, its competitive edges, and its supporting performance measurement systems. Only then, with an understanding of which business processes support the goal and competitive edges and where the constraints lie, can an effective business process be engineered.[6]

This chapter begins with a discussion of the JIT philosophy, techniques comprising the philosophy, and shortcomings associated with the philosophy. A similar presentation is provided for the TQM and TOC philosophies. The chapter ends with a discussion of how the three philosophies can be used simultaneously to achieve bottom-line results.

Numerous books have been written on both the JIT philosophy and its techniques to support world-class manufacturers. Similarly, many books have been written on the approaches to TQM and the statistical tools supporting product and process improvement. For this reason, we will only briefly review these philosophies and their supporting techniques. The TOC philosophy developed by Eliyahu M Goldratt has been less publicized. Therefore, we will discuss its techniques in more detail. We will focus on what are called the *logistics* and *cost world–throughput world paradigms*. We will not discuss the TOC thinking process, which is quite useful in identifying policy constraints but beyond the scope of this book.

THE JUST-IN-TIME PHILOSOPHY

The evolution of JIT in US manufacturing has moved from an inventory control mechanism to a philosophy focused on the elimination of "waste" from all aspects of the business.[7] Celley et al. trace its roots to the efforts of Japanese industrial managers during the 1950s.[8] These managers were assessing the strengths in their emerging postwar industrial system that could provide a foundation for successful worldwide competition. After assessing their strengths, they developed a manufacturing base composed of mature, high-volume, price-sensitive products assembled from purchased parts and components. To meet growing international price competition, both manufacturing and marketing costs had to be reduced on a continual basis. Materials procurement and inventory management then became a focus point for major cost reduction efforts. Thus, the concept of JIT was born.

During its introduction in the United States, JIT was primarily viewed as a new method of inventory control.[9] The definition of JIT has broadened significantly since its adoption in North America in 1980. One of the most widely accepted descriptions of JIT today was presented in a book by Schonberger.[10] He states that the goal of JIT manufacturing is as follows:

> [To] produce and deliver finished goods just in time to be sold, subassemblies **just in time** to be assembled into finished goods, fabricated parts **just in time** to go into subassemblies, and purchased materials **just in time** to be transformed into fabricated parts.

JIT has evolved into an organizational philosophy by which *muda* (Japanese for *waste*) and *mura* (Japanese for *unevenness*) are to be eliminated in all facets of the organization.[11] In a manufacturing firm, each functional area has an important role to play in the support of JIT through the continual elimination of waste and unevenness. Even in nonmanufacturing organizations, application of these concepts can achieve competitive advantages. Given the breadth of JIT applications to industry, a description of its elements is essential.

JIT Manufacturing Techniques

JIT manufacturing techniques also have evolved. Schonberger suggests that JIT is composed of five key ingredients:[12]

1. An inventory control system.
2. Quality and scrap control.
3. A streamlined plant configuration.

4. A production line balancing approach.
5. An employee involvement and motivational mechanism.

Lee and Ebrahimpour state that the components comprising the JIT production system are production smoothing, multifunctional workers, standardization of jobs, and the *kanban* system of inventory control.[13] (Kanbans are cards or other objects used to signal material requirements to preceding operations.) Today, 12 specific JIT techniques have been identified and implemented to various degrees in American manufacturing organizations[14]:

1. Pull method of production (Kanban).
2. Statistical process control.
3. Preventive maintenance.
4. Multiskilled workers.
5. Level scheduling.
6. Setup time reduction.
7. Revised plant layout.
8. Reduced lot sizes.
9. Supplier involvement.
10. Workplace organization.
11. Small-group improvement activities.
12. Management commitment.

Let's briefly review each technique.

Pull method of production. The pull method of production was developed by Toyota Motor Corporation as part of the Toyota production system.[15] Unlike the traditional production philosophy, a subsequent process withdraws parts and other materials from the preceding process as required. Because only final assembly workers can accurately know the necessary timing and quantity of parts required, the final assembly workers begin the "pull" by obtaining the necessary parts and materials from the preceding process. The preceding process then produces the parts withdrawn by the subsequent process. Each part-producing process withdraws the necessary parts or materials from preceding processes further down the line. This pull method results in the elimination of excess WIP, shortening of lead time, minimization of finished goods inventory, and adaptability to changes in demand.[16]

Statistical process control. The origins of statistical process control (SPC) and variability reduction began in the 1920s with Dr. Walter Shewhart of Bell Laboratories. It has been expanded through the work of W Edwards Deming, J A Juran, Armand Feigenbaum, and Genichi Taguchi. SPC is a tool used to measure the variability of a process and determine its capability to produce a particular part.

However, it is important to note that SPC is only a tool to monitor the process and identify special causes of variation, such as tool wear, bad materials, or poor methods. It is not capable by itself of reducing the natural variation inherent within the process.[17]

Preventive maintenance.   Preventive maintenance is the periodic inspection of equipment to identify conditions that may result in machine breakdowns, production stoppages, or other losses. Preventive maintenance allows for the rapid detection and treatment of equipment abnormalities before they cause defects or scrap.[18]

Preventive maintenance consists of two basic activities: periodic inspection and planned replacement of worn parts and components based on the results of the inspection. Daily routine maintenance is also considered a part of a preventive maintenance program.[19]

Multiskilled workers.   *Shojinka* is defined by the Japanese as designing flexibility in the number of workers required at a work station to adapt output to demand changes. Shojinka facilitates maintaining productivity by adjusting and rescheduling workers to support output changes. Three prerequisites must be satisfied to achieve the Shojinka concept: proper design of machinery layout, multiskilled workers, and continuous evaluation and periodic revisions of operating procedures.[20]

U-shaped layouts support the expansion or contraction of the range of job elements for each worker. A job rotation system can be used to develop multiskilled workers over time. Finally, continuous improvement efforts, such as quality circles and small-group improvement activities are used to evaluate current work methods.[21]

Level scheduling.   Changes in demand, product variety, and volume are difficult to cope with in manufacturing environments. The JIT solution is to use level scheduling. In using a level scheduling approach, different products are produced in a mixed fashion with a constant volume over a fixed period of time. Matching production to demand results in lower finished goods inventory, shorter production lead time, and easier fine tuning of production to product mix changes.[22]

Setup time reduction.   Setup reduction is at the heart of the JIT philosophy. Firms can simultaneously increase capacity and productivity and reduce costs. Capacity increases result from the ability to changeover equipment in minutes (or seconds) versus hours (or days). Rapid changeover capability increases overall flexibility, resulting in productivity gains. Other benefits include reduced queue time, reduced inventory levels, smaller lot sizes, and fewer shortages or stockouts.[23]

Revised plant layout.   The first step in revising a plant layout to support JIT is to rearrange the equipment used to machine and finish each family of manufactured items into a new layout called a *cell*. Most traditional layouts locate the machines, processes, and workbenches by function in widely separated areas of the factory. This necessitates moving parts great distances between operations. Cells can be arranged to allow operators to run multiple machines.[24] The results are increased productivity, improved quality, reduced manufacturing floor space requirements, and reduced lead times.

Reduced lot sizes.   According to the concept of economic order quantities (EOQs), labor costs per unit gradually decrease as lot size rises. On the other hand, large lots are accompanied by rising inventory carrying costs. If these costs were plotted, the sum of the two costs would provide the total cost curve. The EOQ would occur at the minimum point on the curve. This concept contains a fundamental flaw: It assumes that set up time is fixed. Dramatic setup time reductions as demonstrated by many Japanese manufacturers (particularly Toyota) allow for substantial decreases in lot size. Cost savings guided by the EOQ concept are superficial.[25] The strategy of lot size reduction results in the elimination of excess WIP, excess finished goods inventory, and long production runs.

Supplier involvement.   Purchasing's responsibilities have increased over the past several years because of significant changes in the business environment, such as raw material shortages, long lead times, inflation, and a decline in quality and productivity.[26]

JIT environments demand consistently high-quality purchased parts. Therefore, supplier involvement is essential to the successful implementation of JIT. Supplier involvement activities include, but are not limited to, frequent delivery of small lots, vendor certification activities, long-term relationship-building activities, and overall support of the customer's JIT effort. Thus, a new purchasing philosophy is needed for the supplier as well as the buyer of materials.[27]

Workplace organization.   U-shaped, cellular layouts are often used in JIT environments. The workplace is transformed into a collection of cells composed of workstations and machines processing families of parts that follow similar flow paths. The following advantages are associated with the use of U-shaped layouts:[28]

1. Increased flexibility and balance.
2. Better teamwork.
3. Increased quality awareness.
4. Better material flow.
5. Simpler material and tool handling.

Small group improvement activities.   Small-group improvement activities (SGIAs) are most effective when conducted by people who work across departments with common objectives linked to the business goals. The result is a natural team that will far surpass the results of individual efforts or the reactive efforts of unfocused teams. These SGIAs can focus on ways to systematically reduce scrap and rework, cycle time, inventory, and other sources of waste. The SGIAs can also improve production processes. Thus, continuous improvement can be achieved in the firm.[29]

Management commitment.   The implementation of JIT requires a cultural change. Corporate leaders must create the organization's culture. An organization's culture will determine the success or failure of any change effort. Management must be committed to creating a continuous improvement ethic throughout the organization. Furthermore, management must be consistent. True commitment surfaces during difficult times, not prosperous times. During both good times and bad, management must be consistent in the implementation of the elements of JIT.[30]

Shortcomings of JIT

Many US firms have reaped tremendous benefits from the adoption of the JIT philosophy. However, many firms have also failed to develop a competitive advantage via JIT. Umble and Srikanth identified four primary shortcomings of the JIT approach:[31]

1. Pull production methods using kanbans are not applicable to all manufacturing environments.
2. Product flow disruptions in kanban environments are catastrophic to the firm's ability to meet customers' delivery expectations.
3. Implementations are often lengthy and difficult.
4. Continuous improvement efforts are systemwide and do not differentiate between constraint and nonconstraint resources.

Kanban limitations.   Pull production using kanbans is limited to manufacturing environments producing a relatively high volume of standardized products or components. The identification of product families that use common components has helped many job-oriented firms to emulate high-volume component production through the use of manufacturing cells. However, this has not been true for all job shop environments. Furthermore, continuous-flow operations (for instance, oil refineries, chemical processing, and so forth) are not suited for the current kanban methodology. Continuous-flow operations are generally capital intensive and are designed to produce products in large batches. In addition, finished goods are not produced in discrete units. It is therefore infeasible to constantly switch from product to product as practiced in JIT environments.

Product flow disruptions.   When a disruption occurs at a workstation in a kanban operation, the product flow of the entire manufacturing system is threatened. Because each workstation is linked via kanbans, as existing kanbans are depleted, those stations downstream from the disruption will no longer receive material and will not be able to produce. Stations upstream from the disruption will also stop working, as kanbans to replenish materials will cease. Thus, the production system stops until the disruption is corrected. During this time, throughput is lost, the production schedule is being missed, and customer shipments can be jeopardized.

JIT implementation difficulties.   Adopting the JIT philosophy requires significant changes to the cultural and manufacturing environments of the company. Resistance to change is a common occurrence when cultural changes are initially introduced. The time required to overcome such resistance will vary, but several years would not be extraordinary. As the manufacturing environment undergoes the necessary transformations for the JIT conversion (such as setup time reductions, quality control improvements, and workforce education and training), disruptions to normal operations must be tolerated. Both patience and persistence are required for a successful JIT implementation. If the firm does not embrace a long-term view of JIT implementation, failure is guaranteed.

Another major implementation difficulty is answering the questions: Where do we begin in the manufacturing process? Should we start with a simple pilot program so that we can develop a series of successes? What about beginning with a limited number of product families? Does it make sense to simultaneously convert the entire manufacturing facility? After the issues have been resolved, the firm must begin to involve suppliers and distributors. Which suppliers and distributors should we begin with and to what degree? Do we have the necessary resources for assisting their JIT efforts? How much time should be allowed for their conversion to JIT principles? All these questions add to the complexity of a JIT implementation.

Unfocused continuous improvement.   A major weakness of the JIT philosophy is its inability to distinguish between constraint and nonconstraint resources for effective continual improvement. The usual approach for determining where to improve the process is to wait until a problem occurs. This reactionary approach does not ensure that the organization's resources are being used in the most effective manner. In a JIT environment, it is unknown whether the improvements result in a local or global optimum. Hence, a company may find that it is expending capital on continually improving nonconstraint resources to the detriment of the entire system.

A second major weakness of JIT is the "shotgun approach" used in directing process improvement efforts. When proactive measures are taken to improve the process, they are done everywhere. Setup reduction programs, statistical process control efforts, total productive maintenance, and multiskilled worker training are done without regard to the types of resources involved. Again, the inability to distinguish between resources that govern the firm's ability to achieve its goal cause JIT implementations to actually waste organizational resources.

THE TOTAL QUALITY MANAGEMENT PHILOSOPHY

The basis for the concept of total quality management (TQM) was articulated by Armand Feigenbaum in describing the principles of total quality control: "To provide genuine effectiveness, total quality control must start with the design of the product and end only when the product has been placed in the hands of a customer who remains satisfied."[32] Joseph Juran is credited for the development of modern-day TQM principles, which include a cross-functional approach to the management of quality. Others, such as W Edwards Deming and Philip Crosby, have also made significant contributions to the TQM philosophy.

Three Approaches to Quality Management

Juran's Approach. Juran defines *quality* as "fitness for use." Juran's approach to quality management centers on three primary activities: quality control, quality improvement, and strategic quality planning.

Quality control systems must be able to address both intermittent and persistent problems for continual quality improvement. Intermittent quality problems are associated with assignable causes detectable through the use of such tools as fishbone diagrams, Pareto analysis, and statistical process control. Persistent quality problems are associated with the inherent or natural variability of the production process and require detailed process analysis, a careful diagnosis of the causes, and an application of permanent solutions.[33]

Three elements are needed in organizations to make progress toward quality improvement: upper management leadership, annual improvement programs, and massive training programs. Juran believes less than 20 percent of quality problems are due to workers with the remainder caused by management. Therefore, all managers must be trained in quality and participate in quality improvement projects. A summary of Juran's ten steps to quality improvement is provided below:[34]

1. Build awareness of the need and opportunity for improvement.
2. Set goals for improvement.
3. Organize to reach the goals.
4. Provide training.
5. Carry out projects to solve problems.
6. Report progress.
7. Give recognition.
8. Communicate results.
9. Keep score.
10. Maintain momentum by making annual improvement part of the regular systems and processes of the company.

The strategic planning process for quality must parallel the firm's other planning processes. These processes must include defining short- and long-term quality objectives, setting organizational priorities, analyzing actual versus planned results, and integrating quality planning into the other strategic objectives.

Deming's approach.   Deming defines quality as a predictable degree of uniformity and dependability at a cost suited to the marketplace. At the core of Deming's approach to quality management for continual product and service improvement is the concept of reducing uncertainty and variability in design and manufacturing processes. Uncertainty and variability reductions are achieved through a continuous sequence of product design, manufacture, testing, sales, marketing and field service feedback, and product redesign. Deming states that higher quality leads to higher productivity, which leads to a sustainable competitive advantage. Deming believes that management is responsible for over 90 percent of all quality problems, so he states that top management must have the primary responsibility for quality improvement.[35]

Deming is an advocate of all employees using statistical quality control techniques and tools such as histograms, fishbone diagrams, Pareto analysis, and control charts. Like Juran, Deming identifies two distinct areas of variation for process improvement. He defines *common causes* of variation as those caused by the natural or inherent variability of the production process. Reductions in natural process variation often require changes in process design. *Assignable causes* of variation arise from external sources not inherent in the process. One can usually detect and eliminate these causes easily.

The essence of the Deming approach to quality management is captured in his now-famous "14 points," briefly summarized as follows:[36]

1. Create a constancy of purpose toward improving products and services and plan products with a view toward the long-range needs of the company.

2. Adopt the new philosophy that no company can compete in the world market until its management discards old notions about acceptable levels of mistakes and defects and provides adequate training and supervision.

3. Eliminate dependence on mass inspection for quality and use statistical controls to ensure that quality is built into the product or service.

4. Reduce the number of suppliers by awarding business based on quality and not on price alone.

5. Recognize the two sources of quality problems: faulty systems and the production workers. Deming suggests that 94 percent of the problems are caused by the systems.

6. Institute modern methods of training, focusing on the prevention of errors and defects.

7. Provide a higher level of supervision that includes accountability for quality.

8. Drive out fear by encouraging open communication so that everyone works toward organizational goals.

9. Break down barriers between departments and promote cooperation.

10. Eliminate numerical goals and slogans that seek improvement without providing methods.

11. Eliminate work standards that provide numerical quotas.

12. Remove barriers that hinder pride of workmanship.

13. Institute a vigorous training program to upgrade current skills and to learn new methods and techniques.

14. Top management must ensure that these points are carried out daily.

Your firm's management can review and implement these points to improve general quality levels.

Crosby's approach. In the Crosby approach to quality management, quality is defined as conformance to requirements. Management is responsible for determining the requirements, and those requirements must become the rule. Crosby believes that prevention, not inspection, is the basis for an effective quality management system. One must first understand the manufacturing process in order to develop prevention systems designed to discover and eliminate sources of error. Crosby is an advocate of *zero defects* as the appropriate performance standard. People must be educated to accept the concept of zero defects as a feasible and necessary standard for competitive success. Finally, Crosby states that the cost of quality is the cost of nonconformance. However, as firms invest in quality improvements and reap financial benefits, the benefits that are realized will far outweigh the initial investment. Thus, Crosby concludes that "quality is free" for such firms.[37]

Elements of Total Quality Management

The total quality management philosophy can be subdivided into three primary components: organizational elements, product elements, and process elements. We will now explain these elements.

Organizational elements. Total quality management requires commitment from everyone in the firm. The philosophy must pervade the company. Everyone must believe in total quality and support it through his or her daily actions. Senior management must create an organizational culture conducive to and supportive of the total quality management philosophy. All aspects of the firm must be examined to determine what changes are required to promote a quality-oriented culture. The actions of all functions within the firm must be integrated on the dimension of quality. Suppliers and customers must become a part of the quality system. The role of the quality professional changes from that of a watchdog to that of a change agent. Quality professionals focus on facilitating quality management processes and procedures throughout the firm. Education and training of quality teams and the proper use of these teams require the involvement of professionals from quality and other functions.

Product elements. Most product elements focus on improving design quality. Quality function deployment (QFD) is a design methodology that incorporates customer requirements (that is, "the voice of the customer") into the initial stages of product design.[38] Customer product requirements are translated into part design specifications. Once part specifications are established, manufacturing processes and vendor requirements are defined. The key to the QFD approach is that the design process begins by listening to the customer to discover the characteristics that constitute a high-quality product. Cross-functional teams from marketing, design engineering, purchasing, manufacturing, and so forth work together starting at the conceptual design stage, thus avoiding the "throw it over the wall" syndrome commonly seen between engineering and manufacturing in many companies. As a part of the QFD process, many tools are employed in the various stages of product design. Concurrent engineering (which uses a *parallel* approach to designing the product and determining manufacturing processes, versus the traditional *serial* approach to product design composed of each function determining its requirements in isolation), design for manufacturability and assembly, Pugh analysis (a structured approach to resolving design conflicts), and other techniques provide a systematic, integrated approach to product design. The use of QFD is credited by Toyota Motor Corporation with reducing automobile manufacturing cost by more than 60 percent via shortened product development cycles.

Process elements. As total quality management is incorporated into the product design process, process improvements are also needed to ensure the delivery of high-quality goods and services to the customer. Several statistical process control tools available for this purpose are: process flow diagrams, check sheets, Pareto analysis and histograms, fishbone (Ishikawa) diagrams, run charts, scatter diagrams, and control charts.[39] Additionally, process capability studies, experimental design and Taguchi methods are used to determine relationships between key specification parameters within the product.[40] Managers and workers must be trained in the proper use of these techniques to improve *all* processes and activities.

Shortcomings of TQM

As in the case of JIT, many US firms have benefitted from the TQM philosophy. Based on a survey of TQM adopters, many firms have not only failed to develop a competitive edge through the TQM philosophy but have also experienced detrimental effects.[41] For example, the Wallace company, a recent Malcolm Baldridge Award winner, has filed for bankruptcy.[42] The firm became so involved with its quality program, it failed to monitor its financial health. Florida Power and Light, a winner of the prestigious Deming Prize, has reevaluated its quality efforts and their impact on its ability to remain competitive.[43] How can the adoption of a total quality management philosophy damage a firm?

Understanding company goals. If a company loses sight of its goal to make money, it will suffer competitively, regardless of the organizational philosophy adopted. We must remember that quality improvements are a *means* to an end, as opposed to ends within themselves. Organizational resources must focus on quality efforts that support the firm's ability to improve current and future throughput (that is, the money generated through sales). Remember, the goal of a company is to *make* money, not to *save* money. You make money by satisfying customers.[44] What quality level does the customer expect? If improving quality will not increase throughput, then what competitive edge will? Time? Product flexibility? Improving quality for quality's sake may sound good in theory, but unless you have unlimited resources at your disposal, effective resource utilization in quality activities is essential to true total quality management.

Unfocused quality improvement. As with the JIT philosophy, a major shortcoming of TQM is its inability to distinguish between constraint and nonconstraint resources for the development of effective quality improvement activities. Because constraints govern the system's ability to achieve its goals, the focus for improving quality should be on the organizational resources that inhibit organizational performance. TQM does not contain a mechanism for defining the *control points* in the business, which allow for a focused approach to quality improvement. It is unclear whether the quality improvements will result in an overall improvement in the organization, or merely improving a local optimum. Again, it is possible for a company to spend money on local quality improvement projects that in reality do not provide overall improvements to the organization.

Recognizing two major points can improve your TQM program. All defects (internal and external) are not equal. First, if an internal constraint exists in your facility, statistical process control should be implemented to ensure that the constraint never creates or works on defective material. In addition, SPC should be used to eliminate the source of defects after the constraint. Defective nonconstraint parts when scrapped represent loss of raw material costs only, whereas defective constraint parts represent loss of significant organizational profit. Second, focus your functional testing and final assembly testing on characteristics deemed critical by your customer. When defects surface, use SPC to identify and eliminate (if possible) the cause of the defects. Once the cause is eliminated, eliminate SPC at that operation. The key is to focus your TQM efforts on operations that provide improvement to your bottom line now and in the future.

THE THEORY OF CONSTRAINTS PHILOSOPHY

In the early 1970s Eliyahu Moshe Goldratt, a physicist, applied a technique for predicting the behavior of a heated crystalline atom to optimizing the numerous variables related to a production work schedule. From this application of physics to the manufacturing arena grew what became known as optimized production technology (OPT). Over the years, the OPT philosophy has been refined, and the focus has moved off of the production floor. Today, OPT has evolved into the theory of constraints (TOC), and it encompasses all aspects of the business. Three TOC manufacturing concepts have caused a logistical paradigm shift. These are the five focusing steps for continuous improvement, the drum-buffer-rope scheduling methodology, and the buffer management information system.

Five Focusing Steps For Continuous Improvement

In the conceptual model discussion in Chapter 3, The Primary Functions and the Organization's Performance Measurement System Model, we compared the five focusing steps and TOC accounting to traditional cost accounting to illustrate the differences in decisions and resulting profits. To effectively use resources to achieve its goal, the firm must first distinguish between constraint and nonconstraint resources. Constraint resources govern your ability to achieve your goal. Thus, it becomes important for you to effectively manage the utilization of such resources. Nonconstraint resources do not directly affect goal achievement, but they do influence the efficiency and effectiveness of constraints.

The first step required to focus your efforts toward goal achievement is to **identify the constraints.** These constraints may be physical or managerial. You may have few physical constraints, which take the form of policies, procedures, and methods.*

Once your constraints are identified, it is necessary to determine how to **exploit the constraints.** This second step, constraint exploitation, applies to physical constraints only. For example, a physical constraint may be exploited by utilizing the resource on products that represent the most profit per use of constraint time for the firm. A managerial or policy constraint should not be exploited, but should be eliminated and replaced with a policy supporting system throughput.

The third step is to **subordinate all other resources** to the performance of the constraint. There are several reasons for this action. First, because constraints govern your firm's throughput and its ability to achieve its goals, resource synchronization with the constraint provides the most effective manner of resource utilization. If your nonconstraint resources are used beyond their productive capacity to support the constraint, they do not improve throughput or goal achievement and are therefore wasted. Besides, your inventory builds up, which hides quality problems and increases lead time. Nonconstraint capacity is composed of **productive capacity**[45] (capacity to support the constraint throughput) and **idle capacity.**[46] Idle capacity is further classified as **protective capacity**[47] (capacity to protect against system disruptions [Murphy's Law]) and **excess capacity**[48] (capacity not currently needed).

---

*Goldratt has developed a technique called a *current reality tree* to identify policy constraints. This technique is not presented here, as it is beyond the scope of this book. For a full description of the current reality tree, see Goldratt's article "What Is the Theory of Constraints?" in *APICS—The Performance Advantage*, June 1993, pp. 18–20.

Second, by definition, nonconstraint resources contain idle capacity. Thus, these resources provide system protection (protective capacity) when problems occur with nonconstraint resources by providing the firm with the ability to catch up to the constraint throughput level. Resource efficiency at the constraint and product flow at the nonconstraints are important. As discussed in step two, the constraint should be scheduled to make the most money for the firm. In managing nonconstraints, your focus is on moving items through the production or business process as quickly as possible.

Finally, as improvements are made to the constraint resources, nonconstraints are able to incrementally increase their capacity utilization relative to constraints in a synchronized manner.

The fourth focusing step, **elevating the constraint,** reinforces the previous point. By concentrating continual improvement efforts on constraint resources, firms will increase their performance. As the constraints are improved, the potential of nonconstraint resources can be better realized. Incremental improvements in constraint resources lead to incremental improvements in overall system performance through the increased effectiveness of all organizational resources. The focused step of continually improving the constraint resource will inevitably lead to another resource or to a policy becoming the new system constraint.

Therefore, the final focusing step is that of **inertia.** It is critical that the organization continually check to ensure the constraint has not shifted. Once you eliminate the existing constraint, you must begin the entire focusing process again. Failure to perform step 5 results in not identifying the new constraints, which may lead to disaster.

The Drum-Buffer-Rope Scheduling Methodology

The drum-buffer-rope scheduling methodology synchronizes the flow of parts and use of resources to produce throughput. After determining the system's physical resource constraint, its utilization rate serves as the *drumbeat* for the entire organization. All other organizational resources should be utilized at a rate to support the constraint. An inventory "time buffer" is established from material release (the gating operation) to the constraint to protect the constraint schedule from the effects of disruptions at nonconstraint resources. The time buffer allows the constraint to continue operation during nonconstraint disruption periods. The constraint must maintain a high utilization rate, since it determines total system throughput. The size of the time buffer is a function of the amount of variation of the nonconstraints preceding the constraint. To ensure that the inventory buffer does not increase beyond the established level, the rate at which additional work is released to the "gating" or first operation in the process must be restricted to the consumption rate at the constraint. This is part of the buffer calculation. A *rope* is tied from the constraint to the gating resource, which *synchronizes* the release of the correct quantity of parts into the system to support customer orders. The rope represents material release (similar to the bill of material explosion and netting operations in a material requirements planning system).

Drum-buffer-rope synchronizes resource and material utilization in an organization. Resources are used only at a level that contributes to the system's ability to achieve throughput. Material is used only to support throughput. Because unplanned, random disruptions are inevitable in any system, drum-buffer-rope provides a mechanism for protecting total system throughput by the use of a time buffer, which also allows an organization to use buffer management to focus continual improvement efforts on operations that exhibit variations jeopardizing throughput or due date performance.

Buffer Management Information System

Time buffers can be used to help identify the causes of disruptions without disrupting throughput. Remember, kanban systems are *reactive,* in that throughput is stopped until the disruption is addressed. Drum-buffer-rope is *proactive;* throughput is protected by a time buffer composed of material at control points while the disruption is addressed.[49] Once the causes of the disruptions are discovered, action can be taken to eliminate these causes. The use of time buffers as an information system for concentrating process improvement efforts is referred to as *buffer management.*

To effectively use time buffers for continual improvement, an organization must first determine the planned content of the buffer for any given day. For example, if a three-day constraint time buffer is used, all the work scheduled for, say, Monday, Tuesday, and Wednesday is planned to be positioned between the gating operation and in front of the constraint resource on Monday morning. If few disruptions have occurred, most of the work will be in front of the constraint because by definition all nonconstraints have extra capacity. Holes in the buffer occur when work planned to be in the buffer at the constraint is missing. The holes are discovered by periodically examining (say, twice a day) the actual against the planned time buffer content. These content profiles are used to identify when and where problems in the planned work flow exist. An immediate concern arises when holes in the buffer are present in the immediate time period. In our example of the three-day buffer, holes in day 1 (region 1) call for immediate action (this is termed the *red zone*). Personnel must determine where the missing work is in its routing and do everything possible to expedite the work to the constraint. A second and significant activity is to conduct an analysis to identify the sources of the disruptions or holes in region 1 to determine the appropriate improvement activities. Holes occurring in day 2 (region 2—the problem-solving zone) of the buffer serve as a focusing mechanism for improvement efforts. The status of the missing work must be determined and closely monitored to ensure that no system delays will occur. If, after time and focused improvement activities, work is seldom missing from days 1 and 2 of the buffer, the buffer should be reduced from three days to two days. This reduction in buffer size reduces manufacturing lead time by one day. Buffer management serves not only as a device for focusing your improvement activities but also as a means for resource activity control. Continually reducing buffer sizes means reducing manufacturing cycle time, which may translate into decreased quoted lead time. Buffer management is discussed in detail in previously cited works.[50]

Shortcomings of TOC

Although the theory of constraints is a very powerful and robust management philosophy, several shortcomings must be considered. The shortcomings exist in two areas: conversion from cost world to the throughput world and tools for continual improvement.

Cost world versus throughput world: a new way of managing. Converting to the TOC philosophy requires a radical change in the cultural and managerial environments of the company. In traditional American firms, cost accounting causes management to focus on the minimization of cost everywhere, which is usually accomplished by reducing cost locally within departments, plants, and divisions. Management then expects that the sum of local cost minimization efforts will yield a firm that is "lean and mean," ready to compete globally.

Under the TOC philosophy, the focus is not on cost minimization (because most costs are somewhat fixed), but on throughput maximization. Thus, profit enhancement, not cost reduction, becomes the key element for managerial decision making. Such a radical change in managerial thinking requires a significant change in the culture of the firm. TOC requires a performance measurement system that links resources and customers' needs and that converts actions into bottom-line profitability. It is almost impossible to successfully implement TOC in one area of a company unless the area contains both the resources and an outlet channel to customers so that improvements can be converted to bottom-line results.

Using buffer management to continually improve nonconstraints without the support or ability to use the resulting increase in capacity to gain more market share (increased throughput) eventually results in cutting nonconstraint resource capacities (laying off employees) to reduce operating expenses. This approach clashes with the concept of continual improvement. Unless throughput can be increased, continual improvement is a mirage. Cost can be reduced only by a small amount without laying off workers and jeopardizing throughput. Workers cannot support an improvement process where the end result is the loss of their jobs.

As with JIT and TQM, an appreciable time period is usually needed to effect such change. In addition, resistance to change may be extremely high because TOC contradicts the traditional management philosophy currently taught in business schools and practiced in most US organizations.

Tools for continual improvement. TOC provides a method of focusing continual improvement efforts but does not offer specific techniques for realizing the improvements. Unlike JIT and TQM, there is no extensive list of prescribed technologies designed to enhance operations. Managers should use the five focusing steps to identify and exploit the constraint, drum-buffer-rope (to schedule key resources), and buffer management to provide information to focus improvement activities. Managers must decide which tools are most appropriate for elevating constraints and reducing variation in nonconstraint resources. TOC provides the focusing power to identify where improvement affects the bottom line, and JIT and TQM provide the tools for improvement (for example, setup reduction techniques, preventive maintenance, statistical process control, and so forth). TOC also provides a problem identification, problem solution (win-win), and solution implementation methodology to identify and eliminate policy constraints.[51]

USING THE THREE PHILOSOPHIES TO ACHIEVE BOTTOM-LINE RESULTS

To achieve bottom-line results, elements of JIT, TQM, and TOC must be integrated into a new philosophy of business management—integrated resource management. You must apply the process of continuous improvement presented in Chapters 1, Why Are You Losing the Battle with Global Competition, and 5, Linking the Primary Functions through Performance Measurement Systems, and repeated in Table 6–1.

TOC provides the means for identifying and managing organizational constraints and nonconstraints once the goal, competitive edges, and performance measurement system are in place. TOC also provides a powerful scheduling methodology—drum-buffer-rope. To implement drum-buffer-rope scheduling, you must determine scheduling actions at each control point (control points are italicized):

1. Identify the *constraint.*

2. Schedule the *constraint* to make the most money for the organization. A Gantt chart of the constraint schedule is sufficient for many manufacturing processes. Software is available for more complex environments.

TABLE 6–1
Process of Continuous Improvement for World-Class Organizations

---

Stage One

---

1. Identify the *goal (or goals)* of the organization.
2. Design a *comprehensive performance measurement system* that tells you when you're moving toward the goal.
3. Implement theory of constraints to *identify the current constraints* to moving toward the goal, implement appropriate actions, and measure constraint and goal results.

Stage Two

---

4. Identify the *competitive edge* for each product and market (price/cost, quality, lead time, and so on) that constrains your organization from reaching its goal through market growth.
5. Design a *comprehensive performance measurement system* that tells you when you are improving on the constraining competitive edge and its effect on profit.
6. Identify and implement *appropriate actions* at the competitive edge constraint and measure the effect of the actions on both the competitive edge and on the organization's goal. In this step if the constraint is broken, go to step 3.

Stage Three

---

7. Identify functional *savings opportunities* that do not impede attainment of the goal.
8. Design a *functional cost measurement system* to determine the impact of local actions on the function and on the organization's goal and its competitive edge.
9. Identify and implement the *actions needed to reduce functional costs and measure the action,* its effects on local measures, and its effect on the competitive edge and in the organization's goal. In this step, if the constraint is broken, go to step 3.

---

3. Determine the size of the *constraint time buffer.* Many firms sum the setup and processing times of the operations performed from the gating operation to the constraint resource and multiply this time by 5 for a starting buffer size. If no holes (missing work orders) appear in region 1 (one-third of the buffer size), and few holes appear in region 2 (the middle third of the buffer), then the buffer is too big—reduce it. If you are continually expediting region 1 parts to the constraint, then the buffer is too small—increase its size.

4. Subtract the length of time for the *constraint time buffer* from the Gantt chart scheduled start time of an order to determine the release time at the gating resource for the specific order.

5. Determine the size of a *shipping time buffer.* The *shipping buffer* pulls parts after the constraint (and parts from the nonconstraints) to the shipping area as completed customer orders. Sizing of the *shipping buffer* is performed as in step 3.

6. The length of time for the *shipping time buffer* is added to the Gantt chart

schedule completion time of an order to determine the shipping date to the customer. This shipping date is quite useful in determining customer order shipment commitment dates.

7. Both *divergent points* (an operation in a part routing where two or more different parts or products can be made from a common part) and *convergent points* (assembly areas requiring buffers) must be scheduled to prevent misallocation of parts to products. The control points to support drum-buffer-rope are as follows: the *constraint;* the *constraint, shipping, and assembly (convergent points) buffers;* the *gating resources;* and *divergent points* in the product structure. These resources usually represent less than 10 percent of total plant resources.

8. All other resources are instructed to work when work is present, and not to worry about it otherwise. Work will arrive later.

Finally, TOC gives focus to a firm's continual improvement efforts. All improvement activities are conducted within the context of the total system versus localized areas. To implement buffer management, you must take the following steps:

1. Determine the proper buffer sizes as discussed in step 3 of the drum-buffer-rope implementation process.

2. Divide the time buffer into three equal regions (1, 2, and 3). Region 1 contains materials to be processed by the constraint in the immediate future, whereas region 3 contains material recently released by the gating resources.

3. Take your Gantt chart of the constraint schedule and start from the present, drawing a time line for the buffer size. The end of the line represents what should have just been released at the gating resource. Divide the time line into thirds. The orders within the time line on the Gantt chart represents the material that should be in each region of the buffer.

4. Take this Gantt chart listing of orders and compare the orders by region with what is actually in front of the constraint for immediate processing. All orders listed in region 1 on the Gantt chart should be present at the constraint resource; approximately two-thirds of the orders from region 2 should be present, and about one-third of the orders from region 3 should be present.

5. If any order from region 1 is missing, immediately expedite it to the constraint. Identify the source of the delay in the order's getting to the buffer. Keep a record of why orders don't arrive in the buffer prior to reaching region 1 status.

6. At the end of a week, conduct a Pareto analysis of the list of causes of delays to determine what resources need improvement and what actions are required. Specific JIT and TQM techniques should be used to improve these resources.

7. As improvement activities are implemented, fewer holes (missing orders) are observed in regions 1 and 2 of the buffer. This lack of expediting means that the buffer is too big. Reduce the buffer size.

8. In some cases, a reduction in buffer size translates directly into a reduction

in product lead time. If this is the case, contact marketing and inform them that the quoted lead time has been reduced (by the amount you reduced the buffer size).

As improvement opportunities are identified through buffer management, a Pareto analysis is conducted to identify which JIT and TQM techniques should be applied to critical nonconstraints to enhance products, services, and processes. The philosophies of waste elimination and cradle-to-grave quality management are compatible with TOC's emphasis on the global optimization of the firm's goal. Managers must combine these philosophies for the creation of an integrative resource management philosophy of business. This philosophy should be based on the effective use of all organizational resources, which should be focused on improved bottom-line performance. Managers must understand the strengths and shortcomings of the various philosophies and, while making decisions, must never lose sight of the real goal of the business. In Chapter 7, Illustrations of Integrative Performance Measurement Systems, we will examine how firms are actually using these philosophies to achieve bottom-line results.

Chapter Seven

Illustrations of Integrative Performance Measurement Systems

In this chapter, we will briefly discuss the case study participants and their measurement systems and linkages. In selecting the firms for this study, numerous manufacturing consultants and production and operations management academics were contacted to identify potential participants. The selection criteria were as follows: (1) The firm had implemented or was currently implementing some combination of JIT, TQM, and TOC; (2) the firm could be considered a world-class manufacturer based on Schonberger's definition[1]; and (3) the firm had recognized that traditional performance measurement systems were inappropriate. Some candidates had started developing their own performance measurement systems and linkages. A previsit questionnaire was sent to each firm. Based on the questionnaire responses and on the willingness to participate, we selected the case study participants.

Each firm was recommended to us by consultants, academics or both who were knowledgeable of the firm and its performance measurement system. The firms recognized problems with their traditional performance measurement systems and its linkages and were in various stages of change both in implementing JIT, TQM, and TOC and in implementing their performance measurement systems and linkages. None had the ideal system presented in Chapter 3, The Primary Functions and the Organization's Performance Measurement System Model. However, each had different elements and linkages reflected in the integrative model. These firms expanded our knowledge in conceptualizing our model.

The study participants exhibited strong linkages between some functions and performance measurement systems but weaker linkages between other functions. The conceptual performance measurement system model developed in Chapter 3 is repeated in Figure 7–1 for reference. This chapter begins with an introduction to the participating firms and then examines how the linkages between the functions and systems were accomplished.

COMPANY CHARACTERISTICS

In describing the company's performance measurement systems, and their use in decision making, we don't want to seem biased toward any company practices or performance measurement systems and will describe only what existed. This discussion should not be considered an endorsement for or a denouncement of any firm.

Characteristics of the six firms are presented in Table 7–1. The six firm participants represented six different industries: Reliance Electric (industrial electronics), Yamaha (recreational vehicles), Northern Telecom (telecommunications), Clark (industrial equipment), Trane (refrigeration and heating equipment), and Hill's® (specialized pet foods). Two of the firms had foreign-based parent organizations— Yamaha from Japan and Northern Telecom from Canada. The remaining firms had parent organizations that were based in the United States.

The number of plants in the divisions ranged from one to four. The Yamaha and Trane divisions had only one plant, which was housed in the same building as the division headquarters. The Reliance Electric division also had one plant, but it was remotely located from the division headquarters. Northern Telecom's Transmission Access Division had two plants. The plant included in the study was located in the same metropolitan area as the division headquarters. Finally, Clark Material Handling and Hill's® Pet Products had four manufacturing facilities each. In both companies, the participating plants were located in the same city as the division headquarters, but not in the same building. The average plant size, based on number of employees, was 350, with a low of 180 (Trane) and a high of 490 (Northern Telecom). Differences in customer bases among the six firms are shown in Table 7–1. Reliance, Yamaha, and Hill's® are primarily make-to-stock manufacturers. The largest percentage of the customer base at Northern Telecom was make-to-stock and assemble-to-order. Trane and Clark are primarily make-to-order manufacturers.

Table 7–1 also illustrates the various manufacturing methods used by the study participants. Reliance utilized a 100 percent batch process, whereas Yamaha and Trane were 100 percent repetitive. Northern Telecom and Clark employed repetitive, batch, and project manufacturing processes. Hill's® manufacturing process was 100 percent continuous.

Information concerning the number of different items in the master production schedule (MPS), the number of levels in the typical bill of materials (BOM), and

FIGURE 7–1

Generalized Performance Measurement System Model to Support Integrative Resource Management

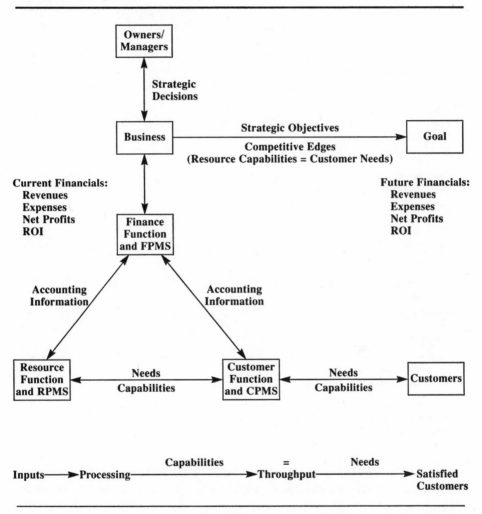

the number of active part numbers in the inventory system was provided by the participating firms. The number of possible items in the MPS ranged from 30 (Yamaha) to 40,000 (Trane). Five of the six firms had no more than 1,000 items in the MPS. Northern Telecom had only one level in the typical BOM, and Yamaha and Trane had five levels. Reliance and Clark contained four levels in their typical BOMs, whereas Hill's® had only three levels in its typical BOM. The quantity of active part

TABLE 7-1
Study Participant Characteristics

Characteristics	Reliance	Yamaha	Northern Telecom	Clark	Trane	Hill's®
Industry description	A	B	C	D	E	F
Number of plants	1	1	2	4	1	4
Plant size (Number of employees)	300+	350	490	300	180	307
Customer base (percentage)						
Make-to-stock (MTS)	100	100		20		100
Make-to-order (MTO)			5	75		
Make-to-stock/ assemble-to-order			90		90	
Engineer-to-order			5	5	10	
Manufacturing type (percentage)						
Repetitive		100	80	75	100	
Batch	100		15	20		
Project			5	5		
Continuous						100
Planning/control characteristics						
Number of items in the master production schedule	290	30	350	1,000	40,000	45
Number of levels in the bill of materials	4	5	1	4	5	3
Number of active part numbers	12,000	5,000	11,000	5,000	1,200	1,500

A: Industrial electronics
B: Recreational vehicles
C: Telecommunications
D: Industrial equipment
E: Refrigeration and heating equipment
F: Specialized pet foods

numbers in the inventory systems ranged from 1,200 (Trane) to 12,000 (Reliance). Four of the six firms had no more than 5,000 active part numbers in their inventory systems.

For a more comprehensive examination on how the study participants implemented many of the concepts outlined in this book, detailed case studies are provided for each firm in Chapters 8 to 13. The cases provide a window into these companies, which allows the reader to see various approaches to achieving manufacturing excellence. None of the study participants exhibited all of the competitive edges and linkages expressed in our model. However, each case study illustrates some combination of the competitive edges and linkages. In Chapter 2, Defining the New Philosophy: Resource

TABLE 7-2
Performance Measurement System Linkages Illustrated by Case Studies

Case study/ chapter number	Strategic objectives	Performance measurement system linkages
Reliance (8)	Cost Quality Delivery	Finance-customer Customer-resource Resource-finance
Yamaha (9)	Cost Quality	Customer-resource Resource-finance
Northern (10) Telecom	Cost Quality Lead time	Customer-resource Resource-finance
Clark (11)	Cost Quality	Customer-resource Resource-finance
Trane (12)	Cost Quality	Finance-customer Customer-resource Resource-finance
Hill's® (13)	Quality Delivery Flexibility	Customer-resource Resource-finance

Management, we defined *strategic objectives* as initiatives directed to affect the long-term health of the firm. We also defined *competitive edges* as product or service characteristics for which the firm strives to achieve advantages in a given market. The study participants used the term *strategic objective* to describe the competitive edges they were striving to attain in the marketplace. Because we did not conduct a customer analysis to ascertain whether these strategic objectives have attained the status of true competitive edges, we will use the participants' term to describe the factors the firms have decided to compete on. Table 7-2 provides information on which case studies illustrate a strategic objective sought by the firm, along with specific performance measurement system linkages. The reader can use this information to select the appropriate cases for a deeper understanding of a particular approach.

Table 7-2 shows that cost (price) was considered a strategic objective by five out of six firms. Hill's® did not acknowledge cost as a strategic objective shared between the division and plant levels. All the study participants identified quality as a strategic objective at the division and plant levels. Reliance, Northern Telecom, and Hill's® identified delivery (due date performance) as a strategic objective, and only Northern Telecom viewed lead time as an objective. Hill's® identified process and product flexibility as a strategic objective, and no participants acknowledged field service, process or product innovation, or product introduction responsiveness as a key strategic objective.

PERFORMANCE MEASUREMENT SYSTEM MODELS TO SUPPORT STRATEGIC OBJECTIVES

Before examining the details related to each strategic objective and linkage, we will provide a framework for performance measurement system models for each strategic objective. The case study data provided the basis for developing these performance measurement system models. The conceptual models were presented in Chapter 3. The models to support strategic objectives provide a summary of current reality as represented by the study participants. The study participants are viewed as being on the path toward continual improvement, and they use the models for assessing progress toward the firm's strategic objectives, as presented in Figures 7–2 to 7–5. These models show linkages between the plant and the division levels for the strategic objectives of cost, quality, lead time, and delivery, respectively. Each model shows the linkage between customers' needs and the specific competitive edge. The customers dictate the criteria and standard the company must achieve to have a competitive edge. The measurement represents the firm's current performance level.

Five of the six firms viewed themselves as being in markets where product price (cost) was a strategic objective. These firms therefore emphasized controlling product costs as an important *performance criterion*.

The price/cost performance measurement system model in Figure 7–2 shows customer feedback on price and the accumulation of costs within the plant accounting system. Price is established in the marketplace by competitors or by customers' direct interaction with the firm's sales personnel. Marketing and sales were the firm's agents in setting price and negotiating sales. This market price is the *performance standard*.

In most instances, the participants used traditional product costing and variances from budget from their accounting systems to assist in establishing a product price. Many participants recognized the accounting problems presented in Chapter 3, The Primary Functions and the Organization's Performance Measurement System Model and Chapter Four, Linking the Primary Functions Through Performance Measurement Systems, and illustrated in the Gedanken exercises in Chapter 5, The Process of Continuous Improvement for World-Class Organizations, but none had developed an alternative cost/price mechanism. The plant cost accounting system would accumulate expenditures related to the resource function and allocate overhead based

FIGURE 7-2
Price/Cost Performance Measurement System Model

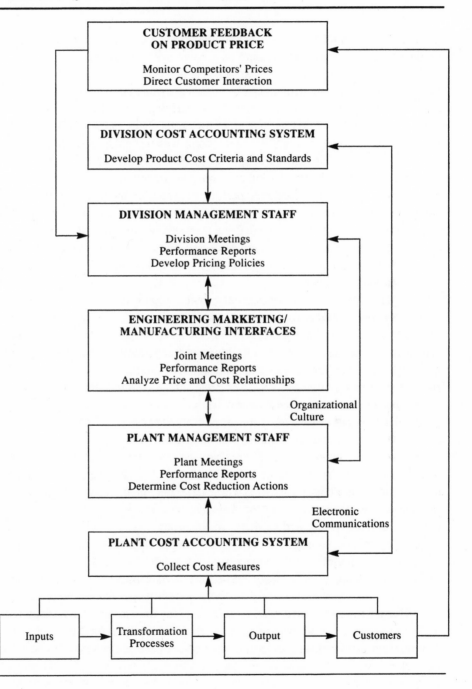

primarily on direct labor to establish a product cost. A profit margin is added to the product cost to establish the measure of product price for the firm.

Division and plant staffs have separate and joint meetings to determine appropriate actions to reduce product costs and gather information on market price. The organizational culture emphasizes cost reduction as a driving force. Performance reports track costs by category and product and provide feedback to both the division and plant staffs. The price/cost information system was technologically the most well developed in most firms. On-line communication systems between plant and division functions existed. Although the information was aligned to support organizational effectiveness, traditional accounting performance measurement systems were used. Again, the participants recognized accounting shortcomings but had no comprehensive alternative methodology. Some firms used several means of linking functions, including reports, meetings, common databases, and telephone conversations. Each firm was involved in implementing JIT, TQM, or TOC to align business processes with performance measures.

The quality performance measurement system model is presented in Figure 7–3. All six firms viewed quality as a strategic objective and linked their performance measurement systems directly to the customer. Customer returns, formal complaints, and surveys were the primary vehicles for identifying customers' quality problems. Feedback was shared by division and plant staffs. Several quality performance criteria such as warranty costs of repair or replacement, returns, scrap, rework, and defects per product were used by each firm and are discussed in detail later. The quality performance criteria must be viewed from the customers' perspective. What quality characteristics are critical to your customers? The standard should also be determined by customers' needs. The performance measure is the firm's current level of performance for that specific criterion. Marketing, field service, engineering, and manufacturing met with customers, with each other, or both to study customers' returns to identify the causes of the defective product. Again, the organizational culture promoted quality and superior workmanship.

At the plant level, several firms had implemented quality audits, functional testing, and so forth to simulate actual customer use. When a defect was identified, statistical process control was used to isolate and eliminate its cause.

The lead time performance measurement system model is presented in Figure 7–4. **Market tolerance lead time** is defined as the amount of time a customer is willing to wait for a product from the time an order is placed until it is delivered.[2] This information is critical in determining whether or not, and where, the firm needs to stock inventory. As indicated previously, a firm can take one of two actions to meet customers' lead time needs. The firm can either attempt to stock items in finished goods, or it can make and ship the item in less time than the market tolerance

FIGURE 7-3
Quality Performance Measurement System Model

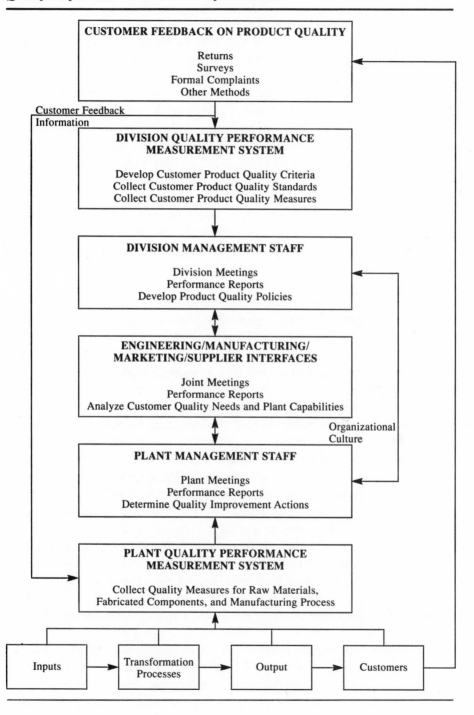

lead time. Traditional management philosophies support the former approach, whereas the JIT and TOC philosophies focus on the latter approach.

Customer interactions, surveys, and knowledge of competitors' quoted lead times are useful in identifying quoted customer time standards. Lead time criteria used at the plant level were manufacturing cycle time and vendor lead time. Measures at the plant level provide feedback on firm performance. Performance reports monitor the firm's progress in reducing quoted lead time. Division, plant, and joint staff meetings are useful in identifying lead time problems and appropriate actions that support lead time reduction. Organizational culture plays a major role in supporting quoted lead time reductions.

The performance measurement system model for due date (delivery) performance is shown in Figure 7–5. When an order is received and a delivery commitment made, the plant must continually monitor order status to ensure successful completion by the due date commitment. Order entry can be done centrally at the division and allocated to plants, or it can be done directly at the plant. Delivery criteria include internal delivery schedules, on-time vendor delivery, and on-time customer delivery. Performance reports and daily meetings at the plant are used to update the progress of each order. Again, organizational culture and an active communication network across functions and levels are essential to improving due date performance. TOC's buffer management information system is a proactive methodology for ensuring on-time shipments.

Several linkage elements are common in each model. The first common element is the need for each organizational level to assess strategic objective performance through a supportive performance measurement system that crosses functional boundaries. Both business processes and their performance measurement systems must not be constrained by functional boundaries. The study participants held separate division and plant meetings to evaluate functional and overall performance results. Another means of evaluation may be used, but the periodic assessment of strategic objective performance is imperative. The second common element is the use of frequent joint staff meetings designed to determine a course of action that supports continual improvement on strategic objectives. Finally, a key ingredient for maintaining an integrative performance measurement system is to create and reinforce an organizational culture conducive to both workers and managers identifying and implementing continual improvement activities focused on the organization's goal.

Several model-specific elements are also presented in Figures 7–2 to 7–5. The cost performance measurement model in Figure 7–2 includes electronic communications between the division and plant cost accounting systems. This is necessary for the timely and accurate transfer of cost information. Customer feedback information is

FIGURE 7–4
Lead Time Performance Measurement System Model

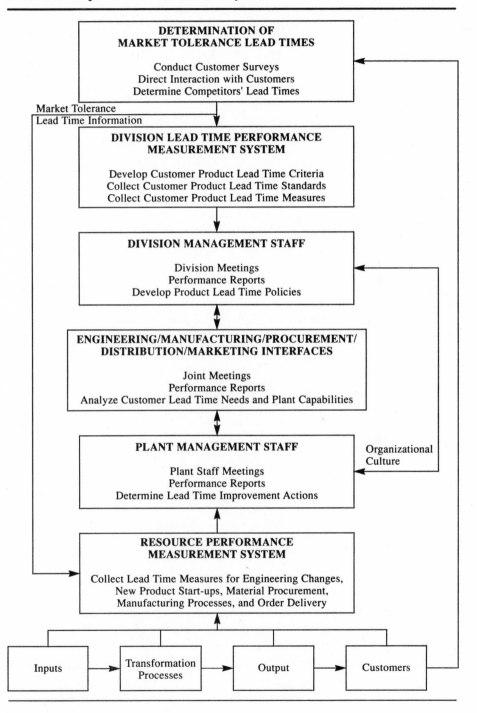

FIGURE 7-5
Due Date Performance Measurement System Model

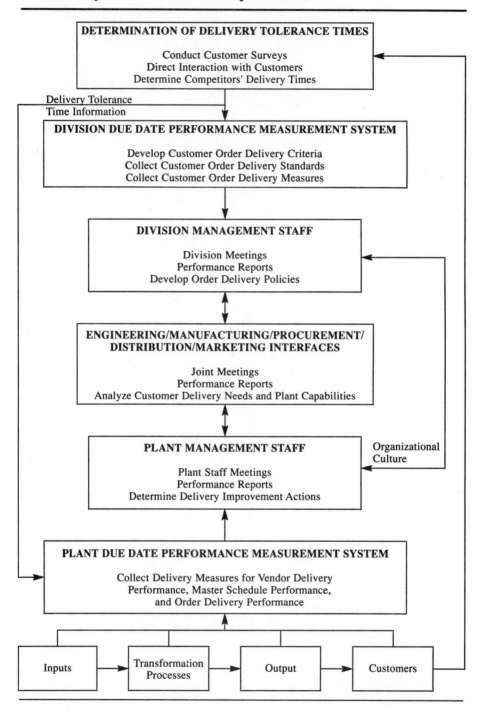

a critical element to the quality performance measurement model presented in Figure 7–3. The information is used to assess current product and process quality performance as well as guide future improvement activities. In the case of lead time and delivery performance, the firm must be capable of measuring its performance in relation to the tolerance level of the customer in a particular market segment. If the firm's lead times do not meet the expectations of the customers (that is, their tolerance level), then the firm cannot compete on this basis. Thus, the lead time and delivery performance models include an evaluation of how well the firm is able to consistently achieve quoted lead times and delivery levels that exceed customers' expectations, leading to a competitive advantage.

Within this framework, let us now examine each of the three performance measurement system linkages to identify how the study participants are completing the linkage.

SYSTEM LINKAGES

Finance and Resource Linkage

None of the six study participants used activity-based costing, direct costing, or TOC accounting to provide linkages between their resource and finance performance measurement systems. The six study participants recognized the problems in using traditional cost accounting systems in world-class manufacturing environments for establishing product price and measuring performance, but had made few changes to their systems. However, each firm used cost to measure resource effectiveness.

Monthly warranty costs were tracked by Reliance to monitor the adequacy and effectiveness of engineering and manufacturing resources. Appropriate resource decisions were based on the warranty claims and associated costs. Engineering development dollars were reported monthly to direct new product development resources. Direct labor resources were converted into dollars by measuring the ratio of net sales billed to customers against the total number of direct labor employees. Increases in the ratio were viewed as denoting an increase in labor effectiveness. Other resource measures linked to the financial system that Reliance used were dollars of product shipped per day, dollars of product shipped per employee, and the ratio of backlog size (in dollars) to sales growth.

Another measure used by Reliance to link its resource and finance performance measurement systems is called pull through. **Pull through** is defined as the ratio of the deviation in actual earnings before interest and taxes from the plan (actual EBIT − planned EBIT) to the deviation in net sales billed to customers from the plan (actual NSB − planned NSB). The ratio is calculated only if the change in NSB is positive. The measure demonstrates the effect of a marginal increase in sales on earnings and employed resources. A positive pull through value indicates that actual net sales were greater than planned and resulted in a marginal increase in earnings. Therefore, the employed resources were successful in accommodating the increase in sales profitably. A negative pull through ratio indicates that, although NSB was larger than anticipated, actual EBIT was less than planned. Therefore, the employed resources were unable to accommodate the sales increase in a profitable manner. The pull through ratio provides Reliance with a metric for assessing the financial impact of marginal sales increases on the employment of organizational resources. A downward trend in the metric may signify resource level inadequacies or a need for increased resource effectiveness.

At Yamaha, material resource effectiveness was measured in scrap dollars and rework costs. The measures assisted in focusing operational resources in quality improvement activities. Projected target costs for new products were established to translate required resources into costs. The accounting organization decomposed new product cost by individual parts and manufacturing processes. The information was used to determine methods for reducing costs without sacrificing customers' requirements. Resources were allocated in areas with opportunities to reduce cost without diminishing value. Yamaha also translated external resource information into financial terms. Inbound freight cost of purchased materials was closely monitored. Vendor cost analyses on purchased materials were conducted monthly to examine the effect of price reductions or increases on profitability.

Northern developed cost improvement programs designed to create techniques that reduced current product cost without sacrificing value to customers. The firm's primary focus was on material resources, because they represented approximately 70 percent of total product cost. Three approaches were used to monitor and control organizational resources employed in current products: product redesign, material substitution, and purchase price variances. Northern computed a cost improvement impact (CI) metric monthly to assess the effect of cost improvements on the profit and loss statement. Cost improvements were determined by deducting program expenses from accrued program savings. Measuring the effectiveness of cost improvement programs through financial impact provided Northern with a direct link between its resource and finance performance measurement systems. The firm also measured monthly purchase price variances (PPVs) to monitor material resources in dollar terms. Weekly scrap and monthly field failure statistics are converted into dollars for deploying engineering, manufacturing, and other functional resources toward activities that improve customer satisfaction.

Clark's resource and finance performance measurement system linkages originated in the new product development process. Projected versus actual product costs were tracked weekly based on preprototyping and prototyping activities. This information guided the actions of project teams. Teams were then engaged in activities that would achieve product cost objectives. For existing products, Clark linked its resource and finance performance measurement systems by measuring the cost per hour to operate its product in the field. This information was periodically collected from dealers and customers. The "cost per hour of operation" measure was used to establish new product design criteria and value engineering targets. Annual cost improvement targets were established for each commodity to manage material resources. Material price variance targets were also set annually for each commodity that incorporated projected cost reductions and forecasted inflation levels to assess the bottom-line impact.

Trane's resource and finance performance system linkages focused on material resource effectiveness. Because labor represented only 4 percent of total product cost, the firm used a simplified cost accounting system that eliminated the need for detailed labor reporting by the manufacturing organization. After a sales order was entered into the material requirements planning (MRP) system and material requirements were generated, the accounting staff generated the material cost for the order. Trane used a multiple-point milestone backflushing system to relieve consumed materials from inventory. In this system, material usage is *backflushed* (calculated and subtracted from existing inventory balances) at milestone points in the manufacturing process, versus single-point backflushing at total unit completion. Once the unit is built and all materials used are backflushed, material costs are then run against the backflush requirements to determine the actual material cost for the order. This material cost information, along with weekly spoilage and scrap dollars incurred per work team, is used to determine how efficiently and effectively material resources are utilized in the completion of an order.

At Hill's® each plant established a total monthly labor pool of dollars based on the actual payroll. An analysis of total planned versus actual labor expenditures is conducted each month to determine labor resource effectiveness. Historically, the measure of manufacturing cost per pound (of product) had been used to assess the performance of production resources. In the past, however, the measure was not used properly, and it promoted detrimental actions. For instance, instead of decreasing manufacturing cost per pound through employing resources in plant quality improvement activities, plant spending was cut. Such actions created an infinite loop such that, as spending continued to decline, poor quality accelerated, which led to more cost increases. The management team at Hill's® now understands how to use the manufacturing cost per pound metric in accordance with other metrics to effectively monitor and control production resources. A total manufacturing cost improvement measure defined as the monthly total actual manufacturing cost divided by the monthly total standard manufacturing cost is also used to examine plant cost improvement efforts. These metrics provides linkages between the resource and finance performance measurement systems.

Finance and Customer Linkage

Linkages between the finance and customer performance measurement systems are necessary for assessing the firm's ability to achieve current and future sales objectives. To achieve linkages between these systems, selected information derived from marketing, sales, and field service must be converted into dollars and integrated into the firm's accounting system. Reliance and Trane exhibited strong linkages between their finance and customer performance measurement systems, but the other study participants did not.

Reliance measures the ratio of monthly actual to planned revenue in each sales region by product line. The performance measurement information is used to evaluate the validity of the regional sales plans and to discover sales trends for product applications. The revenue information is published and distributed monthly throughout the marketing and sales functions. The general manager and the marketing manager meet twice a year with the regional sales managers to discuss actual performance, objectives, competitive edges, and sales plans.

Returned products are disassembled by the Reliance field service staff to determine the cause of failure. The results of the failure analysis are amassed in a database, and a report is sent to division and plant management staffs. The report includes total monthly warranty dollars and warranty cost trend lines by product line. Thus, revenue and warranty cost information collected by the customer system is shared with the finance system to facilitate the effective use of marketing, sales, and field service resources. Revenue performance information can be used to focus the activities of these three areas toward specific actions necessary for improving current sales trends. Warrant cost information is useful in determining areas of improvement and in guarding against losses in future sales levels caused by dissatisfied customers. The information can also be used to reveal opportunities for increasing future sales through product enhancements.

Marketing engineers at Trane assist customers in developing product specifications, and they determine a price range for a given product configuration. The prices are established by estimating a product cost associated with any of the 40,000 standard product configurations offered by Trane. Product costs are developed by the accounting organization using a financial model. Trane can convert customer requirements collected by the marketing organization directly into dollars based on the level of resources necessary to meet customers' needs. Customers are then charged a price reflective of the cost of resources required to complete the order, plus a profit margin.

Trane products are primarily sold to building contractors in a competitive bidding process. Therefore, the firm must be able to effectively use its organizational resources on every order to win the order and make a profit on it. Linkages between the finance and customer performance measurement systems are critical for the firm to stay in business. Without this linkage, the firm may be unable to compete with the bids of its competitors. Even worse, it may find itself winning bids, but never achieving profitability. The finance and customer performance measurement system linkages provide an informed evaluation of the firm's ability to service customers' needs with current organizational resources at a profit.

Clark and Hill's® used market-driven pricing to establish product price versus the traditional cost-driven approach, although they both employed a standard cost accounting system. While both firms monitored the behavior of actual cost via the accounting system, competitive pressures in the marketplace, not cost data, determined product prices. Clark and Hill's®, therefore, use market-driven versus cost-driven pricing.

The other study participants were also sensitive to competitive pricing pressures and made price adjustments as dictated by market forces. Similarly, with the exception of Trane, each of the firms used direct labor as a basis of overhead allocation to develop product costs. Although the firms were aware of the traditional accounting problems (direct labor costs continue to decrease relative to direct material and overhead), only minor actions had been taken to address them at the time of this writing.

Customer and Resource Linkage

Along with converting customers' needs into financial terms, companies must translate these needs into product and process design and manufacturing requirements. World-class manufacturers ensure a match between the products and services offered and each targeted market segment. Mismatches between products, services, and markets lead to the ineffective use of company resources. All the study participants exhibited strong linkages between the customer and resource performance measurement systems.

The engineering-manufacturing-marketing connection is viewed as critical to the success of Reliance Electric Design, manufacturing, and marketing staffs hold joint product concept design meetings with customers to identify and anticipate customers' needs. These staff members also hold field application workshops. These functions conduct joint customer interviews to develop a better understanding of actual customers' expectations prior to product design and manufacturing.

Field failure information collected by the field service staff is used to trace field failures to specific design characteristics or manufacturing processes. This information is used to direct design and manufacturing activities to eliminate the defect source. In this manner, design and operations resources immediately affect the firm's competitive success in the marketplace. In design, improving products to eliminate field failures is given priority. Engineering changes are also made to reduce failures. Manufacturing personnel target improvement efforts at specific processes or materials, versus the shotgun approach used by companies when implementing TQM and JIT. It is not surprising that many firms that have "successfully" implemented TQM and JIT using the shotgun approach have yet to see any increase in profits. In many instances the firms failed to develop a linkage between customers' needs and the necessary resources and processes to meet those needs.[3]

Yamaha's quality control department collects product information through the field service organization. The information is analyzed by the quality control department, and feedback is provided to the appropriate internal Yamaha departments, suppliers, or distributors. The feedback is used as a basis for focusing continual improvement efforts and for determining the type and level of organizational resources needed for improvement endeavors.

Yamaha also integrates customer performance information into its RPMS via daily inspections of packed units and periodic endurance tests on assembled products. Each day a packaged unit ready for shipment is selected, isolated, visually inspected for packaging appearance, unpacked, and then visually and functionally inspected. The intent is to accumulate information that simulates what the customer sees upon receiving the product. This customer information is also used for defining what the improvement areas are, what resources are required, and where the resources should be applied. Endurance tests on assembled products are conducted in on-site tests tracks and off-site test areas to collect and evaluate customer performance information.

Northern Telecom's quality function also compiles market information for its field service area. The quality function examines and distributes information to the other functions. As in the case of Yamaha, the information is used to effectively improve processes for customer satisfaction. Customer and resource performance measurement system linkages in Northern Telecom are critical to the firm's ability to maintain its reputation as a technological leader. Northern Telecom provides its customers with state-of-the-art products, which often set the standard in the telecommunications industry.

Northern Telecom also simulates what customers may see upon product receipt.

Personnel in the quality department place an order through the firm's normal ordering process. The units are delivered to a quality team that unpacks them, sets them up, and conducts tests. Any nonconformity found during receiving and unpacking is registered as a defect. In addition, a 10 percent sample is audited every week. To validate the audit team's findings, the results are compared with those of customers who install the identical equipment. The customer results are forwarded to the quality department and compared with the audit team's results. The information is again used to focus on activities that improve customers' satisfaction.

The manufacturing planning staff of Clark works directly with marketing in developing new product designs and improved product manufacturability. Manufacturing engineers work as a team with marketing professionals to define future customers' needs. The teams conduct customer surveys and discuss current products with customers. These inputs are used in developing new product specifications. The teams also conduct value analysis on competing products. The joint collection of customer information by manufacturing planning and marketing facilitates linkages between the customer and resource information systems aimed at providing next-generation products that meet or exceed customers' expectations. The linkage provides management information for making intelligent decisions on resource requirements for developing and producing new products.

Customer and resource performance measurement system linkages also support current product offerings as demonstrated by Clark. Plant product engineers are responsible for resolving field and customer service issues discovered by marketing or field service. The engineers receive detailed information on problems and correct the situation via product or process changes. Thus, incoming customer performance information is directly linked to appropriate plant resources for direct customer benefits. This customer and resource linkage reduces customer dissatisfaction and identifies areas where continual improvement is required. With specific customer information, the proper resources can be employed to guarantee the desired result. Clark also simulates field conditions by operating each product before shipment.

The marketing function at Trane provides the primary link between its customers and resource performance measurement systems. Marketing engineers furnish technical assistance to the sales force and aid customers in developing product specifications. Marketing also provides order requirements to product engineering for configuring the bill of materials (BOM) for the order. Finally, the master scheduling of orders into the production system is conducted by the marketing staff. Master production schedule (MPS) performance is used to assess manufacturing's ability to meet customer-driven schedule commitments. Measures of MPS performance are collected and shared across production departments and other functions to monitor and control the effective use of organizational resources in supporting customer delivery commitments. Buffer management is also used both to assure due date performance, and to focus continual improvement efforts.

Trane's marketing function is responsible for ensuring that the organization is capable of meeting customer order specifications. Before an order is accepted, marketing engineers determine whether all customer specifications are achievable using available resources. In situations where a unique configuration or specification is requested, a review board decides whether to accept the order. These procedures match customer requirements and organizational resources to ensure the desired profitability, market growth, and customer satisfaction. Customer and resource performance measurement systems at Trane are thus synchronized toward achieving the company goal.

Hill's® has defined dependability in servicing customer orders and in equipment operations as a competitive edge. For Hill's® to achieve dependability in both areas, customer and resource performance metrics must be complementary, owing to the capital-intensive nature of its industry. The firm also has an overall objective of maximizing asset effectiveness. This objective translates into utilizing all organizational resources to their full potential such that the operation is able to support the capacity demands of the market. Hill's® key dependability measures are case fill rate, defined as the monthly percentage of customer orders filled (indicators of dependability to customers) and the percentage of unscheduled downtime (an indicator of equipment dependability). The case fill rate and unscheduled downtime measures focus managerial actions on critical areas.

An independent quality laboratory evaluates the acceptability of Hill's® finished products. Customer information from the lab is used to guide internal quality improvements, which lead to enhanced customer satisfaction. This information is compared against detailed resource performance metrics collected in the manufacturing process to determine the source of inconsistencies that require corrective action. The customer and resource performance measurement system linkage provided through independent lab information safeguard against the delivery of unsatisfactory products to customers and direct resources toward customer-focused improvement opportunities. Most of the linkages tie customers' needs to resource capabilities. Performance measures are at the customer level. Products are subjected to tests simulating actual use. Field failures are analyzed to identify the source of the problem. The firm's emphasis is on meeting the current and future customers' needs.

Performance Measurement

Organizational culture, meetings, performance reports, and charts linked performance measurement systems at the division and plant levels for the firms. A summary

TABLE 7-3
Summary of Performance Measurement System Linkages on Strategic Objectives

Linkage Mechanism	Reliance	Yamaha	Northern Telecom	Clark	Trane	Hill's®
Corporate culture		C		C	C	
Visual display of measurements		C	C		C	
Plant staff meetings	D	D	D	D	D	D
	M	M	W	W	W	W
				M		
Division staff meetings	M	M	M	W	W	
				M	M	
Joint staff meetings	M	M	M	M	M	Q
Periodic performance reports	M	M	W	D	M	D
			M	W	Q	M
				M		Q

Linkage Frequency: C = continuous
D = daily
W = weekly
M = monthly
Q = quarterly

by firm is provided in Table 7-3. The frequency of reporting for the firms is also displayed in this table as being continuous, daily, weekly, monthly, or quarterly. The linkages are accomplished through corporate culture, visual displays for performance measures, formal division and plant staff meetings, formal joint staff meetings between division and plant management, and periodic performance reports. Specific details on how these techniques were used by the firms to achieve performance measurement system linkages on the strategic objectives are provided in the case studies (Chapters 8 through 13).

Closing the Loop

Synchronized performance measurement systems provide managers with the information required to evaluate the effectiveness of resources in achieving the organization's goal. Linkages between the performance measurement systems close the loop between the company's goal, customers' needs, and organizational resources. If the system is properly aligned, one can detect misalignments between the company's goal, customers' needs, and organizational resource performance; and resources can be allocated to correct such misalignments. The effectiveness of resources across functions is captured in the performance measurement system and is linked across all three measurement dimensions: customers and resources, resources and finance, and finance and customers.

The customer and resource linkage consists of the customers' needs (related to the competitive edges of price/cost, quality, lead time, due date performance, and so on) flowing in one direction, and resource capabilities to support these competitive edges flowing in the other direction. The resource managers must be aware of both the measurement criteria and standards to support the customers' needs for each competitive edge. What product or service characteristics are important from a customer's perspective? Finally, the measures must represent the actual results.

The link between the resource and finance performance management systems is based on accounting information. Today, the options are traditional cost accounting, ABC accounting, and TOC accounting. We have already discussed numerous problems of traditional costing systems and described ABC and TOC accounting. Using TOC, we also illustrated the difference between fixed and variable costing concepts in arriving at valid business analyses.

Three major weaknesses exist in these six firms and most traditional performance measurement system: the use of traditional cost accounting; the customer and finance linkage; and investment decisions to support competitive edges. First, traditional cost accounting leads to incorrect decisions. Second, the customer and finance linkage should translate market opportunities into revenue streams based on resource capabilities, not based on product cost. Traditional and activity-based accounting systems provide product cost rollups (an attempt to capture and summarize all cost associated with producing a product) as a basis for pricing. In contrast to traditional full absorbtion costing, TOC accounting provides an estimate of variable cost per unit and requires the CPMS to estimate product price based on market forces. Throughput can then be computed as price minus variable cost to identify whether the firm would be better off by accepting the order. The third major weakness is the inability to translate changes in competitive edge factors into valid operating expense and throughput streams. For example, if we improve product quality from a 5 percent to a 3 percent defect rate, how does this affect investment, operating expenses, raw materials, and sales?

In Chapter 1, Why Are You Losing the Battle with Global Competition?, we discussed the business environment and traditional management decision making. In Chapter 2, Defining the New Philosophy: Resource Management, we defined the elements of the resource management philosophy and provided definitions of key terms supporting this concept. In Chapter 3, The Primary Functions and the Organization's Performance Measurement System Model, we provided an integrative, closed-loop performance measurement system model that facilitates holistic managerial decision-making processes at each organizational level and within all functions. Our measurement system model is based on the global goal, not local performance criteria. Functions no longer benefit from actions and behaviors resulting in local optimization. In Chapter 4, Linking the Primary Functions through Performance Measurement Systems, we defined the linkages to support an integrative performance measurement system. In Chapter 5, The Process of Continuous Improvement for World-Class Organizations, we detailed a process of continuous improvement.

In Chapter 6, Actions to Achieve Bottom-Line Results, we briefly reviewed and provided references for the philosophies of JIT, TQM, and TOC. We described the TOC accounting system, the five focusing steps for identifying and managing a physical constraint, the drum-buffer-rope scheduling methodology, and buffer management. We discussed how JIT and TQM must be focused using TOC to implement projects that affect profitability. In this chapter, we summarized the results of six detailed case studies of firms identified as having reengineered their measurement systems to link business processes to strategic objectives. These firms are attempting to synchronize the activities of their business functions effectively to meet customers' needs. We described the numerous measures used by these firms. Some measures are correct, and others still reside in cost-world thinking. We again warned readers of the problems of using traditional cost accounting measures. "Customer satisfaction at a profit" should be your organization's motto.

The remaining six chapters provide the details of the strategic objectives, actions, and measurement systems of firms that are on a path of sustaining world-class organizational status.

Chapter Eight

Reliance Electric Industrial Controls Division

This chapter illustrates how linkages between the three performance measurement systems and functions can be accomplished: finance and customer; customer and resource; and finance and resource. The firm's strategic objectives are cost, quality, and delivery, which are monitored by the performance measurement system.

COMPANY BACKGROUND

The industrial controls division manufactures programmable logic controllers used by firms in the chemical, rubber, paper, metals, food processing, utility, textiles, and wastewater industries. The organization's customer base is 100 percent make-to-stock. All products are made intermittently. Approximately 30 percent of the product is shipped on an interplant basis to other Reliance facilities worldwide. Division headquarters are located in Cleveland, Ohio. The manufacturing facility is in Athens, Georgia. The Athens plant actually contains two focused factories within one structure: an industrial controls operation and an electric motor operation. Total plant employment is over 300, which includes approximately 40 percent salaried and 60 percent hourly workers. Of the more than 180 hourly workers, approximately 80 percent are classified as direct and 20 percent as indirect labor. The Athens plant produces 290 model numbers, uses seven planning bills of materials, and has 12,000 active part numbers in the inventory system. There are approximately four levels in the typical bill of materials (BOM) for a given product line. Currently, the plant is utilizing elements of MRP, MRPII (manufacturing resource planning), JIT, and TOC to plan, monitor, and control the production process. We conducted interviews with the following individuals:

- Industrial Controls Division general manager.
- Division marketing manager.
- Division engineering manager.
- Division controller.
- Plant manager of the Athens Facility.
- Operations manager industrial controls.
- Manufacturing manager.
- Materials manager.
- Plant accounting manager.
- Production engineering manager.
- Test engineering manager.
- Customer service manager.
- Quality assurance manager.

DIVISION ORGANIZATION

The division is functionally structured and consists of financial, marketing, and engineering organizations. The functional managers report directly to the general manager. The industrial controls division is part of Reliance's electrical operations group. Sales is housed in a separate division. One sales force sells all the products produced by Reliance Electric, including industrial controls. The division organizational structure is illustrated in Figure 8–1.

STRATEGIC OBJECTIVES

The electrical components group has embarked on a strategy to increase business through productivity improvements. The strategy includes the following elements:

1. Continuing to develop world-class manufacturing capabilities within each division and plant.

2. Instituting employment programs that foster professional growth and develop working relationships with academic institutions for state-of-the-art technical and managerial assistance.

3. Providing employee incentives that allow all employees to share in the profitability of the organization.

FIGURE 8–1
Organizational Structure of the Industrial Controls Division

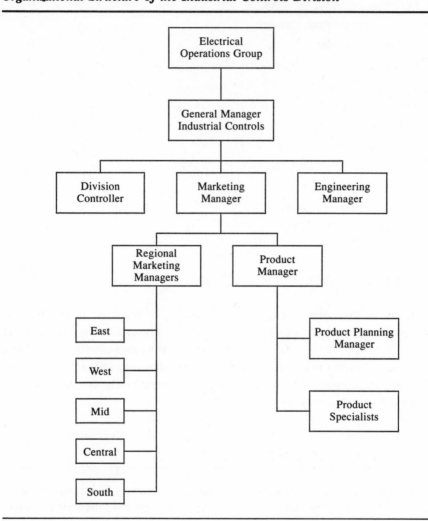

Each operating division within the electrical operations group has a mission statement. The mission statement for the industrial controls division is as follows:

Mission: To be a leader with digital-based control products that provide expanded solutions to customer needs and that enhance the desire to do business with Reliance.

The industrial controls division has also instituted a growth strategy consisting of the following objectives:

- *Sales growth:* promote international sales in existing businesses; increase sales to Reliance affiliates and external customers; increase promotion and advertising activities.

- *Technological leadership:* maintain technological leadership by increased investment in research and new product development.

- *Human resources capability:* attract superior technical and managerial talent; promote continual professional growth of all employees; continue to invest in the education and training of employees.

DIVISION FUNCTIONS

General Management

The engineering-manufacturing-marketing interface is viewed as critical to the success of the industrial controls division by the general manager. Engineering and manufacturing work together very closely on getting new products into the plant and on solving problems within the production process. When the plant has a problem in manufacturing a particular product, more times than not the answer is somewhere in the engineering-manufacturing interface. The problem may not be in the component itself, but the engineer who designed the product has the insight to allow him, in working with plant personnel, to get to the root problem and then solve it. The marketing-manufacturing interface has become increasingly important in light of the firm's recent 30 percent sales growth rate. Issues related to plant loading, inventory stocking policies, and manufacturing cycle times must be discussed between the two functions. The general manager is a prime promoter of the various disciplines working together and enjoys the challenge of tearing down traditional functional boundaries.

The industrial controls division has chosen to focus its R&D and selling efforts on the high end of the market; products using digital technology. The development of the mission statement is generally left up to division management. The division has an annual formalized strategic planning process. A presentation of the plan, which begins with the mission statement, is made to group management. The general manager tries to involve as many people as possible in the strategic planning process, including plant management.

Once the formal part of the process is completed, he then begins an educational process whereby meetings are conducted at the division and plant levels to present the plan. The information is also shared with all employees at both levels of the firm. In addition, joint marketing-engineering meetings, which include developing and reviewing the division mission statement, product development plans, marketing plans, and some of the philosophies on running the business, are held in Cleveland twice a year. The general manager is a strong believer in total employee involvement and plays an active role in promoting the concept through his own actions.

Quality, product innovation, process innovation, and field service are viewed as the key areas for competitive advantage. The general manager considers lead time and delivery as a part of quality. In his view, you are not doing a quality job for customers unless you give them the product when they want it. Field performance statistics are collected on customer returns; returned industrial controls division products are sent to a facility in Columbus, Ohio, for replacement and tracking of field results. The products manufactured by the industrial controls division are considered "replacement" merchandise (this means that failed circuit boards in returned units are replaced instead of repaired).

In Columbus, the products are disassembled to determine the reason for failure. The results of the failure analysis are accumulated in a database and a circuit board analysis report is sent monthly to the Athens quality assurance manager. The report contains a description of the failures and a listing of the replaced parts for individual orders. The report also includes total monthly warranty dollars, warranty cost trend lines by product line, the mean time between failures (MTBF) for products and components, and the replacement frequency for each component. This information is fed back to the lowest level of the industrial controls organization to which the quality assurance manager can trace the failure. R&D staff also receives field failure information on a regular basis for product development and improvement.

Internally, all products and circuits are put through a test operation. The test operation provides information on whether a product or circuit has passed or failed, and why. This information is captured directly in an in-process database. The prior day's test results are reported in a 7:30 AM meeting held daily at the plant. The meeting is composed of all plant staff members. During the meeting, test results from the previous day are analyzed, and a course of action is decided. Field failure and internal failure information help focus attention on products and materials having high failure rates so that the appropriate actions can be taken collectively by division and plant personnel.

Another quality measure closely monitored by the general manager is guarantee costs. Guarantee costs are costs incurred during the warranty period of a sold product (in other words, warranty cost). R&D spending on product innovation is also scrutinized. Although the degree of product innovation and the level of R&D investment may not be directly related, the general manager feels that it gives an indication of how much the division is investing in the future of the business. Division and plant financial statements are generated and reviewed monthly. Key areas for consideration are earnings, return on investment, inventories, and receivables.

The general manager's key use of performance measurement data is to assist in guiding the organization toward continuous improvement. The standard for performance is the attainment of world-class capabilities, which are driven by the division mission statement. The overall performance criterion is customer satisfaction. Currently, customer satisfaction is informally measured by the number of credit memos the division controller receives. However, the quality assurance manager is creating more formal measures. The organization thus attempts to focus its energies in the direction of value-added activities that support the customers' needs.

Regarding the future direction of performance measures, the general manager states that he would first like to develop a culture conducive to measurement. He would also like to develop a standard and accepted way of doing things to make measurement easier. Product development speed is an area where future measures will be developed, as well as in the number of engineering change orders generated. Finally, a metric in the area of product innovation is desired. The general manager believes that measures will have to change as improvements are made in the business. Performance measures must evolve with the business.

Marketing

There are 10 marketing professionals in the industrial controls division. Four individuals concentrate on the management of the product, and five focus on managing field opportunities (see Table 8–1). Both groups report directly to the marketing manager. The organization is in the process of adding a third dimension, seven or eight control specialists who will report to marketing, but who will actually be based in seven different sales offices across the United States. The product manager is responsible for developing business plans, forecasts, price determinations, and deviations and assisting Athens plant management in determining the monthly plant load. In effect, he is in charge of the product line profit and loss statement (P&L) for the two major industrial control products built in the Athens facility: AutoMate (a traditional programmable logic controller) and AutoMax (a distributed control system).

Reporting to the product manager are a product planning manager and two product specialists. The product planning manager is a technically oriented person who develops product specifications on new products and talks to large users and original equipment manufacturers (OEMs) to ensure that Reliance is developing products that the customer genuinely wants, instead of simply developing "devices." He also is involved in evaluating third-party vendors. Two product specialists provide toll-free product support. There were plans to add a third specialist at the time of this writing.

The five remaining individuals are regional marketing managers for the sales divisions. Industrial controls divides the United States into five sales divisions: east, west, midwest, central (which comprises essentially the states surrounding the Great Lakes), and south. These five sales divisions are further broken into 20 sales regions, with a total of 300 salespeople. Because the sales force is organized this way, five years ago the marketing manager assigned some of the senior marketing people to these areas to support the sales regions. The regional marketing managers are based in Cleveland and spend about 80 percent of their time traveling.

A key task of the regional marketing managers is the development of region sales plans. Once a year, generally in January, the marketing and sales management meet and map out a strategy in the local markets for industrial control products. They assign new distributors, look for new distributors, target companies for presentations and tours of the Athens facility, conduct training seminars, and introduce new products to the sales force.

The regional marketing managers are seasoned professionals who are technically trained (electrical engineers or computer scientists), with some also holding MBAs. Many have worked for competitors such as Westinghouse, General Electric, or Texas Instruments. These managers also have industry specializations based on industrial experience and expertise. For example, one regional marketing manager has many years of experience in the rubber industry. He therefore focuses on bringing Reliance's package solutions or individual hardware to that industry. Another regional marketing manager is a metals specialist by virtue of 15 years at Armco and Kaiser Aluminum.

Product innovation, quality, timeliness, and cost are considered the most critical elements to the business, based on current goals and objectives. Performance in the marketing department is measured by comparing monthly actual to planned revenue results in each sales region by product line. Specific revenue measures used are actual bookings and billings as a percentage of the regional sales plan values, and actual bookings and billings as a percentage of last year's values during the same period. The performance measurement information is used to assess the validity of the regional sales plans and to identify sales trends for product applications. The information is published and distributed throughout both the marketing and sales departments.

To ensure that field personnel understand the overall mission and strategic thrust of the division, the general manager and the marketing manager meet twice a year with the regional sales managers to share their strategic plan and talk specifically about the division's mission. They describe actual performance, discuss goals, and describe the results of the agreed-on plan. Also discussed are the development of a quality culture, world-class manufacturing concepts, product design issues, and customer technical support. Specific confidential product marketing strategies are also shared. The marketing manager believes that the mission statement is the foundation on which all actions are built.

Engineering

The engineering department has seven functional groups, which report to the engineering manager. The functional groups are hardware development (two groups), software development (two groups), computer system support, system engineering, and technical writing. Each group contains 10 to 12 people and is managed by a group-level supervisor. Representatives from engineering are involved in the formal monthly meetings, which are usually held in Athens. The meetings are either one or two days in duration and consist of two phases. Phase 1 is focused on the introduction of new products. Here, representatives from engineering talk to Athens management about any issues relating to specific products that have recently been put into production. Phase 2 is directed toward what is called continuing engineering or support issues, that is, anything related to existing products.

The engineering manager distributes an agenda to the participants before the meeting. The meeting thus provides an opportunity for members of both engineering and plant staffs to discuss product-related issues face to face for consensus and resolution. Primary plant involvement is with industrial engineering, test engineering, and manufacturing, with some input from purchasing and material control when required. A critical performance criterion discussed in the meeting for new products is first-pass yield results. Before the responsibility to produce a new product is transferred to the Athens plant management, the product must first achieve a first-pass yield rating over 90 percent. Until this performance standard is met, engineering and plant staff share the responsibility of monitoring the process and executing actions for achieving an above 90 percent yield.

About four years ago the engineering department switched from being primarily paper oriented to working with personal computers. At that time personal computers were installed on every engineer's desk. The main effect of this action was in the hardware engineering area because, before that time, all the hardware engineering and schematics were drawn manually. By moving these tasks to a computer, hardware development engineers were able to capture the essence of the design on the computer in a form that would allow them to extract a computer-readable BOM file from a schematic drawing. This then prompted a project to take the BOM generated from the engineering computer and transmit it into the manufacturing computer.

Engineering does not intend to tell the plant how to structure or route its materials, but both groups would like to eliminate the mistakes that occur and the time that elapses with a manual transfer. Another benefit derived from the project is that division engineering employees will have access to a screen in the manufacturing computer, which will give them the current production status of a printed circuit board involved in an engineering change order. When division engineering wants to make a change to the BOM, it must be concerned with that particular item's stage in the manufacturing process. Upon installing the new system, division engineering will be able to relate the change order document to the status of the part in the plant. A two-way flow of information, beneficial to both engineering and the plant, is thus created.

The engineering manager cites quality as the most important competitive edge for industrial controls, followed by process and product innovation, delivery, and process and product flexibility. In terms of performance measurement, the department uses a project scheduling package for tracking performance against project milestones and completion dates. Currently, there are no performance measures for engineering change notices or new product development. All department personnel fill out monthly time sheets so that project hours can be collected; an analysis of project hours will promote the understanding of effort being spent on a particular project. Besides the number of engineering hours and development dollars (which appear on the selling, general, and administrative [SG&A] expense line of the operating statement), very few formal measures are used in the division engineering function. The engineering manager believes that part of the challenge in the department is to foster a creative atmosphere. He tries to walk the line between creating a bureaucratic structure and allowing the department to function as a group of free spirits.

Accounting

The cost accounting system is currently driven by direct labor hours. All plant overhead is allocated on this basis. Once a year, purchasing revises material standard costs. New labor rates are applied to routings, and new overhead rates are applied to the labor to derive standard cost. One of the problems associated with the cost accounting system is that it is driven by direct labor. The direct labor standard hours produced continue to decline as labor is taken out of the operation. Currently, direct labor represents only 3 percent of the total product cost. With increased capital investment on the shop floor, the department is faced with allocating more and more overhead based on an ever-shrinking pool of direct labor standard hours. The division controller states that the cost accounting system will have to be updated to catch up with 1990s technology.

Although the division utilizes a traditional full-absorption accounting system, which tracks direct labor efficiencies and machine utilization, division staff does not utilize the information to make decisions. The division controller states that labor efficiency is only as good as the industrial engineering standards, which have not been updated in at least 10 years. The focus is on how much money can be made. Capital investment justifications still utilize the measures of net present value and return on investment, but incremental volume gains also play an important role in the investment decision. The hurdle rate for new investments is 40 percent, and 20 percent for replacement over a three- to four-year horizon. Capital projects are also monitored to see how well the investment is achieving its financial returns objective.

The division controller cited quality as the most important competitive edge for the division, followed by cost, delivery and lead times, and field service. The key performance measures of inventory management are inventory turns based on sales and stock service level. The standard for acceptable stock service is 93 percent. The objective is high inventory turns with good stock service levels. Plant productivity is measured by net sales billed per employee (NSB/employee). The net sales billed for the month is divided by the total plant head count for the same period. Increases in the NSB/employee ratio indicate relative increases in productivity, whereas decreases signify productivity declines. Another more subtle measure used is backlog size relative to sales growth. If the backlog is relatively flat or decreasing during increasing volumes, then chances are good that productivity is also increasing and is not an issue. If backlog is building, however, then productivity needs to be addressed.

Other measures that are monitored and reported are cratings per day (dollars of product shipped per day), cratings per employee (dollars of product shipped divided by total plant head count), guarantee cost, and R&D spending. Performance data are reported on a monthly basis and distributed primarily to plant and division staff members. All financial information is expressed in total dollars and as a percentage of NSB (except sales bookings). Furthermore, all financial information is compared to planned results. In general, the measures used at the division are understood by the entire organization. To ensure this understanding, division accounting has conducted training sessions with the marketing department on how to read its financial statements. This training will also be carried out in the engineering department.

PLANT FUNCTIONS

The plant operation consists of functionally structured departments. An operations manager for the industrial controls operation and an overall plant manager responsible for the Athens facility are both located in Athens. Other plant staff functions are manufacturing, management information systems, materials management, accounting, production engineering, test engineering, customer service, and quality assurance. The plant staff departments are shared resources between the two manufacturing facilities. However, all functional department managers report directly to the plant manager, including the operations manager for industrial controls. The organizational structure of the industrial controls plant is presented in Figure 8–2.

Manufacturing Operations

The layout of the Athens plant allows material to flow from one end to the other. Receiving is on one end of the plant, followed by a stockroom and subassembly areas. Material then flows toward the other end of the facility for final product shipment. In the circuit area, which is one of the high-volume subassembly operations, the flow is U-shaped. The facility layout and material flow are illustrated in Figure 8–3. There are approximately three horizontal departments that feed a series of vertical departments. Horizontal departments include sheet metal fabrication, circuit assembly test, and some subassembly areas where the subassemblies are specialized from a processing or testing standpoint.

Vertical departments consist of individuals building products that will leave the plant and go to an outside customer, as opposed to the horizontal departments, which provide materials for internal use. Vertical departments are viewed as product lines or business areas. Every department has one or more supervisors, depending on the number of people and the size of the operation. Each supervisor manages not only the hourly workers, but also his own material handlers, who have the responsibility of gathering any material together for that circuit board and then stocking it on the line. Production workers are held responsible for quality. In-process inspectors test subassembles and report to the supervisors. Thus, business unit supervisors manage all the functions necessary for getting the product from raw material to shipping.

Manufacturing performance is measured from raw materials issuance to the customer order shipment. The plant uses input-output measures to track raw material and WIP inventory. The Athens plant management examines the dollars of inventory in and out, along with monthly changes. Inventory turns and absolute inventory dollars are monitored. Inventory valuation includes raw material, direct labor and manufacturing overhead costs. Inventory turns are completed by dividing net sales

FIGURE 8-2
Organizational Structure of the Industrial Controls Plant

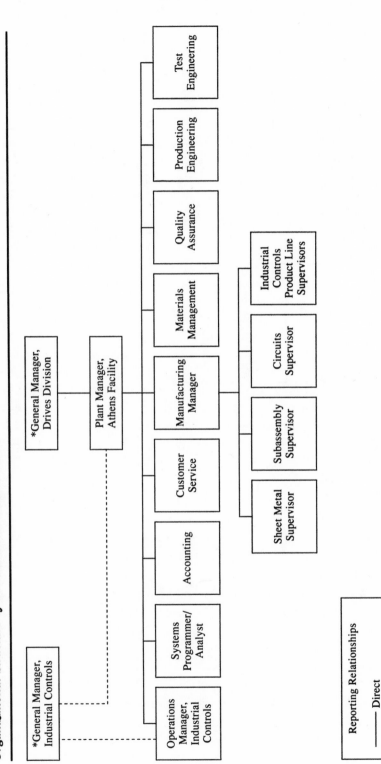

FIGURE 8–3
Athens Plant Facility Layout

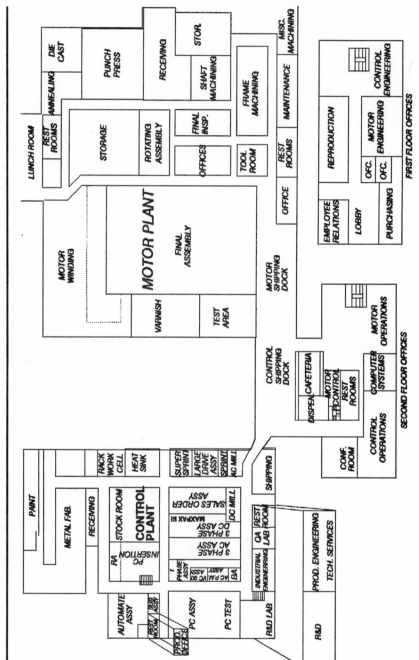

billed (NSB) by the inventory investment (NSB/inventory investment). Management also examines net sales billed per employee (NSB/employee). The NSB per employee is used as a measure of plant productivity and is derived by dividing total monthly plant head count into the net sales billed for the same period.

Labor efficiencies for each horizontal and vertical department are still reported monthly by the accounting department, but are not used. The operations manager suggested, however, that such information may be useful for the management of bottleneck resources. Athens plant management also measures the dollar amount of merchandise shipped on a daily basis. Shipping dollars to date are compared against the monthly shipping goal daily. This has helped eliminate the "end of the month" syndrome that takes place in many plants. Another measure that is examined is known as *pull through*. Pull through is the ratio of the deviation in earnings before interest and taxes (actual EBIT − planned EBIT) in a given month to the deviation in net sales billed (actual NSB − planned NSB) for the same period. The ratio is calculated only if the deviation in NSB is positive. The percentage should be high, as no additional resources were added to generate the additional profits. A positive pull through value indicates that actual net sales were greater than planned and resulted in a marginal increase in earnings (EBIT). A negative pull through ratio indicates that, although net sales were larger than anticipated, the actual EBIT was less than planned and resulted in a loss of profitability.

Other measures used at the plant level are vendor delivery performance (number and percentage of units delivered on time), daily yields on boards, weekly failure analysis, material utilization via scrap measurement, and warranty costs. Two measures that are reported directly to the division and group levels are delivery performance against schedules and in-stock service levels. Delivery performance is measured by comparing the quoted delivery date to the number of units shipped against the order. The performance standard is for all orders to be shipped within two weeks of the promised date. A two-weeks-late report is generated biweekly and distributed to plant, division, and group management staffs. Furthermore, the total number of units late for any amount of time is reported to plant, division, and group management staffs monthly.

The in-stock service level (that is, the in-stock percentage of items in the warehouse) performance standard is 93 percent. The Athens plant currently does not measure lead time. Athens plant management has not installed a new performance measurement system but has added measures to the existing system. The operations manager believes that the strategic objectives of quality, delivery, and cost are essential to the survival of the business. However, he also thinks that product innovation, lead time (which includes product design and development), and product and process flexibility are strategic objectives on which the plant can compete.

All production workers have been trained in statistical process control (SPC), with some having attended advanced SPC classes. Some small-group activities are also in place, led by the supervisor in most cases, typically with a quality focus. Training is conducted during regular business hours. Most education and training activities are voluntary with the exception of SPC. Education and training for nonmanagement plant salaried employees have also been conducted in the principles and concepts of world-class manufacturing.

Manufacturing Planning and Control

The industrial controls plant utilizes a regeneration material requirements planning system, which is updated weekly. The base system was purchased from the Martin Marietta Corporation between 1982 and 1983. A plant staff programmer has modified the system for report generation. No changes have been made to the system logic. Affiliates who purchase products from the industrial controls division have direct access to the MRP system in Athens, and can actually enter customer orders on the Athens plant system for direct shipments.

Kanban cards are being used in certain areas of the facility to manage parts fabrication and assembly. The kanban system is linked to the MRP system through the use of blanket orders. The rule is not to commit material until the kanban card is received. A blanket order (long-term vendor contract) is negotiated for a given quantity to cover some period of time. The consumption of the material is driven by the kanban system. The blanket order is relieved only of the material actually consumed. Thus, the blanket order is "partially" relieved until it is entirely consumed.

An MRP subsystem allows for the batching of material based on need, not on economic order quantity (EOQ). The facility does not use EOQ formulas for lot sizing. They make the assumption that setups are approaching zero, thus allowing for lot sizes to get as close to one as possible. The kanban system allows for material releases from producing work centers to consuming work centers based on actual usage. The system is being used between primary feeder areas (subassembly lines) and the final assembly area. The goal is to use kanban to pull material through the subassembly and assembly areas with MRP functioning as a planning tool.

The MRP system does not contain a capacity requirements planning (CRP) module, so plant load is reviewed based on a rough-cut capacity plan of the master production schedule (MPS). The manufacturing manager and his supervisors review the required hours by work center for potential capacity and material problems. If a problem is anticipated, management looks at each planning bill. The majority of the plant management staff have been educated in TOC, and employees incorporate such thinking into their decision-making processes. Plant management is currently discussing the adoption of drum-buffer-rope (DBR) for scheduling parts fabrication and assembly on the production floor. Although they have not formally implemented the concepts of TOC, plant managers look for bottleneck operations and treat them differently from nonbottlenecks. When a bottleneck operation is discovered, plant management uses various techniques to maximize its throughput: smaller transfer batches, running the operation on breaks and during lunch, setup reduction methods, and so on. Operations that are not considered bottlenecks receive management attention only as required.

BOM accuracy is at least 95 percent. It is measured in several ways. Numerical control (NC) tapes are compared to material planning tapes every six months to detect errors. Manufacturing engineering conducts quarterly audits of blueprints and compares them to the BOM. Finally, line managers check prints against the BOM on an exception basis, when part shortages for an item are reoccurring. The errors seen on the BOM are human entry errors. All BOMs contain the necessary items for manufacturing the product. Once the project to transmit BOMs electronically from division engineering to the BOM file in the plant MRP system is completed, the accuracy rate is expected to approach 100 percent.

Materials Management

The materials management function is involved in new product introductions, parts availability and scheduling, purchasing, material receiving, expediting, and vendor certification. This department interacts with line management by defining material requirements, advising on possible material substitutions or deviations, and defining ship-to-stock vendors. Materials received from ship-to-stock vendors are directly placed in the stockroom without inspection. There are about 12 certified ship-to-stock vendors. The Athens plant also has 20 JIT vendors of electronic components. These vendors supply material to the plant in a just-in-time fashion. There is a major difference between ship-to-stock and JIT vendors. Ship-to-stock vendors supply materials that do not require inspection, but they have not altered the delivery relationship. JIT vendors supply the Athens plant with materials in a just-in-time manner, but their materials still require inspection.

Vendors supporting the Athens plant consist primarily of large-scale electronic component manufacturers, such as Motorola, National Semiconductor, and Texas Instruments. A base of smaller electrical component manufacturers supply specialty items. Eight distributors procure parts that Reliance cannot buy directly from manufacturers. Reliance buys some specialty sheet metal from several job shops.

Vendor qualification for ship-to-stock certification is conducted by a team composed of representatives from purchasing, R&D, and quality, along with the materials manager. Material planners manage the routine problems associated with parts within their planning code responsibility. However, if repeat quality problems occur, the quality function gets involved. The Athens plant establishes long-term relationships with its vendors, partly out of necessity. Once a part is specified and certified, it takes extensive engineering effort to change it. In many cases the plant will buy a family of parts from a single source of supply. Sole sourcing helps to stabilize and standardize the manufacturing operation. Reliance has also found that sole suppliers are more responsive to its needs.

Vendors visit the Athens facility on a regular basis. Many visits are just customer calls to cultivate new business. Vendors also visit to see whether they can identify material cost reduction opportunities or redesign their parts to make them easier for Reliance to build. Material planners also have the opportunity to visit vendor locations for similar reasons.

Inventory accuracy was estimated to be in the low 90 percent range and is complicated by Reliance's point-of-use stocking process. Parts are located at their points of demand. Thus, in order to get an accurate count, it is necessary to count all the parts in all the locations and subtract the known requirements that are being built. However, parts that are on the shelf may already be allocated and must be netted out. These physical inventory totals are then compared to the inventory records annually. The plant is currently not using cycle counting. Athens plant management is evaluating the use of cycle counting on finished goods located in the distribution warehouse. The distribution center is a separate facility located in Athens. Distribution center inventory is still part of the division inventory until it is sold. Not all distribution inventory is part of plant inventory, however, because it includes purchased inventory for resale.

The materials manager believes that quality, product innovation, delivery, and lead time are the strategic objectives on which the plant competes. A key measure in his area is the total number of inventory turns, which includes raw material and work-in-process (WIP). This ratio is based on net sales billed. All inventory valuation includes raw material, direct labor, and manufacturing overhead costs. Total plant inventory is targeted between $10 and 20 million, of which approximately 33 percent comprises raw and WIP. The department closely monitors daily part shortages and on-time delivery performance. Shortages are tracked on a graph by part number and as a percentage of daily parts usage. Part shortages are also tracked by orders. The information is used to discover part shortage trends that may relate to vendor performance.

Inventory turns have increased fourfold in the last four years. The on-time delivery performance percentage has gone from the high fifties to the nineties in the same time period. Delivery performance is measured monthly and is defined as the ratio of actual to planned scheduled shipments for the period.

Accounting

The same accounting system is used for the Athens facility and division headquarters. Division financial statements reflect products sold from plant production and resale, whereas plant financial statements reflect only what was produced and sold from plant operations. The accounting system is a direct labor-based system, with its primary components being raw material, labor, and overhead costs. New standards for material purchases and direct labor are developed once a year. An overhead study is conducted each year to determine the rates at which to value the direct labor. The plant controller views the accounting function as a support organization. The objective is to provide the information that is needed to enhance total business performance. The plant controller cites quality, product innovation, cost, and field service as the most critical areas of competition for the plant.

Production Engineering

Production engineering supports existing manufacturing processes, defines the appropriate manufacturing processes and equipment for new products, and is indirectly responsible for equipment maintenance. With direct labor representing only 3 percent of the product cost, production engineering has become more process-oriented, as opposed to a more traditional orientation toward work methods and time standards.

In product introductions, production engineers are a part of the design team. They are responsible for deriving process routings, costing, and BOM structuring. This group also lends technical support to the quality department, as there are currently no quality engineers. Maintenance support is procured either from the motor plant or from outside contractors. However, maintenance for the industrial controls operation is ultimately the responsibility of production engineering. The production engineers are assigned product families based on their expertise. They are expected to do a mixture of what is traditionally viewed as manufacturing, industrial, and design engineering tasks relative to their product lines. Production engineers are also involved in vendor qualification or ship-to-stock program audits. Their role is to examine the vendor's manufacturing process to assess how well the process is being controlled.

Production engineers are heavily involved in teaching world-class manufacturing techniques to production workers. Tools such as SPC, preventive maintenance, and setup reduction are taught to the operators. Once the procedures are mastered, the engineer's role now changes to that of a facilitator. As production workers develop ideas for tool design, manufacturing methods, and setup improvement, the engineers are expected to evaluate the ideas, modify them when necessary, and help the workers to implement the ideas. The department is trying very hard to harness the mental capabilities of the entire work force.

The production engineering manager believes that quality is the primary competitive area of the industrial controls facility, followed by cost, delivery, and product innovation. The key, in his view, is to give the customer the highest value-added per dollar. Furthermore, the production engineering manager views the workers on the production floor as his customers. The department's focus is therefore on how well the manufacturing processes are defined or designed and how well manufacturing technology is employed to reduce inventory and operational expenses while increasing total plant throughput. The production engineering manager believes that a good manufacturing engineer should save about twice his annual salary in cost reductions. In 1990, the department set a year-end goal in the range of $250,000 to $300,000 for cost reductions. The actual result was an annual savings amounting to approximately 120 percent of the year-end goal. These cost reductions are measured and recorded monthly.

Test Engineering

The primary focus of test engineering is to provide test engineering instructions, procedures, and equipment to manufacturing and to make sure that the equipment is able to test products adequately. The department is involved with manufacturing in new product introductions to ensure that production personnel understand the test procedures and use of the equipment. Test engineers also support existing products by reviewing equipment and test procedures and making changes as necessary. They help verify whether component vendors or third-party vendors on new products are supplying parts that meet the technical requirements. When components or outsourced products fail, test engineering will generally assist the supplier directly in solving the problem.

The test engineering manager believes that quality, cost, and delivery are the key areas of competition for the industrial controls operation. A crucial performance criterion in this department is the on-time placement of test equipment in the production facility for new product introductions. If the equipment is not in place, the product cannot be produced. The ability to install test equipment in a timely manner directly affects delivery and plant throughput. The performance measure is the timely delivery of the test equipment. The performance standard requires that test equipment be installed on schedule.

Customer Service

The goal of customer service is to support the plant in satisfying customers' needs. Industrial controls is a 100 percent make-to-stock business. Customers are supplied directly from finished goods inventory. Customer service personnel enter customer orders into the order entry system. The order entry system is linked to both the MRP and accounting systems. Bills of lading (legal contracts between the shipper and carrier for the movement of designated freight) are then created via the accounting system and picked up by the crating and shipping department, which then pulls, boxes, and ships the order. Next, customer service posts and authorizes those shipments in the order entry system for the generation of invoices via the accounting system. Customer service also helps the production supervisors and material planners in changing manufacturing priorities to meet particular order situations in which some products may not be available to meet a certain shipment date. Customer service also assists the marketing function in the administration of special pricing agreements.

Customer orders can be placed in several ways. Some customers electronically place orders directly into the system. These customers can also view plant completion dates of existing orders and stock availability. Orders can be placed via fax, telex, mail, or telephone. Three customer service personnel enter orders for industrial controls. Reliance is studying the use of electronic data interchange (EDI) for order entry. EDI is the direct computer-to-computer exchange of standard business documents (purchase orders, trade and freight invoices, bills of lading, and so forth) between two separate companies. The current on-line system provides readable screen or printed output to the user, whereas EDI also updates computer files automatically.

The customer service manager believes that quality, product and process innovation, delivery, and lead time are critical to the success of the plant. Key areas of performance for the department are customer shipments and service levels in finished goods inventory, which are examined daily. The department also monitors the number of finished goods stockouts daily. Invoice errors are measured and causes ranked. Another performance measure is the percentage of orders placed via the on-line order entry system. Initially, the percentage was virtually zero. At the time of this writing, approximately 25 percent of all orders are placed electronically. The information is tracked graphically. A future measure for the customer service area is the elapsed time between receipt of an order via fax, mail, or telephone and its placement in the order entry system. This process currently takes two to three days.

Quality Assurance

The quality assurance function at the Athens plant consists of a quality assurance manager, a components quality engineer, and several process auditors. The process auditors are former quality inspectors who are now responsible for proactively discovering current or potential problems in the manufacturing process. Quality inspectors are no longer used in the Athens plant. The components quality engineer has the task of continuously monitoring and improving the quality of purchased components by working directly with component vendors. When internal or field failures occur because of purchased components, the components quality engineer works directly with his counterparts at the vendor facility to determine an appropriate course of action. The quality manager is viewed almost as an internal consultant. He provides long-range strategy for quality to the organization, as well as guidance in education and training.

Education and training in quality management techniques at the Athens plant started in 1984. The educational process started at the top with the general manager, followed by division and plant staff, and has been ongoing with production and office personnel. The training consists of a two-week course on basic statistical quality control philosophies and techniques. To avoid knowledge gaps within the organization, a rule was established that employees cannot attend the course unless their supervisor has already attended or is currently attending. Currently, one-week SPC courses are conducted on-site every six weeks by an external consultant. An advanced course in statistical methods is also taught; it covers correlation, experimental design, and Taguchi loss functions. The quality manager teaches the concepts of quality function deployment (QFD) at various levels of the organization. He firmly believes that quality is the plant's most important competitive advantage, but that cost and delivery are also important.

PERFORMANCE MEASUREMENT SYSTEMS

Division management has a business review meeting once a month (usually lasting one to two days) with plant management to review the previous month's business performance. Performance areas reviewed at the monthly meeting include bookings, backlog, net sales billed per employee (NSB/employee), earnings before interest and taxes (EBIT), guarantee cost (warranty cost), days of sales outstanding (DSO), inventory dollars, inventory turnover, cash generated, return on capital employed, sales by distribution channel, gross margins, service level, and plant cost. All financial results are presented both in dollars and as a percentage of NSB. Year-to-date financial results are also included in the financial statements. Written reports are presented by division and plant staff managers in the form of graphs, trend lines, or any other format deemed appropriate.

Important interactions also occur between division engineering and manufacturing concerning troubleshooting and new product development. Reliance considers its products as the lifeblood of the business, so it works very hard at keeping the engineering-manufacturing relationship strong. Another critical relationship exists between division marketing and the Athens plant. The industrial controls division has experienced a growth rate of approximately 30 percent in the past several years. Thus, plant capacity is of primary concern to marketing. Shifts in product mix, manufacturing cycle times, and inventory policies are critical to satisfying customer delivery expectations in a make-to-stock business. The engineering-manufacturing-marketing linkages have proven to be critical to the success of the business unit. The performance measurement systems used at the division and plant levels are given in Tables 8-1 and 8-2 respectively.

PERFORMANCE MEASUREMENT SYSTEM LINKAGES

Plant costs are a critical performance criterion for the Athens plant. These costs consist of returns and allowances, standard cost of sales, material price variance, other material variances, labor variances, overhead incurred, overhead recovery, overhead variance, inventory adjustments, guarantee cost, miscellaneous manufacturing costs, interunit markup, procurement, storage, shipment, and testing costs, manufacturing administration, and sales order engineering costs. Plant costs reflect the activities of the facility during the month and are collected by the cost accounting system.

To support the division's mission of customer satisfaction, the quality manager has been actively involved in developing a means for keeping the organization abreast of customers' needs. Quality assurance is currently conducting training sessions for design engineers, marketing, and manufacturing staff on how to perform a customer interview. The skills acquired in these training sessions will be used in product design meetings with the customer and in field application workshops devised to avoid customers from misapplying the product. Customer interviews are conducted by design engineers, marketing, and manufacturing staff to better determine what actual customers' needs are prior to the design and manufacturing phases. Customers' interviews during field application workshops are held to discover whether the product is performing in a satisfactory manner. Follow-up interviews with customers are also conducted to monitor customer satisfaction levels. Quality assurance is currently developing an instrument to use during customer interviews for measuring the level of customer satisfaction.

Capability studies have been conducted on most of the major equipment in the plant. This equipment is monitored using statistical process control charts, which are posted by the equipment. A quality information system database maintains quality information on a part from the time it is received. The part is also monitored throughout the production process. All test information is collected daily and formally reported on a weekly basis. A 7:30 AM meeting provides a forum for discussing actions required of plant personnel, based on yesterday's test results.

On a monthly basis, a first-pass circuit yield report is produced by quality assur-

TABLE 8–1

Industrial Controls Division Level Performance Measurement System

Performance Criterion	Performance Measure*	Performance Standard
Financial	Bookings	Financial plan
	Billings	Financial plan
	Sales by distribution channel	Financial plan
	EBIT	Financial plan
	Accounts receivable DSO	Financial plan
	Backlog	Financial plan
	Gross margins	Financial plan
	R&D expenditures	Financial plan
	Return on capital employed	Financial plan
Quality	Guarantee cost	Improving trend
	MTBF—products	Engineering specs
	MTBF—components	Engineering specs
	Component replacement frequency	Improving trend
Inventory†	Inventory dollars	Financial plan
	Inventory turns	Financial plan
	Excess inventory	Above projected three-year usage
	Obsolete inventory	No usage in three years
Plant	NSB per employee	Improving trend
	Number of credit memos	No credit memos
	Backlog size to sales growth	Improving trend
	Cratings per day	Improving trend
	Cratings per employee	Improving trend
	Stock service level	93%
	On-time delivery	All deliveries within two weeks of promise date
	Plant cost	Financial plan
	BOM accuracy	>95%
	Stock service level	93%
	On-time delivery	All deliveries made within two weeks of promise date
	Plant cost	Financial plan
	Cost reductions per production engineer	Twice annual salary
	On-time delivery of test equipment	On-time delivery
	Percent of orders received on-line	>25%
Engineering	Engineering hours by product	Planned project hours
	Engineering development dollars spent	Financial plan

*Performance measures are reported monthly unless otherwise specified.

†Inventory valuation includes raw material, direct labor, and manufacturing overhead costs.

TABLE 8–2
Industrial Controls Plant Level Level Performance Measurement System

Performance Criterion	Performance Measure*	Performance Standard
Financial	Bookings	Financial Plan
	Billings	Financial Plan
	Sales by distribution channel	Financial Plan
	EBIT	Financial Plan
	Accounts receivable DSO	Financial Plan
	Backlog	Financial Plan
	Gross margins	Financial Plan
	R&D expenditures	Financial Plan
	Return on capital employed	Financial Plan
	Pull through	Positive value
Quality	Guarantee cost	Improving trend
	MTBF—products	Engineering specs
	MTBF—components	Engineering specs
	Component replacement frequency	Improving trend
	Circuit yields	>95%
	Number of soldering failures	No failures
Inventory†	Inventory dollars	$10.5 million
	Inventory turns	Financial plan
	Excess inventory	Above projected three-year usage
	Obsolete inventory	No usage in three years
	Dollars of inventory in versus dollars out	Improving trend
	Monthly inventory change	Improving trend
	Daily parts shortages	No shortages
	Inventory accuracy	>90%
	Stock levels	Quantity for 93% service level
Plant	NSB/employee	Improving trend
	Backlog size to sales growth	Improving trend
	Crating per day	Improving trend
	Cratings per employee	Improving trend
	BOM accuracy	>95%
	Stock service level	93%
	On-time delivery	All deliveries made within two weeks of promise date
	Plant cost	Financial plan
	Cost reduction per production engineer	Twice annual salary
	On-time delivery of test equipment	On-time delivery
	Percent of orders received on-line	>25%
Vendor	Daily parts shortages	No shortages
	Performance to schedule	On-time delivery

*Performance measures are reported monthly unless otherwise specified.

†Inventory valuation includes raw material, direct labor, and manufacturing overhead costs.

ance; this report ranks all the circuits produced over the past six months in six different categories, based on level of complexity. The circuits are categorized so that quality comparisons can be made for similar circuits. The first-pass circuit yield report shows the number of circuits tested, the first-pass yield, and the cause of failure (failure categories used are component, workmanship, or other) in a given month by circuit number. Also included in the report (by circuit number) are the number of circuits tested year-to-date, the year-to-date number of circuit failures, year-to-date first-pass circuit yields, the average first-pass circuit yield for last year, and the three-month first-pass circuit yield.

The report is distributed to the test engineering manager, production engineering manager, manufacturing supervisor, operations manager, plant manager, and quality assurance manager. First-pass circuit yields currently average 95 percent. In soldering, several years ago the failure rate was in the area of 3,000 parts per million. Currently, the plant is averaging 125 failed parts per million. This rate is on a volume of 250 billion soldering jobs per year. Performance measurement system linkages in the areas of plant costs and quality are thus assisting the industrial controls division in maintaining world-class manufacturing capabilities within the organization.

LESSONS LEARNED

The Reliance Electric case provides several lessons on the development of performance measurement linkages between systems and functions on a firm's strategic objective.

Finance and Customer

Performance measurement information is needed to assess the financial impact of planned and actual sales activities. Reliance measures actual to planned monthly revenue results in each sales region by product line. Specific revenue measures used are actual bookings and billings as a percentage of the regional sales plan values, and actual bookings and billings as a percentage of last year's values during the same period. The performance measurement information is used to assess the validity of the regional sales plans and to spot sales trends for product applications. Specific activities to facilitate the linkage include biannual meetings between the general manager, marketing manager, and regional sales managers to discuss actual performance, goals, objectives, competitive edges, and the sales plan. Also discussed are world-class manufacturing concepts, product design issues, and customer technical support.

Customer and Resource

The engineering-manufacturing-marketing interface is viewed as critical to Reliance's success. Design, manufacturing, and marketing personnel hold joint product concept design meetings with customers to keep abreast of customers' needs. Field application workshops devised to avoid customers' misapplication of the product are also held jointly by design, manufacturing, and marketing personnel. Customer interviews are conducted by design engineers, manufacturing and marketing to better determine what customers' needs actually are prior to the design and manufacturing phases. Returned products are disassembled to determine the failure mode. The results of failure analyses are accumulated in a database, and a circuit board analysis report is sent monthly to the quality assurance manager. The report contains a description of the failures and a listing of replaced parts for individual orders. The report also includes total monthly warranty dollars, warranty cost trend lines by product line, the MTBF for products and components, and the replacement frequency for each part. The information is used to trace field failures to specific design flaws or manufacturing processes. Field failure and internal failure information is used to focus organizational resources on continual improvement efforts for products, processes, and materials that cause failures.

Finance and Resource

Reliance Electric uses a traditional full-absorption accounting system that tracks many of the common measures found in such systems, such as direct labor and machine efficiencies and utilizations. Although these measures are collected, they are not used for purposes of decision making. A key metric for monitoring labor is the ratio of net sales billed to the number of employees. Another resource performance metric is the ratio of backlog size to sales growth. Both measures attempt to assess the financial impact of the current level of resources employed. The pull through metric (deviation in EBIT/deviation in net sales billed) allows the firm to examine the effect of a marginal increase in sales on earnings. A positive pull through value indicates that actual net sales are greater than planned and resulted in a marginal increase in earnings (EBIT). A negative pull through ratio indicates that, although NSB was larger than anticipated, actual EBIT was less than planned. Thus, the resources employed to generate the incremental gain in net sales billed did not result in higher earnings. This case illustrates how firms can begin to develop linkages between their performance measurement systems and across functions to become a world-class competitor.

Chapter Nine

Yamaha Motor Manufacturing Corporation of America

The case illustrates how to develop linkages between the customer and resource performance measurement systems and functions. Yamaha has the strategic objectives of cost and quality and established performance measurement criteria, standards, and metrics to meet these objectives.

COMPANY BACKGROUND

The Yamaha Motor Corporation (referred to as Yamaha Japan) is a worldwide manufacturer of internal combustion engine products with headquarters in Japan. Yamaha Japan has established manufacturing, sales, and distribution organizations outside of Japan around the world to better serve target markets. The Yamaha Motor Corporation of the United States (referred to as Yamaha USA or YMC USA) is a sales and marketing company established in California during the 1960s to distribute and sell Yamaha products in the United States. Yamaha Motor Manufacturing Corporation of America (referred to as Yamaha Motor Manufacturing or YMMC) produces golf carts and water vehicles for the US market. The manufacturing organization is located in Newnan, Georgia, and began its first commercial production in June 1988. The firm's customer base is 100 percent make-to-stock, and the manufacturing process is repetitive (high volume, few models). Products manufactured by YMMC are sold directly to Yamaha USA for sales and distribution to retail outlets. Total YMMC employment is 470. There are approximately five levels in the typical bill of material for both the golf cart and water vehicle product lines, and 5,000 active part numbers in the inventory system. Yamaha Motor Manufacturing uses elements of material requirements planning (MRP) and just-in-time (JIT) to plan, monitor, and control the production process.

FIGURE 9–1
Yamaha Motor Corporation Organizational Structure

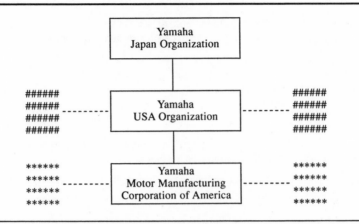

#Denotes existence of other sales and distribution organizations worldwide.

*Denotes existence of other motor manufacturing organizations worldwide.

Interviews were conducted with the following individuals:

- Product engineering manager.
- Quality control manager.
- Manufacturing engineering manager.
- Operations manager.
- Production control manager.
- Material control manager.
- Purchasing manager.
- Information systems manager.
- Accounting manager.
- Human resources manager.

The organization structure of the Yamaha Motor Corporation is presented in Figure 9–1.

STRATEGIC OBJECTIVES

Yamaha Japan is involved in a globalization process in each major market segment worldwide to enhance its overall customer sensitivity and ability to interpret market needs. The firm wants to design, develop, refine, and market internal combustion engine products that fit the needs of specific markets. The following objectives have been established to support Yamaha Japan's globalization strategy:

- Establishment of global information networks to allow all locations to share common databases for improved timeliness of information worldwide.
- Establishment of profitable manufacturing sites outside of Japan within regional markets worldwide.
- Globalization of manufacturing processes using generic systems (CAD, CAM, etc.).
- New product development through concentric diversification around the core product, internal combustion engines.
- Increased sales, reduced product cost, reduced fixed cost, and achievement of long-term profitability.

A major objective of YMMC is to develop technical and manufacturing independence from Yamaha Japan within several years. The tactics for achieving this objective include the following:

- Developing further the manufacturing know-how of the Newnan facility.
- Continuing to strengthen the YMMC organization using enhanced information systems, advanced technical capabilities, and world-class management practices.
- Developing a presence in the United States by producing products whose quality is equal to or exceeds those manufactured in Japan.

Yamaha Motor Manufacturing has already managed to achieve product quality levels equal to those of similar products made by Yamaha Japan. Other key YMMC objectives that directly support the globalization strategy include these:

- Continuing to develop world-class manufacturing capabilities at the Newnan facility.
- Developing new products specifically for the US market that exploit the firm's core manufacturing competence (internal combustion engines).
- Continuing to develop organizational capabilities for faster and more accurate customer response in the US market.
- Providing manufacturing capabilities in the United States that enhance the long-term profitability of Yamaha.

YMMC has a written policy in the lobby area stating that the organization will work to create and maintain an attitude of pride about jobs, products, and company.

The policy also states that YMMC will maintain relentless dedication to excellence and will not compromise the quality and reliability of Yamaha products.

YMMC DEPARTMENTS

Operations

Manufacturing is composed of five separate operating units. Three are involved in fabrication operations, and the other two operating units assemble products. Fabrication operating units include plastics (molding and forming operations), welding, and paint. The two assembly operating units are organized by product line: one line assembles golf carts, and the other assembles water vehicles. Maintenance and distribution (plant stockroom) operating units are also located in the manufacturing area but are not under the direct responsibility of the operations manager. (Manufacturing engineering is responsible for the maintenance operating unit, and production control manages the distribution operating unit.) Area leaders help the operating unit develop the motivational instincts and interpersonal skills necessary for team building within the operating units. Production workers are hourly employees, but there are no time clocks in the facility. Time sheets are completed by the workers daily. The work force is flexible, and individuals are moved between production operating units as required.

The manufacturing facility layout is cellular and uses an overall manufacturing flow concept. Manufacturing's goal is to "flow" the materials through the various operating units, adding value to them at each phase. As one completed golf cart or water vehicle is produced by an assembly operating unit, an unfinished assembly enters the line. MRP is not used in the production area for shop floor scheduling or control purposes, but strictly as a tool for material planning. Thus, JIT elements such as "pull" production, quality at the source, level scheduling, small lot sizes, and cellular layouts are used to plan, monitor, and control the manufacturing operation.

The operations manager views the manufacturing function as the "customer" of all other supporting departments. He states that the "product" of the supporting departments is customer service and that the primary customer being served is the manufacturing area. With this in mind, the operations manager believes that his primary responsibilities to YMMC are to control the labor utilized in production and to ensure that all manufacturing processes are operating to established standards. He believes that by maintaining a customer-supplier relationship internally as well as externally, each department will better understand its role and will develop stronger interrelationships.

Each of the five unit supervisors collects and monitors daily performance measurement information on product quality, labor usage, and performance to the master production schedule (MPS). Other performance measurement areas are safety, labor cost, material expenses, and new products. The specific criterion measures used in the production department are as follows:

Plant safety.

- Number of OSHA-recordable injuries.
- Number of lost-time accidents.
- Number of lost-time days.

Product quality.

- *First-pass ratio:* percentage of material that meets all product specifications the first time through the manufacturing process.
- *Scrap dollars:* dollar value of materials ruined in-process.
- *Warehouse holds:* number of products that, for whatever reason, were shipped from the facility to a distribution warehouse and returned for rework.

Business cost measures.

- *Labor cost:* represents approximately 20 percent of total product cost; comparison of monthly actual to budgeted labor cost.
- *Materials/consumables expenses:* comparison of monthly actual to budgeted expenses.

Direct labor usage.

- *Direct labor efficiency (DLE):* ratio of standard output time (standard time per unit × units produced) to the actual production time used.
- *Direct labor utilization (DLU):* ratio of actual production time used to the total time available.
- *Direct labor productivity (DLP):* ratio of standard output time to total time available, or DLE × DLU.

MPS performance.

- *Performance to scheduled volume:* ratio of daily scheduled production volume to actual production volume.
- *Performance to scheduled mix:* ratio of daily scheduled production mix to actual mix.
- *Manufacturing throughput:* daily number of units manufactured through

each phase of the operation (assembly, inspection, and shipping); units are tracked via bar coding.

New products.

- Achieve planned efficiencies and quality levels for new products three weeks after release to operations.

Plant safety measures are collected weekly for each of the five operating units and are reported monthly. First-pass ratios are calculated daily for each unit, as well as monthly for the entire plant. Direct labor efficiency, utilization, and productivity are determined for each manufacturing operating unit on a daily basis, and monthly for the plant. Because the operation manufactures two product lines simultaneously, the operations manager is concerned about achieving daily product mix targets and production volume objectives. Thus, daily performance to scheduled volume and scheduled mix are closely monitored. He states that the performance measures employed in operations are designed to enhance manufacturing competence in YMMC for increased product diversification.

A production meeting is held each morning to discuss what stands in the way of the daily manufacturing schedule. The attendees include the unit supervisors, production control manager, material control manager, quality control manager, purchasing manager, maintenance supervisor, and operations manager. Overall manufacturing performance is discussed in the monthly management review meeting. This meeting is attended by the department managers, vice presidents, and the president of YMMC. Plans for improving manufacturing are developed based on performance measurement information. Before the meeting, a monthly operations report summarizing performance measurement data in chart and graph form is distributed to the president, vice presidents, and department managers. General trends are emphasized. A streamlined version of the operations report referred to as the "items of interest report" is distributed to YMC USA and YMC Japan monthly. The focus of this report regarding operations at the Newnan facility is on the big picture. This report highlights key activities summarized by functional area, along with key milestones. The report also contains statistics on permanent and temporary worker head count by cost center. The primary vehicle for reporting YMMC business performance to YMC USA and YMC Japan is the monthly YMMC summary report. The report contains performance information on delivery, downtime, productivity, scrap, first-pass ratios by product line, and safety. Specific information on content areas included in the report follows:

Delivery-production summary table. This table displays planned to actual shipments for the previous month with variation from plan by model number and for the total; the same information is given year-to-date by model number and for total deliveries. The table also displays the number of units being held from delivery at YMC USA and YMMC owing to rework or missing parts.

Downtime graph.   The downtime graph is a bar graph displaying monthly downtime in minutes by product line (golf carts and water vehicles). It includes the management by objectives process (MBOP) goal to which the monthly results are compared and shows total downtime minutes for the current reporting month, the previous three months, and the previous year by product line. Downtime minutes are converted into the number of equivalent units missed or not produced owing to downtime by each unit in the manufacturing area (distribution, weld, assembly, paint, others), or by the vendor for the month and year-to-date. The total number of units not produced owing to downtime is displayed for the month by product line.

Productivity table and graph.   This material is a tabular display of manufacturing hourly head count for each unit in production and maintenance for the current reporting month and the previous three months. A breakdown of the number of permanent and temporary workers in each unit is provided for the current reporting month and the previous three months.

Scrap graph and tables.   This part of the report is a bar graph displaying monthly and previous year scrap dollars categorized as caused by either in-house mistakes or vendor performance. It is illustrated in thousands of dollars and shows the current reporting month and previous three months. The bar graph includes the MBOP goal to which the monthly results are compared and displays current month and year-to-date scrap in thousands of dollars for the golf cart assembly, water vehicle assembly, paint, weld, plastic, distribution, and other units. In addition, the graph shows the current month and year-to-date scrap dollar totals caused by either in-house or vendor mistakes. It also displays scrap dollar values as a percentage of standard material cost by unit (for the same units as mentioned previously) for the current month and the previous three months.

First-pass ratios for golf carts and water vehicles.   These ratios are given in separate graphical displays and compared with its quality control goal. Information is given for the current reporting month, the previous three months, and the previous year. The graph indicates for the months shown the percentage of first-pass misses that were uncontrollable or controllable. Included is a tabular display of first-pass ratio percentages by model number for the current reporting month and the previous three months. The graph also shows the first-pass goal by model number, an explanation of failures by model number, and the previous year's first-pass ratios by model number. The total first-pass ratio for the reporting month and the previous year compared to an overall goal are displayed.

Safety. Safety information is shown on a bar graph displaying the total number of OSHA recordable and nonrecordable injuries for the current reporting month, the previous three months, and the previous year. This section of the report also includes a tabular display of OSHA recordable and nonrecordable injuries by unit for the current reporting month and previous three months. Total injuries for the current reporting month and previous three months are provided.

Material Control

The purpose of the material control department is to support the daily material needs of the fabrication and assembly units. Initially, the primary objective was to establish American vendors. Material control is now focused on supplying the daily material needs of the operation.

Material control uses MRP to define manufacturing material requirements by loading orders into the master production schedule (MPS) and exploding through the BOMs to generate vendor purchase orders. The department interacts daily with other departments as described:

- *Purchasing:* vendor quality issues, delivery performance problems, and so on.
- *Incoming receiving:* material quality issues, vendor shipping errors, and so forth.
- *Quality control:* material quality problems, material disposition issues, and so forth.
- *Production control:* schedule changes, schedule adjustments, and so on.
- *Distribution:* parts shortages, among other issues.

The purchasing department is initially responsible for all materials relating to new products. Once a part successfully completes the pilot production runs, responsibility is then forwarded to material control to oversee on a production basis. The material control department interacts with product engineering if, during production, a problem is encountered relating to material or engineering specifications.

The material control manager cites quality, cost, and delivery as the essential areas for long-term strategic success. The following performance measures are monitored by the department:

- *Production line delays.* The department tracks daily the number of times an assembly line is delayed owing to a lack of vendor parts.

- *Purchased parts inventory levels.* Each material control specialist has targets for the parts he controls; each possesses established guidelines or target inventory levels for his weekly monitored area responsibility.

- *Scrap dollars.* The department measures weekly the amount of scrap dollars absorbed by Yamaha owing to vendor defects and measures weekly the dollar amount of scrap charged back to vendors.

- *Vendor delivery performance.* The material control department tracks vendors' daily on-time deliveries.

- *Vendor errors.* The department tracks daily the number and type of vendor errors discovered by incoming inspection, such as missing purchase order numbers, wrong part numbers, overshipments, undershipments, and so forth.

- *Freight rates and freight costs.* The department monitors monthly freight rates and costs for inbound transportation of purchased parts. This information is used to develop cost reduction targets.

A material control report containing all monthly performance measurement results is distributed each month for review and plan development to all manufacturing department managers and the vice president of manufacturing.

Purchasing

The purchasing manager uses the management by objectives process (MBOP) to set targets for the purchasing budget, new product cost, and vendor relations as a company policy. He believes that a vendor problem should be viewed as a Yamaha problem, and that YMMC must help the vendor overcome difficulties when possible.

The purchasing manager believes that cost, field service, and quality hold the keys to sustainable competitive success for YMMC. Performance measures used in the department are as follows:

- *Forecast accuracy.* This is a comparison of monthly forecasted to actual expenditures for purchased parts. The objective is to minimize deviations between actual and forecasted expenditures.

- *Target cost for new products.* New product costs requested by the YMC USA sales organization are broken down into individual parts or processes by accounting, manufacturing engineering, and purchasing personnel. Buyers are responsible for working with product engineering on achieving projected target product cost.

- *Value analysis.* A cost reduction target is set annually and is shared with product engineering and purchasing.

- *Vendor measures.* These include daily on-time delivery performance by vendors, weekly vendor-related scrap dollars, and monthly vendor cost analysis. The purchasing department examines the effect of vendor price reductions or increases on profitability.

The purchasing manager believes that MBOP helps foster teamwork within the purchasing department as well as between other functional areas through the establishment of common objectives that support overall business goals.

Information Systems

The main information system consists of an IBM System 38, which is used to collect and maintain manufacturing and financial information. Over 60 individual personal computers, two CAD workstations, and a separate network in the human resources department for processing payroll and personnel information are located throughout the office and plant area. The information system department is viewed as a service organization to all other departments. The department's primary responsibility is to maintain the main system. Another critical responsibility is handling requests for either system modification or development. The information systems manager has each department prioritize its own requests. He then reviews all requests and prioritizes them for the information systems department based on the following criteria:

- *Companywide impact.* Which requests have the greatest influence on achieving corporate and business level objectives?

- *Bottom-line impact.* Will the request either reduce costs or increase revenues?

- *Productivity impact.* Will the request make it easier for individuals and departments to accomplish their daily tasks?

An overriding theme in prioritizing requests is determining how the request will satisfy the daily, as well as the long-term, business requirements. The information systems manager states that the MBOP helps him make such determinations.

The Newnan facility is linked to Yamaha Japan's global communication network and to the YMC USA sales office in California. Sales orders are developed by Yamaha USA, which are translated into a master production schedule by production control. Once an order is released to the factory, the unit is tracked by the information system through each stage of the manufacturing process. Terminals are located at the end of assembly, inspection, and shipping areas. Information moves along with the unit via bar coding. When a unit is assembled, it receives a serial number with a bar code that is scanned and recorded into the main system. A record is thus created showing that the unit has passed through the assembly stage.

The unit then goes to inspection, where it will either pass or fail. The serial number is again scanned and the results of the inspection are entered into the system. For units that fail inspection, the system also keeps track of the number of times it has failed, for the calculation of first-pass ratios. Information on failures is maintained on personal computers, which are being linked to the main system. After the unit passes inspection, it goes to the shipping area, where it is packed. The serial numbers are scanned to enter information such as the individual unit packed in a given case, the cases loaded on a given truck, and the number of units shipped on a particular day. The bar coding system allows for daily reports displaying quality, MPS, and shipping performance in real time.

The information systems manager cites quality, product and process flexibility, and cost as the most critical areas for competitiveness. Departmental performance measures include performance to project schedules and the achievement of the objectives developed in the MBOP. The information systems department plays a vital role in the globalization process through the enhancement of systems capabilities at the Newnan facility.

Accounting

Yamaha Motor Manufacturing uses a traditional full-absorption cost accounting system whose elements include direct labor, materials, and overhead. Monthly financial reports are generated and distributed to all managers, highlighting performance in the following areas:

- *Labor variance tracking.* Performance regarding labor efficiency, productivity, and utilization is collected and reported weekly for each unit.
- *Material variance tracking.* Raw material and purchased components price results are tracked daily.
- *Material usage tracking.* Variances caused by scrap, shrinkage, engineering substitutions, or changes are reported.

The accounting manager believes that quality, delivery, and field service hold the keys to the strategic success for YMMC.

Human Resources

Key areas of performance measurement in the human resources department are as follows:

- *Safety.* HRD examines the number of OSHA recordable accidents, number of lost-time accidents, and number of lost-time days.
- *Turnover.* Employee turnover is compared monthly to the national industry average.
- *Absenteeism.* Employee absenteeism is compared monthly to the national average.

The Newnan facility has a safety committee that meets monthly to examine safety performance and develops action plans for safety improvements. The executive committee, composed of the president and vice presidents, reviews absenteeism with the human resources manager on a monthly basis.

The human resources manager states that quality, product and process flexibility, and product and process innovation are the primary areas of focus for YMMC's long-term success.

PERFORMANCE MEASUREMENT SYSTEMS

The performance measurement systems used at Yamaha Motor Manufacturing are maintained functionally within each department. Many of the measures are monitored daily using graphs, trend lines, and reports from individuals who are held accountable for the performance results. Performance measurement information exchanges between functions and across organizational levels are accomplished through periodic performance reports and interfunctional meetings.

PERFORMANCE MEASUREMENT SYSTEM LINKAGES

A key mechanism for accomplishing performance measurement system linkages between departments and across organizational levels at Yamaha Motor Manufacturing is MBOP and frequent meetings. This goal-setting procedure allows departments to establish continuous improvement targets based on the philosophies of total productive maintenance (TPM) that are consistent with and support overall corporate and business level strategies. MBOP also helps integrate functional efforts by establishing interdepartmental improvement targets, which leads to shared performance measures.

Formal functional meetings and periodic performance reports also play a crucial role in performance measurement system linkages. The daily production meeting provides a means to link functional systems used by material control, quality control, manufacturing engineering, purchasing, and operations.

Status meetings headed by product engineering with representatives from other departments allow for continuous interfunctional input into the product development process. These inputs directly affect performance measurement relative to new product development. This procedure is also used by manufacturing engineering for capital projects and process development and improvement. Process development review meetings provide a vehicle for interdepartmental inputs on manufacturing engineering projects and serve as a forum for project schedule evaluation, which affects project performance measurement system criteria, metrics, and standards.

The monthly quality workshop aids in focusing the manufacturing organization on determining the root cause of quality problems so that corrective actions designed to eliminate their future occurrence can be developed. Quality review meetings held monthly keep the entire organization informed of current quality issues and the game plan for solving them.

The most important interorganizational meeting is the monthly management review meetings between the department managers and the executive committee (president and vice presidents). The management review meeting is used to develop action plans for overall business improvement based on the performance results displayed in the operations and items of interest reports. Other periodic reports that provide performance measurement system linkages include these:

- *Financial reports:* contain monthly financial results of the YMMC operation; distributed to all managers.

- *Material control reports:* contain material control performance measurement results for the month; sent to all managers in the manufacturing organization.

- *Quality summary report:* monthly report consisting of graphs illustrating the following information: first-pass ratios and defects per hundred units for golf carts and water vehicles, scrap and rework dollars, and Pareto analysis of quality problems in each of the five manufacturing operating units. Also contains a brief, written explanation of the current status of key quality issues; report is sent to Yamaha Japan.

- *Field quality summary report:* monthly report on what countermeasures are being taken by YMMC regarding quality problems in the field; report is sent to YMC USA.

- *Serial number performance summary reports:* contains monthly and year-to-date information regarding performance to schedule, the number of units assembled, the number of units passed through inspection, the number of units passed through inspection on the first attempt, the first-pass ratio, the number of units packed, and the number of units shipped. The report is generated monthly and distributed to all department managers.

- *YMMC summary report:* graphical report displaying current, year-to-date, and previous year performance concerning delivery schedules, downtime, productivity, first-pass ratios by product line, and safety; sent monthly to Yamaha USA and Yamaha Japan.

- *TPM performance to schedule report:* contains monthly performance to schedule on TPM activities in a Gantt chart spanning a six-month time frame; shows progress for four key events: education (management and operators), 5s activities (standards for a clean workplace), *kaizen* (improvement) suggestions and small-group activities. It also outlines key activities accomplished in previous month and TPM focus for current month.

YMMC's methods of achieving performance measurement system linkages between departments and organization levels are congruent with corporate and business level objectives and will help the organization maintain a process of continual improvement.

LESSONS LEARNED

The Yamaha Motor Manufacturing case illustrates how performance measurement system linkages between systems and functions can be achieved on the strategic objectives of cost and quality.

Customer and Resource

Yamaha creates customer performance measurement information internally using periodic endurance tests on products that simula⸱⸱ field conditions. This information is used to focus organizational resources on product improvements critical to long-term customer satisfaction. Thus, a link is developed between customer's needs and the organizational resources required to fulfill those needs. In addition, the quality control department collects market information from the field service organization in California. The information is analyzed monthly, and feedback is provided to the responsible areas (vendors, functional departments, or both). This customer and resource link ensures effective resource deployment.

Finance and Resource

Yamaha uses a traditional full-absorption accounting system that focuses on labor, material variances, and material usage. In the operations function, material resources are examined in financial terms through the measures of scrap dollars and rework costs. Also scrap dollars caused by vendors are monitored. Warranty costs are used to link design and operations resources to the financial system. Because labor is 20 percent of Yamaha's total product cost, direct labor efficiency, utilization, and productivity metrics for each operating unit are collected to focus organizational resources on achieving cost objectives. Another key cost element is freight charges from the import of purchased parts from Japan. The material control department actively seeks methods to reduced freight costs. Finally, the purchasing department works directly with product engineering on achieving projected target product cost. Vendor cost analyses are conducted to examine the effect of vendor price reductions or increases on profitability. The case provides a vehicle for examining how customer-resource and resource-finance linkages can be used to facilitate strategic objective accomplishment.

Chapter Ten

Northern Telecom, Inc. Transmission Access Division

This case is another illustration of how linkages between the customer and resource performance measurement systems and functions can be achieved. Cost, quality, and lead time are the strategic objectives of the transmission access division. Performance measurement systems for these objectives were established to continually improve these areas.

COMPANY BACKGROUND

Northern Telecom Ltd. is recognized worldwide as a technological leader in the telecommunications industry with headquarters in Toronto, Canada. The company is composed of several independent subsidiaries: Northern Telecom Electronics (NTE); Bell-Northern Research (BNR); Northern Telecom World Trade (NTWT); Northern Telecom Canada (NTC); and Northern Telecom, Inc. (NTI). NTI has headquarters in Nashville, Tennessee, and is organized by groups on a product line basis. The firm consists of the following four groups:

1. *Switching:* produces a wide range of central office digital switches.

2. *Business communications:* provides telecommunication systems for business applications, such as PBX and NORSTAR systems.

3. *Data networks:* produces software for corporate telecommunication networks and develops network plans for satisfying total company voice and data communication requirements.

4. *Transmission:* provides telecommunication systems that transport voice and data messages between central office switches (telephone exchanges) over long-distance lines, and provides systems that allow access to the central office switch by home or business subscribers over local lines.

FIGURE 10-1
Organizational Structure of Northern Telecom, Ltd.

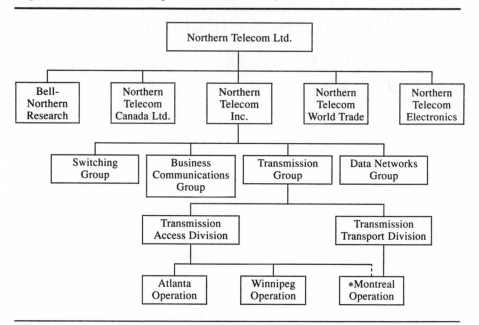

*Facility manufactures products for both divisions.
Note: Not all divisions and plants shown.

The transmission group is further subdivided into two divisions, which are also organized by product line. The transmission transport division manufactures systems designed to link long-distance telephone exchanges, and the transmission access division produces telecommunication systems that link home and business subscribers to local exchanges. Transmission access division products are manufactured in three facilities in the following locations: Stone Mountain, Georgia; Winnipeg, Manitoba (Canada); and Montreal, Quebec (Canada). Division headquarters is located in the Atlanta Technology Park in Norcross, Georgia. The organizational structure of Northern Telecom, Ltd. is given in Figure 10-1.

The transmission access division produces digital loop carrier systems (housed either in a telephone switching center or a cabinet), which concentrate 554 subscriber lines into eight high-capacity lines, which are then connected to the local central office switch. The division also produces a range of channel bank units. It released a new product in 1991, known as "AccessNode," which utilizes fiber-optic technology. This technology was already being used in transporting voice and data messages between central office switches, but not between the central office switches and local subscribers. The product represents the most significant technological breakthrough in the telecommunication industry since the introduction of digital technology, also led by Northern Telecom.

The division's customer base is 90 percent make-to-stock and assemble-to-order, 5 percent make-to-order, and 5 percent engineer-to-order. The manufacturing processes are 80 percent repetitive (high volume, few models), 15 percent batch (products are made intermittently), and 5 percent project (product is designed and engineered for a specific customer).

The Winnipeg plant produces channel bank units, primarily for Canadian telephone companies. The Stone Mountain plant manufactures a digital product known as the DMS-1 urban subscriber loop carrier, and the Montreal facility produces products for the transmission access division on a subcontract basis. (The Montreal plant is actually part of the transmission transport division.) Stone Mountain also produces the new fiber-optic product known as Fiber World AccessNode.

The Stone Mountain facility has a total employment of 490, which includes 398 hourly workers and 92 salaried employees. Of the 398 workers, 306 are classified as direct and 92 as indirect labor. The plant operates on three shifts. All manufacturing operations are performed on the first and second shifts, and the third shift only conducts assembly tests and system integration "burn-ins." (Units run under normal operating conditions for 44 hours to detect failures.) Approximately 11,000 active part numbers comprise the inventory system, and the typical bill of material is one level. The Stone Mountain facility uses elements of material requirements planning (MRP), just-in-time (JIT), and total quality control (TQC) to plan, monitor, and control manufacturing processes. Interviews were conducted with the following individuals:

- General manager of operations.
- Director of cost improvements.
- Director of planning and scheduling.
- Direction of manufacturing (current products).
- Director of purchasing.
- Director of quality.

DIVISION ORGANIZATION

The transmission access division is headquartered in Norcross, Georgia. The division uses a functional organization and consists of operations, marketing, quality, technology, and information systems. The functional directors report directly to the division

FIGURE 10–2
Transmission Access Division Organizational Structure

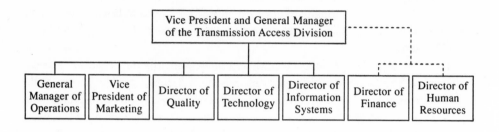

vice president. Financial and human resources directors report to transmission group management, with indirect reporting responsibilities to the division vice president. The organizational structure of the transmission access division is presented in Figure 10–2.

STRATEGIC OBJECTIVES

NTI has developed strategic objectives focusing on the following areas:

- New product introduction and product changes.
- Procurement.
- Manufacturing process improvement.
- Operations planning and scheduling.
- Product delivery cost.
- Installation and field service.
- Education.
- Customer service.
- Business systems and tools development.

Companywide core programs have been established to support these areas for the development of a product delivery process capable of providing NTI with the competitive advantages of being able to move more rapidly, flexibly, and predictably than NTI competition; to consistently deliver a changing portfolio of new products that are on time, that possess superior quality, and that exhibit "mature" first cost; and to be responsive to customer application requirements.

The goals, objectives, and tactics of the NTI core programs are as follows:

A. New product introduction and product changes.
   Goal: To provide superior design quality while limiting recurring design changes.
   Objectives:
   a. Reduce overhead cost associated with design changes as a percentage of sales by 50 percent.
   b. Achieve a "mature first cost" (110 percent of final product cost) within six months of the manufacturing start date by doing the following:
      1. Releasing quality designs with no modifications necessary during the manufacturing phase.
      2. Implementing cost reduction activities at the design feature and capability introduction stage.
      3. Achieving a 95 percent composite process yield capability on all new products.
      4. Starting with low component cost.
   c. Meet new target time intervals for each design phase 95 percent of the time.
   d. Shorten design change cycles.
   Tactics: Design, manufacturing, installation, and customer support issues will be addressed jointly early in the design cycle. Traditional value analysis and value engineering techniques will be coupled with design and test simulations, computer-assisted design (CAD) tools, and electronic design transfer.
B. Procurement.
   Goal: To properly balance the interrelated factors of quality, availability, cost, investment, and pricing to achieve competitive advantages in procurement.
   Objectives:
   a. Attain a total defect rate better than 100 parts per million (PPM) from suppliers.
   b. Maintain on-time deliveries from suppliers and correct order quantities with no more than a 0.1 percent event failure rate.
   Tactic: Utilize fixed finished goods schedules (one month) that "pull" material from suppliers directly to assembly with responsive lead times.
C. Manufacturing process improvement.
   Goal: To establish "flow processes," in which cycle time approaches process times that can be measured in hours instead of weeks.

Objectives:
a. Reduce manufacturing cycle times to hours with a maximum duration of 14 days.
b. Achieve a 95 percent composite yield on all processes.
c. Attain a 100 percent on-time delivery level of final product to installation or customer.

Tactics:
a. Integrate JIT and TQC philosophies and techniques into the manufacturing operations with an emphasis on quality.
b. Instill process understanding, pruning, and simplification along with computer-integrated manufacturing (CIM) on the factory floor.
c. Develop process technology and testing innovations.
d. Use fixed monthly production schedules to provide production smoothing.
e. Create high-velocity production lines with quick changeover capabilities to reduce manufacturing cycles.

D. Operations planning and scheduling.

Goal: To provide effective management of the customer order throughout the business cycle to achieve inventory and customer service objectives.

Objectives:
a. Meet established customer request date 95 percent of the time.
b. Eliminate NTI configuration errors from 95 percent of all jobs.

Tactics:
a. Conduct a full analysis of the order entry interface and production scheduling system.
b. Develop the following product forecast accuracy capabilities:
   1. > 20 percent deviation for 90 days.
   2. > 10 percent deviation for 60 days.
   3. > 0 percent deviation for 30 days.

E. Product delivery cost.

Goal: To minimize the cost of delivering product to the customer using fewer transactions and less reporting.

Objectives:
a. Reduce the required number of transactions by 50 percent.
b. Reduce support overhead cost as a percentage of sales by 50 percent.

Tactics:
a. Analyze the appropriateness of current product delivery cost; simplify overhead, administrative and infrastructure support to reduce cost.
b. Adapt support structure to JIT and fast flow processes, which require fewer transactions and less reporting.

F. Installation and field service.

Goal: To deliver a complete and operating product to NTI customers as cost effectively and in as timely a manner as possible.

Objectives:
a. Reduce installation interval by 50 percent.
b. Reduce field failure rate to 0.5 percent annually.
c. Maintain product engineering change effectivity dates and documentation that are 100 percent complete and on time.

Tactics:
a. Design for installation, reduce time intervals for each design phase, and increase customer service.
b. Develop a close and improved linkage with customers.
c. View product installation as an extension of the factory with as much of the product as possible completed before shipment to the installation site.

G. Education.

Goal: Change the business processes of the company to allow it to work more effectively.

Objectives:
a. Proactively achieve "mature" first cost on new product introductions instead of focusing on product cost reductions after the introduction.
b. Develop a process focus instead of a product orientation.
c. Develop pull instead of push processes throughout the organization.

Tactic: Implement operations education and training programs to help effect behavioral changes by doing the following:
a. Utilizing the NTI building blocks approach to business processes.
b. Focusing on key strategic and tactical skills required to implement core programs.
c. Capturing and documenting current organizational strengths.
d. Strengthening links between divisional programs.

H. Customer service.

Goals:
a. To focus NTI's product delivery process on satisfying the customers' needs.
b. To achieve "preferred supplier" status in the telecommunications industry.

Objectives:
a. Establish service improvement activities in all core programs to provide cross-functional solutions that significantly enhance NTI's service image.
b. Develop a continual improvement process that aligns NTI's service metrics with the value system of the customer.

Tactics:
a. Conduct regular customer satisfaction surveys.
b. Establish service metrics for service responsiveness, product performance, delivery performance, customer training, and documentation.
c. Maintain a continual review and development of the service metrics to ensure alignment with customer data, customer satisfaction surveys, and the customer value system.
d. Maintain a timely response to each service issue in order to keep the NTI commitment of "doing what we say we do."

I. Business systems and tools development.

Goal: To provide instantaneous access of accurate information at the point of use.

Objective: Create an information system network with high-quality electronic transfer of information between design, marketing, manufacturing, administrative, installation, service, and distribution organizations on a timely basis while providing the capability for universal user access (including suppliers) with appropriate security.

Tactic: Development of a network environment for information transfer (called T-NET), utilizing an open network architecture with standard interfaces capable of linking together all NTI business systems.

Division Objectives

The mission of the transmission access division is to support Northern Telecom, Ltd.'s technological leadership position in the telecommunications business by developing state-of-the-art products that set the standard for the industry. Thus, the division plans to harvest its mature product line of digital products and increase the volume of business by introducing fiber-optic products. The objective is to maximize current market share, so that the marketplace will be more willing to accept new products. To do this, the division has focused on improving customer satisfaction through quality and delivery improvements while reducing product cost. Furthermore, the current products will be kept relatively stable, with minimal capital investment and limited design changes. Current product profits are used to offset R&D expenditures for fiber-optic products, although the amount of funding required by the division to develop these products necessitated a significant corporate investment. NTI views the fiber-optic products as its greatest business growth opportunity in the 1990s and beyond.

Manufacturing Objectives

Manufacturing operations at the Stone Mountain facility play a crucial role in supporting the harvesting of mature digital products and growth of fiber-optic products in the division. The organization must effectively manage a product line phase-out, which may take from 3 to 10 years before complete discontinuation, while also supporting the growth of the new product line. Specific manufacturing objectives necessary to make the transition are as follows:

- Incorporate elements of the JIT/TQC philosophy into the manufacturing of current products. Key elements of the philosophy include flow manufacturing, quality at the source, point-of-use inventory stocking, employee involvement, and continual improvement processes.

- Reduce overall manufacturing costs using cost improvement activities to enhance current product profitability and market penetration potential.

- Minimize capital investment, design changes, and new product features on the current product base.

- Install high-velocity flow lines for the production of fiber-optic products consistent with the JIT/TQC philosophy.
- Use the most sophisticated, state-of-the-art manufacturing and test equipment for producing the new product.
- Continue to interface the design engineering and manufacturing organizations during the prototyping and volume production activities in the Stone Mountain facility.

STONE MOUNTAIN ORGANIZATION

The Stone Mountain operation is functionally structured and consists of cost improvement, planning and scheduling, purchasing, manufacturing, and quality organizations. The functional directors report to the general manager of operations. The Winnipeg plant manager also reports to the general manager of operations at Stone Mountain. The director of quality at Stone Mountain reports to the division vice president. Each functional head has a staff responsible for specific subareas. The organizational structure of the Stone Mountain operation is presented in Figure 10–3.

STONE MOUNTAIN FACILITY FUNCTIONS

Operations

The general manager of operations is directly responsible for manufacturing and related activities in the Stone Mountain and Winnipeg facilities. He also has shared responsibility for the Montreal operation with his counterpart in the transmission transport division. Marketing is a separate organization within the division and jointly participates in the order forecasting process. For the Stone Mountain operation, marketing forecasts each "module," which comprises the DMS-1 urban subscriber loop carrier system: printed circuit board line cards and carrier assemblies, printed circuit board common equipment and power assemblies (also called "circuit packs"—supply system management and power to the units); and purchased bays or cabinets that house the systems (wired and tested in the equipment shop area of the plant). Modules are then produced in a make-to-stock manner and stored in the finished goods stockroom. Approximately 70 percent of Stone Mountain's production volume is sold as modules, as opposed to configured systems. Standard orders for complete systems are assembled to order from finished goods stock. Systems requiring nonstandard features are either made to order or engineered to order.

FIGURE 10–3
Organizational Structure of Stone Mountain Operation

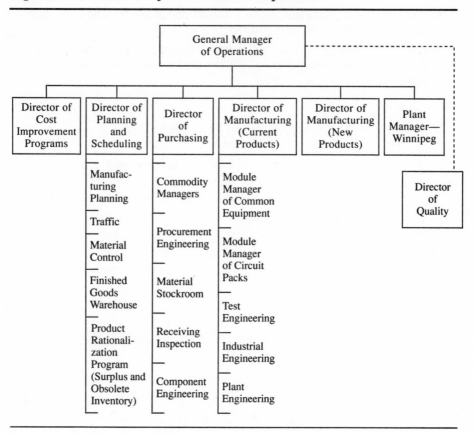

The general manager of operations believes that the FiberWorld AccessNode product line will have the same effect on the telecommunication industry that the automobile had on the transportation indurstry. For example, all the telephone conversations taking place in the city of Atlanta, in any given moment could be transmitted over one optical fiber; hundreds of thousands of television signals could be transmitted to subscriber living rooms with the clarity of a live show. NTI experienced a significant shortening of its traditional product development cycle for the FiberWorld product. The firm took 10 years to bring its digital switching product line from conceptualization to volume production. However, NTI took approximately three and a half years to bring the AccessNode product, which is technologically more complex, into full production. The shortened product development cycle is attributed to better cross-functional coordination in the initial stages of design. The projected demand for the new product required that the Stone Mountain facility had high-volume production capabilities shortly after the 1991 introduction. Therefore, the product was designed for manufacturability and superior quality.

Although the FiberWorld product is a major technological breakthrough in the telecommunications industry, the general manager of operations realizes that the marketplace's transition from digital to fiber-optic products will be evolutionary. The firm has already made agreements with several current customers to position them for the transition. Subscribers (businesses and homes) must be switched from copper wire to glass fiber to utilize the technology. The division is currently involved in a project with Bell South, whereby a subdivision in suburban Orlando (Heathrow) has been completely wired with fiber-optics using NTI technology. The project serves as a living example of the capabilities of fiber-optic technology. However, the transmission access division expects to ''migrate'' the product into the marketplace in an evolutionary manner.

The general manager of operations views delivery, quality, and product and process innovation as critical to the strategic success of the division. He believes that the firm has a social responsibility to produce telecommunication products that are highly reliable and have superior quality. The dependency that North Americans have on telephone networks for health emergencies and other crucial services dictates the need for reliable systems. Equipment produced by NTI was functional during the San Francisco earthquake and Hurricane Hugo. Key measures monitored by the operations general manager are as follows:

- *Financials.* Monthly financial results in the areas of earnings, capital spending, inventory investment, accounts receivable, expense containment against budgets, and surplus and obsolete inventory levels are monitored; also examined earnings before interest and taxes and before R&D expenditures (EBIT before R&D) to assess the true profitability of the division.

- *Quality.* The weekly percentage of defects found on an out-of-box inspection of line cards, common equipment, and bays and cabinets is monitored; units are ordered from the shop by the quality department, unpacked, and inspected.

- *Customer service.* Weekly on-time delivery percentage based on the customer request date is monitored.

Cost Improvement

The goal of the cost improvement program is to develop methods that reduce cost on current products without reducing value to the customer. The program focuses primarily on material cost because it comprises over 70 percent of the total product cost. Labor costs represent approximately 7 percent of the total product cost. A greater emphasis was placed on overhead savings during the new product introduction in 1991. However, the current product will be manufactured for a minimum of three to four years after the new product introduction. Therefore, material cost improvements are an important element of the division's harvesting strategy (the phasing out of mature digital products).

Three approaches are used to reduce material cost on existing products: product redesign, material substitution, and purchase price variances. The technology employed in the current product offering is mature and has reached a point where the expense associated with redesigning the circuitry is unjustifiable for a product at this stage of its life cycle. Thus, product redesigns are not a major contributor to the cost improvement effort. Material substitution, which entails changing circuit board devices (capacitors, resistors, and so on) instead of changing the board itself, is providing the division with substantial material cost savings. The most significant savings in material cost are coming from the competitive purchasing programs, which involve participation of the supplier in identifying cost savings opportunities. It is measured by the actual purchase order price per unit minus the base (standard) cost per unit multiplied by the total number of units of the commodity purchased (referred to as the purchase price variance, or PPV).

The transmission access division uses a standard costing system in which material, labor, and overhead rates are established annually. Labor efficiency is no longer tracked, and only one labor rate is used for the entire Stone Mountain facility. The accounting system of Stone Mountain is electronically linked to the division, group, and corporate level systems. Separate profit and loss (P/L) statements are developed monthly for each plant, division, and group, and consolidated into a corporate financial statement. Individual financial statements for US and Canadian operations are also developed monthly. PPV is a line item on the P/L statements that reflects directly on the bottom line.

Annual material cost standard adjustments reflect the cost improvement program results of the previous fiscal year. To ensure that the cost improvement programs reflect true cost reductions, the director has instituted a number of program requirements. For example, cost improvements are not counted until the target cost (based on value analysis and value engineering techniques) for the commodity has been reached. Reductions prior to achieving the target cost are considered cost avoidance, not cost savings. The cost associated with implementing a cost improvement program is deducted from its savings. In addition, material substitution cost improvements are not counted until the old material has been completely exhausted and the new material is being used.

The cost improvement process is managed through monthly meetings chaired by the director of cost improvement programs. The meetings are multifunctional and include representatives from design engineering, manufacturing, quality, engineering, production, planning and scheduling, purchasing, business systems, marketing, and finance. The functional directors usually attend, as do selected staff members. The meeting is spent examining the results of completed programs, assessing the status of cost improvement programs in progress, and developing ideas for new programs.

Cost improvement is measured by individual program, impact on product cost (using cost models), and net bottom-line impact. A cost improvement program status report is compiled monthly; it highlights the division's progress on all major cost reduction efforts. The report is consolidated monthly and is forwarded to NTI management in Nashville. At the plant and division levels, a detailed cost improvement analysis is furnished monthly to Stone Mountain directors, managers, and staff members. The report serves as a working document to track cost improvement progress. The document details prior cost, new cost, and monthly and year-to-date savings for each commodity affected by cost improvement programs.

The director of cost improvement programs cites quality, delivery, and lead time as essential to the long-term success of the division. Key performance measures monitored by the director of cost improvement programs and other operations staff members are as follows:

- *Cost improvement (CI) impact.* This is a monthly measure of the effect of true cost improvements on the P/L statement; cost improvements are offset by program expenses. The figure is given in the monthly CI status report.
- *Purchase price variance (PPV).* This monthly measure is defined as the actual material purchase order price per unit minus the base (standard) cost per unit, multiplied by the purchased quantity. It is reported monthly in the PPV major items report, which displays the PPV value for each purchase order by supplier. Twelve-month and year-to-date PPV totals are also displayed by category (preprocessed and finished goods). The gross variance total is netted against cash discounts and other outlays (rework, premium charges, setup cost, and so forth) to determine the net PPV value.

Planning and Scheduling

The planning and scheduling function plans the material requirements and schedules shop orders for the Stone Mountain and Winnipeg plants. Transmission access division products manufactured in the Montreal plant are scheduled by the Montreal organization. The planning and scheduling department receives monthly marketing forecasts on end-item products (circuit packs, bays, and cabinet assemblies) covering a rolling 12-month period. The forecast is then matched against production capacity, loaded into the master production schedule, and converted by the MRP system into requirements utilizing super BOMs. The material requirements are given to buyers in purchasing to procure the necessary amount of material to support production. Manufacturing planners in the planning and scheduling department work with production managers on developing daily production schedules. The intent is to achieve linearity (that is, no schedule deviations) in the manufacturing process. A daily production meeting is held to discuss performance against the weekly manufacturing targets. The meeting is attended by the directors of planning and scheduling, manufacturing, and purchasing, along with manufacturing planners and production managers.

The Stone Mountain plant is undergoing a JIT conversion process, which significantly affects the planning and scheduling function. The elimination of the semifinished goods area has allowed the department to drop an interim planning step. Significant reductions in manufacturing cycle time have made the manufacturing environment more dynamic and allow customer orders to be scheduled within shorter time frames. Before JIT was instituted, manufacturing orders were released as "kits" to the production floor. Now, material releases are controlled by a two-card kanban system. Kanban sizes are established by multifunctional teams, which included production workers, based on the current run rate of the operation. The business systems department has also developed a kanban software package, which is used to determine the optimal kanban size for various plant operations. Point-of-use inventory stocking is being used on a limited basis as the facility moves toward the elimination of receiving inspection on incoming materials and certified suppliers.

The director of planning and scheduling believes that quality, delivery, and lead time are the keys to the strategic success of the division. Measures monitored within the department are as follows:

- *Conformance to daily production schedules.* This measurement monitors positive and negative deviations from the daily production schedule; it is discussed in daily production meetings.
- *Customer service.* This is monitored by examining the weekly on-time delivery of central office and merchandise orders against the customer request date, order promise date, and the standard order lead time.
- *Manufacturing cycle time.* The manufacturing cycle time is monitored weekly against established targets. It is discussed in the production meetings.
- *Scrap cost.* This is a weekly measurement of scrap dollars as a percentage of material cost. The figure is reported monthly.
- *Shipping performance.* This measure is monitored by examining the weekly performance to the shipping schedule and total dollars shipped.

- *Customer service measures.* These measures monitor the weekly on-time delivery percentages for central office orders (orders for either total systems or modules) and for merchandise orders (spare parts orders for existing systems). On-time delivery percentages are tracked against three criteria: customer request date, order promise date, and delivery against standard lead time. Delivery against standard lead time is an internal measure used to assess whether the customer request and order promise dates are within the standard delivery lead time for the items.
- *Inventory performance.* Surplus and obsolete inventory dollars and quantity are monitored weekly; inventory turns are monitored monthly in general and weekly by specific departments; finished goods inventory is monitored weekly.
- *Departmental budget performance.* Monthly actual versus planned departmental expenditures are monitored by all department heads.

Manufacturing

The Stone Mountain plant manufactures three products, or *modules*, which are sold separately or as complete units. The modules are printed circuit board line cards, printed circuit board circuit packs (also known as common equipment), and bay and cabinet assemblies. The plant is integrating the concepts of JIT and TQC into its daily operations. An external consultant held four-day workshops for division senior managers and other white-collar workers that included a hands-on demonstration of the effect of switching from batch to flow manufacturing on a production operation.

The JIT implementation on the manufacturing floor began in a high-volume area of the facility containing few parts. The conversion has now moved into the low-volume areas of the plant with numerous parts. Before the JIT implementation process, plant material flow began with material releases from component stockrooms to the manufacturing departments. The products were manufactured in separate assembly areas and stored in semifinished goods stockrooms. The semifinished goods were then routed to the systems integration department, which was discovered to be the bottleneck operation in the manufacturing process. After systems integration, the products were stocked in the finished goods stockroom. Today, material releases are triggered by the two-card kanban system, the semifinished goods area has been eliminated, and systems integration areas have been created for each module. These actions have resulted in manufacturing cycle time reductions of 67 percent, 50 percent, and 43 percent for common equipment, line cards, and bays and cabinets, respectively.

The director of manufacturing cites quality, delivery, and lead time as key areas for achieving advantages in the marketplace. The following performance measures are used in the manufacturing area:

- *Direct labor utilization.* Total plant direct labor utilization is measured weekly; the measure is defined as the ratio of current hours to available hours, where

  Current hours = Standards hours − Improvements to methods

  Available hours = Payroll hours − (Holiday + Sick + Personal + Short-term disability time)

  Available hours include production, training, meeting, setup, and rework hours; labor utilization targets are established for line cards, common equipment, and the bay and cabinet modules. The figure is displayed in bar graphs showing monthly actual versus target values, with trend lines for the 12-month period; it is posted on the production floor.

- *Out-of-box (OOB) defectivity.* This is a weekly measure of the percentage of defectivity of OOB units inspected. The percentage is calculated for each module (line card, common equipment, and bays and cabinets); the percentage of defective modules is divided by the total number of modules (for example, OOB% defectivity / Line cards = [number of defective lines cards/total number of line cards] × 100%). OOB percentage of defectivity targets are established for module type. The figures are displayed in bar graphs showing monthly actual versus target values, with trend lines for a 12-month period; they are posted on the production floor.

- *Systems integration (SYS) defectivity.* This is a weekly measure of the percentage of defective modules inspected after systems integration; the percentage is calculated for each module type (line card, common equipment, and bays and cabinets). Targets are established for each module type. The figures are displayed in bar graphs showing monthly actual versus target values with trend lines for a 12-month period; they are posted on the production floor.

- *Defects per frame.* This figure measures the weekly number of defects per frame as the ratio of frame defects to the total number of bays or cabinet frames; it is displayed in a bar graph showing monthly actual versus the target value with a trend line for a 12-month period and posted in the equipment shop area.

- *Customer service.* This measures weekly on-time delivery percentages for each module based on the manufacturing plan. On-time delivery targets are established for each module. Figures are displayed in bar graphs showing monthly actual versus target values, with a trend line for a 12-month period; they are posted on the production floor.

- *Manufacturing cycle time.* The manufacturing cycle time is monitored weekly against established targets and is discussed in the production meetings.

Purchasing

The purchasing department is responsible for all procurement activities at the Stone Mountain facility. Departmental duties include material purchasing, incoming material auditing, material storage, and supplier qualification. Component engineers qualify manufacturing materials and work with suppliers on improving quality levels while reducing cost. Commodity managers purchase approved production materials and cultivate supplier relationships. Material stockroom and receiving personnel inspect incoming materials and stock them for future use. Although the purchasing department is self-contained from a procurement standpoint, it has daily interactions with the planning and scheduling and design engineering functions. Commodity managers work closely with manufacturing planners on issues regarding purchased components. Procurement engineers interact with design engineers on design changes and the documentation required to support new product introductions.

The adoption of the JIT/TQC philosophy is substantially affecting the purchasing department. Through the creation of a supplier reduction program, the number of suppliers has decreased by 50 percent over a 12-month period. The Stone Mountain operation is receiving more frequent deliveries from suppliers in smaller lot sizes. A supplier certification program has been established to eliminate or significantly reduce incoming material audits and the use of material stockrooms. The NTI purchasing staff have created supplier certification guidelines to be followed by division purchasing organizations. A supplier must meet three criteria for certification:

- *Quality.* The supplier must meet the quality standards established for the commodity class by the NTI purchasing staff.
- *Delivery.* The supplier must meet the delivery requirements of zero days late and no more than four days early.
- *Service.* Suppliers are evaluated on their day-to-day business relationship with the division on invoicing, quotations, lead time, and responsiveness.

Within each criterion are specific elements on which suppliers are scored by the supplier certification team. Weighting factors of 45 percent, 45 percent, and 10 percent are then applied to the accumulated quality, delivery, and service scores, respectively. If the supplier achieves the appropriate certification score, the division then follows the recommended guidelines from NTI purchasing on awarding of the certification, the duration of the certification, recertification requirements, and so forth. NTI purchasing awards annual corporate contracts to suppliers who furnish commodities used across product lines. These contracts allow division purchasing staffs to procure the commodities at reduced rates, depending on the total dollar volume purchased. NTI purchasing receives monthly outgoing quality level reports from suppliers with corporate contracts on each commodity. The report is forwarded to the divisions to use as a check against the actual incoming quality levels received during the period. As the number of certified suppliers increases, the purchasing department will begin to eliminate incoming material inspections. The department will also increase the level of point-of-use inventory stocking on the production floor and eliminate material stockrooms.

The purchasing department has played an active role in cost improvement programs within the Stone Mountain facility, providing over 50 percent of the cost reductions through favorable PPVs. The director of purchasing is aware that the PPV measure could be abused if buyers reduce prices at the expense of material quality, delivery, or service. As a counterbalance to the PPV measure, the purchasing director monitors supplier certification and supplier reduction progress by the material buyers. These concerns will be even more important to the fiber-optic products because the division plans to reach mature cost at the onset of production rather than through material cost improvement programs.

The director of purchasing believes that cost, delivery, and quality are essential to the success of the transmission access division. Performance measures monitored within the department are as follows:

- *Incoming quality levels.* Daily incoming material quality levels are determined through lot acceptance sampling; a 96 percent acceptance plan is used to inspect incoming lots; if no failures have occurred with a supplier for 27 consecutive lots, then a "skip lot" inspection plan is used (sample every other lot); the figures are reported monthly.

- *Supplier certification.* This figure measures monthly the number of certified suppliers based on quality, delivery, and service criteria.

- *Purchase price variance (PPV).* This is a monthly measure defined as the actual material purchase order price per unit minus the base (standard) cost per unit multiplied by the purchased quantity; reported monthly in the PPV major items report displaying the PPV value for each purchase order by suppliers. Twelve-month and year-to-date PPV totals are also displayed by category (preprocessed and finished goods). The gross variance total is netted against cash discounts and other outlays (rework, premium charges, setup costs, and so forth) to determine the net PPV value.

- *Supplier reductions.* This is a monthly measurement of the number of suppliers for each commodity. The target is to develop single sources for each commodity where feasible.

- *Supplier outgoing quality levels.* These are monthly measures of outgoing quality levels of suppliers with NTI purchasing corporate contracts. Figures are forwarded to the division purchasing organizations to compare against actual quality levels received.

Quality

The quality function serves as the focal point for the development of TQM systems. Quality staff members facilitate weekly quality task force meetings in which action plans for specific quality problems are developed. The teams are composed of design engineers, test engineers, shop floor managers, and production workers. Pareto analysis, cause and effect diagrams, SPC charts, and brainstorming techniques are used by the teams to discover the root cause of the problem. The quality department conducts periodic product and process audits to ensure that quality standards are maintained. Customer complaints are also handled directly by the quality department. Finally, the quality department serves as the "gate keeper" during new product development cycles.

NTI has defined seven critical milestones (referred to as "gates") in the product development process. It is the responsibility of the quality department to provide the independent resource for critically assessing whether the "deliverables" associated with a gate are acceptable. The decision to accept the deliverables at a given gate is made in milestone meetings attended by the division vice president and his staff (which includes the quality director), along with the functional directors. After reviewing presentations on the new product, the attendees arrive at a consensus that either the gate has been successfully completed or that acceptable plans are in place to resolve outstanding issues. Upon meeting the gate requirements, the new product introduction proceeds to the next phase.

Statistical process control (SPC) is widely used throughout the manufacturing operation. Process and quality engineers jointly decide which operations require SPC, based on the critical parameters associated with the process. SPC data are collected both automatically and manually on the production floor. In the case of processes utilizing automatic data collection capabilities, such as wave soldering, automatic insertion machines, and test equipment, control charts can be accessed in real time using terminals located throughout the plant. SPC data are collected and charted by hand in the manual assembly areas. Experimental designs based on Taguchi methods are used to continually reduce process variability, instead of focusing only on problem areas.

Product quality performance measures used by the quality department were developed from the customers' perspective. The out-of-box (OOB) quality metric is used as a continual monitoring device to check what the customer sees upon product delivery. The quality department places orders for complete systems and modules through the normal ordering process. The units are delivered to the quality audit team, which unpacks them, sets them up, and conducts tests. Any nonconformity found during the receiving and unpacking process (for instance, illegible packing labels, incorrect packing labels, scratched face plates) is recorded as a defect. All defects are equally measured, whether they are simply visual or involve a major circuit failure. A 10 percent sample is taken weekly to assess OOB quality. To validate the findings, the division compares results with customers who install their equipment into a controlled environment and duplicate the OOB inspection procedure. To date, the results are practically identical.

Other key measures used to monitor product quality from the customers' perspective are customer complaint statistics, field failure rates, and the customer satisfaction index. The customer satisfaction index is an annual measure based on customer survey responses computed by NTI staff members. Each year, the division submits to NTI management a list of customers to be surveyed. NTI staff then mails surveys to the customers and asks them to rank the divisions from 1 to 5 (1 means unsatisfactory; 5 is excellent) on the performance areas of billing accuracy, product quality, on-time delivery, product reliability, and so on. The values are summed to determine the customer satisfaction index for the division. The measure is reported annually to the division management staffs.

The quality director cites quality, delivery, and field service as crucial areas for success. The following performance measures are monitored by the quality department:

- *Out-of-box (OOB) defectivity.* This is a weekly measure of the percentage of defectivity of out-of-box units inspected. The percentage is calculated for each module (line card, common equipment, and bays and cabinets). The percentage of defective modules is divided by the total number of modules (for example, OOB% defectivity / Line cards = [number of defective lines cards/total number of line cards] × 100%). Targets are established for each module type. Figures are displayed in bar graphs showing monthly actual versus target values, with trend lines for a 12-month period; they are posted on the production floor.

- *Systems integration (SYS) defectivity.* This is a weekly measure of the percentage of defective modules inspected after systems integration. The percentage defective is calculated for each module type (line card, common equipment, and bays and cabinets), and targets are established. Figures are displayed in bar graphs showing monthly actual versus target values, with trend lines for a 12-month period; they are posted on the production floor.

- *Defects per frame.* This is a weekly measure of the number of defects per frame as the ratio of frame defects to the total number of bay or cabinet frames. The information is displayed in a bar graph showing monthly actual versus the target value, with a trend line for a 12-month period; it is posted in the equipment shop area.

- *Field failures.* The percentage of field failures per year of in-service product is monitored monthly by customer, system, and circuit pack module. Field failure data are collected by the service group; marketing supplies statistics on the number of in-service units in the field.

- *Customer complaints.* Measured monthly are the number of customer complaints received, the number closed, the number open, the average age of the complaints (that is, the average amount of time the complaints have existed), and the age of each individual complaint. Figures are reported in the monthly operations review meetings.

- *Customer satisfaction index.* This figure is an annual measurement computed by NTI staff members. NTI headquarters sends questionnaires to customers for each division; customers rank the divisions in various categories on a 1 to 5 scale, and a customer satisfaction index is computed and reported to each division.

PERFORMANCE MEASUREMENT SYSTEMS

The performance measurement systems used at the Stone Mountain facility are maintained by each department. The measures are collected by function and consolidated into monthly reports by the functional directors. Manufacturing and quality performance measures are displayed in tables, charts, and graphs throughout the production area. The information is used to monitor performance trends and to unveil new opportunities for improvement. Cost improvement performance results are supplied to plant personnel in monthly cost improvement analysis reports. The reports serve as working documents that reflect the bottom-line effect of cost improvement programs.

The Stone Mountain facility utilizes essentially one performance measurement system, integrated at the plant and division levels. This integration is partly due to the plant and division operations staffs being located in the same building. The close daily working relationships between the organizational levels have created a unified performance measurement system within the facility. A distinguishing factor between the levels exists, however, on the utilization and monitoring frequency of the shared measures. The plant uses the measures on a daily basis for real-time decision making, whereas division management focuses more on weekly and monthly performance trends to develop tactics for continual improvement. Division management also uses measures received from external sources focusing primarily on long-range performance issues, such as field failure rates, supplier outgoing quality levels, and customer service indices. A summary of the performance measurement system used in the Stone Mountain facility is presented in Table 10–1.

PERFORMANCE MEASUREMENT SYSTEM LINKAGES

Performance measurement system linkages between the plant and division levels are accomplished in several ways. Visual displays of performance measures in the form of graphs, tables, and charts in the production area provide focus to the entire Stone

TABLE 10–1

Stone Mountain Facility Performance Measurement System

Performance Criterion	Performance Measures	Performance Standards
Quality	Daily incoming material quality level	96% acceptance
	Weekly OOB defectivity percentage	Line cards = 0.21% Common equipment = 0.48%
	Weekly system integration defectivity percentage	Line cards = 0.25% Common equipment = 1.5% Bays and cabinets = 3.0%
	Weekly defects per frame	0.61 defects/frame
	Monthly percentage of field failures	0.08%/month
	Monthly number of customer complaints open	All customer complaints closed
	Average age of customer complaints (monthly)	Average age < 60 days
	Age of individual customer complaints (monthly)	Age < 120 days
	Monthly supplier outgoing quality levels	Meet or exceed commodity acceptance standard
	Annual customer satisfaction index	CI = 75 (Max = 100) (NTI standard)
Customer and service delivery	Daily production schedule	No schedule deviations (linearity)
	Weekly shipping schedule	Meet customer requirements
	Weekly on-time delivery/ customer request date	98% on-time
	Weekly on-time delivery/ promise date	100% on-time
	Weekly on-time delivery/ standard time	100% on-time
Supplier performance	Weekly supplier on-time delivery	0 days late 4 days early (maximum)
	Monthly number of certified vendors	Vendor certification objectives
	Monthly number of suppliers per commodity	Supplier reduction objectives
Cost	Weekly scrap cost as a percentage of material cost	Financial plan
	Monthly PPV/CI	Cost improvement target for each program
	Monthly departmental budget variances	Financial plan

TABLE 10-1 (*continued*)
Stone Mountain Facility Performance Measurement System

Performance Criterion	Performance Measures	Performance Standards
Lead time	Weekly manufacturing cycle times	50% annual reduction
	Weekly vendor lead times	Within NTI purchasing guidelines
Profitability	Monthly P/L's	Financial plan
	Monthly EBIT before R&D	Financial plan
Productivity	Weekly direct labor utilization	Line cards = 96%
		Other areas = 70%
Inventory	Weekly surplus/obsolete inventory dollars	Financial plan
	Weekly inventory turns	Financial plan

Mountain operation. Multifunctional daily production meetings offer a forum for performance measurement exchanges between directors, managers, and production workers. Weekly quality task force meetings ensure a cross-functional approach to solving quality performance problems and assist in implementing divisional quality objectives. All Stone Mountain employees attend a monthly state-of-the-business meeting to review business performance. The monthly cost improvement analysis report also provides performance linkages between the two levels by detailing the effect of plant cost improvement programs on the bottom line. The commonality of measures displayed between the plant and division performance measurement systems at the Stone Mountain facility unifies the two systems.

The primary vehicles for achieving performance measurement system linkages between division, group, and corporate (NTI) levels are the monthly operations review meetings, the monthly financial results package, and the monthly activity report. Operations review meetings allow division management to present monthly performance results to NTI group and corporate management staffs, as well as exchange performance measurement information across functional areas. Opportunities for future improvements are also assessed in the meetings. The financial results package provides NTI group and corporate management with division profit and loss statements, balance sheets, cash flow statements, overhead analyses, and functional spending summaries. The package also includes cost improvement program performance results. Monthly reports contain consolidated performance metrics for each functional area, highlighting performance trends and progress against NTI and divisional objectives.

NTI also has measures that are distributed to the divisions. A supplier outgoing quality level report on suppliers with corporate contracts is forwarded monthly from NTI staff to division purchasing organizations. The customer satisfaction index is also forwarded from NTI staff to division organizations on an annual basis. Thus, the firm has a two-way flow of performance measurement information, which is the result of the corporate staff's effort to better assist operating divisions.

Several other methods are used to develop performance measurement system linkages between the plant, division, group, and corporate levels of the organization. The use of a totally integrated accounting system allows for financial visibility from the plant to the parent (Northern Telecom, Ltd.) level of the company. A weekly summary of quality metrics published by the director of quality is distributed to the division manufacturing staff. A detailed description of the methods the transmission access division uses to create performance measurement system linkages follows:

- *Visual measurement displays.* This method allows a visual assessment of daily performance measures and weekly performance trends on key indicators. It assists in the development of cross-functional and interorganizational linkages by focusing management efforts on the highest-priority items.

- *Daily production meetings.* The directors of planning and scheduling, manufacturing, and purchasing meet daily with manufacturing planners and production managers to discuss performance against weekly production targets and to develop the means to achieve schedule linearity in the manufacturing operation.

- *Weekly quality task force meeting.* Meetings of multifunctional teams comprising design engineers, test engineers, shop floor managers, and production workers are held weekly and are facilitated by quality department personnel. The teams develop methods to determine the root causes of quality problems and programs for eliminating the causes.

- *Weekly quality summary.* Quality metrics are summarized by the director of quality and distributed to manufacturing management, the division general manager, and group and corporate staff members.

- *Monthly state-of-the-business meetings.* These are presentations to all Stone Mountain employees by the division management staff on overall business performance.

- *Monthly cost improvement analysis report.* This report provides the plant with detailed information on the effect of each cost improvement program on division profitability. It serves as a working document for monitoring plant cost improvement progress.

- *Monthly operations review meetings.* Division management staff present performance results to group and corporate management. Information is exchanged across functional areas, and improvement opportunities are jointly explored.

- *Monthly financial results package.* This provides information on the division's financial performance to group and corporate management on profitability, cash flow, asset management, spending, and cost improvements. Division results are consolidated at the group and corporate levels and forwarded to the parent organization.

- *Monthly activity report.* Division directors summarize key activities and performance metrics monthly. Information is consolidated into a monthly activity report distributed to group and corporate management.

- *Monthly supplier outgoing quality report.* NTI management compiles quality statistics on the outgoing quality levels shipped by suppliers with corporate contracts. Reports are distributed to the division purchasing organizations and are used to check against actual quality levels received during the period.

- *Annual customer satisfaction index ratings.* NTI headquarters mails questionnaires to selected customers for each division annually; customers rank the divisions in various categories on a 1 to 5 scale (1 means unsatisfactory, and 5 is excellent). A customer satisfaction index is computed and reported to each division.

The methods employed by the transmission access division to achieve performance measurement system linkages will assist the organization in its continued effort to contribute to Northern Telecom's technological leadership position in the telecommunications industry.

LESSONS LEARNED

This case shows how strategic objectives can be achieved by linking performance measurement systems and functions.

Customer and Resource

To facilitate a customer-resource link on the strategic objective of quality, the quality department developed a product quality performance measure from the customers' perspective. The out-of-box (OOB) quality metric is used to continually monitor what the customer sees upon product delivery. A 10 percent sample is taken weekly to assess OOB quality. To validate the findings, the transmission access division compares results with customers who install its equipment in a controlled environment and duplicate the OOB inspection procedure. Information is fed back into the manufacturing operation so that problems can be corrected. The information is also shared with other functions if the problems originated in a nonmanufacturing area. This process allows resources to be deployed effectively to improve quality in areas important to customers. In addition, field failure information collected by the service group is forwarded to the quality department to promote the effective use of organizational resources and to facilitate product and process improvements.

Finance and Resource

The transmission access division uses a traditional full-absorption accounting system that focuses on material resources. Because material cost represents more than 70 percent of total product cost, the firm is constantly developing methods to reduce material cost on current products without reducing value to customers. Three primary approaches are used: product redesigns, material substitutions, and PPV control. The division closely monitors the effect of true cost improvements in resource usage on the P/L statement. To ensure an accurate assessment, all cost improvements are offset by the program expenses necessary to realize the improvement. Other methods for linking material resource usage to the financial system are the monitoring of scrap costs as a percentage of material cost, and inventory dollars of surplus or obsolete materials and finished goods. Field failure statistics are also converted into financial terms to link material resource deployment to finances. This case provides another vehicle for examining how customer-resource and resource-finance linkages can be used to help achieve strategic objectives.

Chapter Eleven

Clark Equipment Company Clark Material Handling Business Unit

This case illustrates how linkages between customer and resource performance measurement systems and functions can be accomplished. Cost and quality are the strategic objectives of the business unit. Performance criteria, standards, and measures were established for these objectives to promote continual improvement in these areas.

COMPANY BACKGROUND

The Clark Equipment Company is a worldwide manufacturer of capital goods equipment, with headquarters in South Bend, Indiana. The company consists of four autonomous business units:

- *Melrose Company* is a manufacturer of loaders, trenchers, and hydraulic excavators for construction, industrial, and agricultural applications.

- *Clark Components International* produces transmissions, torque converters, and axles for heavy-duty off-highway vehicles.

- *Clark Automotive Products Company* manufactures automotive, truck, agricultural, and off-highway axles and transmissions, primarily for Brazilian markets.

- *Clark Material Handling Company* produces a full line of electric and internal combustion forklift trucks.

In 1989, Clark Equipment's North American and European material handling businesses were consolidated into a new business unit renamed Clark Material Handling.

By reorganizing into a single global business entity, the firm is positioned to more effectively take advantage of available synergies on a worldwide basis and enhance its international competitiveness. Clark Material Handling is headquartered in Lexington, Kentucky, with production facilities in the United States, Germany, and South Korea. The firm has also entered into a joint venture with the Korean-based Samsung Company. Samsung supplies Clark Material Handling with internal combustion forklift trucks that are manufactured in Korea and modified in the United States by Clark. Clark Material Handling products are distributed through an independent dealership network. The North American network is the largest in the industry.

Clark Material Handling's customer base is 75 percent make-to-order, 20 percent make-to-stock, and 5 percent engineer-to-order. The manufacturing processes are 75 percent repetitive (high volume), 20 percent batch (products are made intermittently), and 5 percent project (product is designed and engineered for a specific customer). Three solely owned manufacturing facilities currently produce forklift trucks at the following locations: Lexington, Kentucky; Ashville, North Carolina; and Mulheim, Germany. A new facility in Danville, Kentucky, began operations in 1991. The Lexington plant has a total employment of 300, which includes 240 direct and 60 indirect employees. All employees are salaried. The plant is a one-shift operation that produces 2,000- to 10,000-pound capacity electric forklift trucks. The Lexington plant also modifies internal combustion forklift trucks manufactured in Korea for the North American market.

There are 1,000 active part numbers in the inventory system and approximately four levels in the typical bill of material. The facility employs elements of MRP, JIT, and TQM to plan, monitor, and control production processes as well as the overall business. Interviews were conducted with the following individuals:

- Vice-president of manufacturing planning.
- Vice-president of product engineering.
- Director of quality and reliability.
- Manager of business development.
- Director of finance.
- Director of purchasing.
- Area manager of the Powrworker product group.
- Manager of current product engineering at the Lexington plant.
- Manager of quality assurance at the Lexington plant.
- Plant controller at the Lexington plant.

FIGURE 11-1
Clark Material Handling Company Organizational Structure

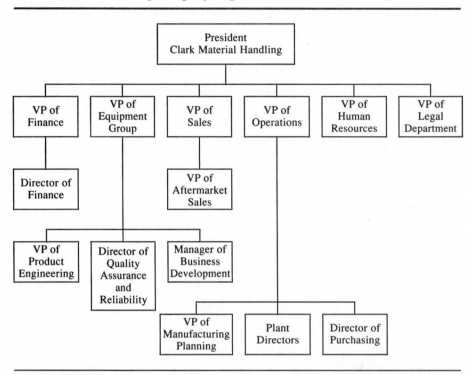

Note: Not all directors and managers are shown.

BUSINESS UNIT ORGANIZATION

Clark Material Handling is functionally structured and consists of operations, engineering, marketing, financial, and legal organizations. The functional vice presidents report directly to the business unit president. Each vice president has a staff composed of directors and managers who focus on specific subfunctional areas. The vice president of the equipment group is responsible for worldwide engineering and marketing activities. Plant directors report to the vice president of operations. The organizational structure of Clark Material Handling is presented in Figure 11-1.

STRATEGIC OBJECTIVES

The Clark Equipment Company has a corporate strategy composed of the following elements:

- To manufacture products that are technically superior, cost efficient, customer responsive, and quality driven and that provide high levels of customer value, increase the value of each shareholder's investment, and enhance company profitability.
- To foster domestic and international market growth in all business units through research and development expenditures for internal product development, and the acquisition of product lines or entire businesses that strategically benefit existing Clark operations.
- To be recognized as a world leader in the businesses in which it competes internationally.

The strategic mission, objectives, and principles governing managerial actions within Clark Equipment are presented here:

Mission:

- Design, manufacture, and market the finest equipment in the world for Clark customers.
- Provide the most satisfying careers for Clark employees.
- Earn high returns and growth for stockholders.

Objectives:

- Continue to develop best-in-the-world design engineering skills on a global scale.
- Continually improve world-class manufacturing capabilities in all manufacturing operations.
- Continue to develop best-in-the-world marketing and sales capabilities worldwide.

Principles:

- Conduct business with honesty and integrity.
- Provide value to Clark customers.
- Behave responsibly with respect to the environment and the safety of employees.
- Maintain high ethical standards internationally.

Business Unit Objectives

The mission of Clark Material Handling is to design, manufacture, market, and service a broad line of competitive forklift trucks containing features, cost, and quality attributes that provide unparalleled customer and user satisfaction in all markets. The mission statement also includes providing superior financial returns to stockholders, continuing to build on established capabilities, and building customer satisfaction into each product. The president of Clark Material Handling annually presents a five-year strategic plan to Clark Equipment management to ensure that its contents are consistent with and responsive to the needs of the corporation.

To support the five-year goals and objectives, Clark Material Handling employs several tactics in the areas of product design, customer satisfaction, quality, and procurement. A summary of key tactics follows:

Product design:

- Redesign internal combustion engine products using engineering projects that utilize value engineering to provide product cost reductions and enhance return on investment.
- Design "world trucks" containing a large proportion of common parts and designs capable of penetrating international markets with the flexibility for regional changes to satisfy specific market needs.
- Enhance customer value by identifying features desired by the customer and providing them at an acceptable price.
- Provide a more pleasant environment for the end user of Clark forklift trucks (that is, include ergonomic considerations in product designs).

Customer satisfaction:

- Use the Malcolm Baldrige National Quality Award review process as a means to improve and increase levels of customer satisfaction through superior product quality.
- Focus on the firm's ability to rapidly respond to customers' needs in the field.
- Continue to work with dealers to ensure that they are satisfying customers' needs.
- Provide customers with on-time deliveries.

Quality:

- Qualify for the Malcolm Baldrige National Quality Award within the next five years.
- Continue to develop total quality management systems throughout the company.

Procurement:

- Utilize joint international sourcing for North American and European operations to achieve maximum benefits with suppliers on a worldwide basis.
- Continue to use certified suppliers.

An important tactic Clark uses to integrate international operations and functional organizations on strategic issues is multifunctional global planning boards. The planning boards are an effective way of ensuring that functional plans are consistent and coherent throughout the organization. Clark Material Handling has assembled general, manufacturing, product, quality, distribution and aftermarket, and administration planning boards, which are designed to address specific strategic issues that the firm faces.

The general planning board consists of the president of Clark Material Handling Company, four key North American vice presidents, and four key European vice presidents. The manufacturing, product, quality, distribution and aftermarket, and administration planning boards are composed of several Clark Material Handling vice presidents and directors from North America and Europe. The president of Clark Material Handling chairs the quality planning board. Many planning board members reside on more than one board in order to facilitate information flow among the boards. Periodic joint planning board meetings are held to resolve issues that require the members' combined efforts. The functional representations and composition of a board is based on its strategic focus. An illustration of the planning board structure and strategic focus is given in Figure 11–2.

Manufacturing Objectives

During the 1980s, Clark Equipment was faced with tremendous competitive pressures from Japanese capital goods manufacturers, causing a near collapse of its forklift business. One of the survival strategies employed by the firm to stabilize and transform the business was to reduce its level of vertical integration and consolidate existing manufacturing operations. Inefficient operations were closed in Battle Creek, Michigan, and Georgetown, Kentucky, and combined into the Lexington plant. A new facility in Danville, Kentucky, began operations in 1991. Current manufacturing operations have been dramatically streamlined from previous levels, primarily consisting of assembly, paint, and testing activities. A critical manufacturing objective for the firm is to strategically assess the appropriate levels of value-added activities within each plant, justifiable by quality, return on assets, and customer response time considerations.

Manufacturing objectives established for Clark Material Handling plants are summarized as follows:

- Increase incrementally the level of vertical integration in selected manufacturing operations based on the following criteria: increased quality control capabilities, enhanced return on assets, and improved customer responsiveness.

FIGURE 11–2
Clark Material Handling's Multifunctional Global Planning Boards

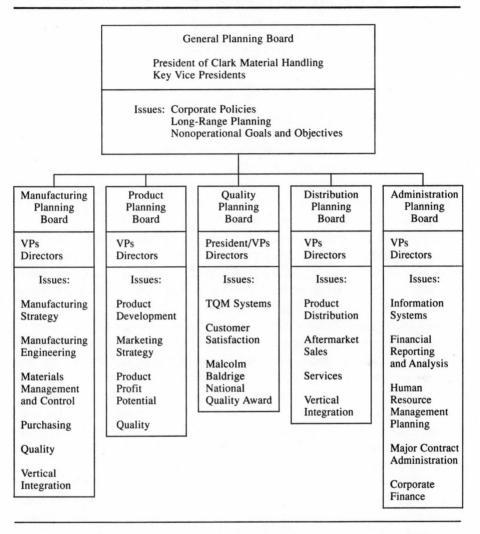

- Incorporate advanced manufacturing technology into selected manufacturing operations based on quality, return on assets, and customer responsiveness criteria.
- Develop and implement quality plans that enhance quality system capabilities in all manufacturing operations. A major element is the use of statistical process control (SPC) on selected operations.

- Develop a participative work environment in the manufacturing facilities, utilizing the JIT concepts of self-managed work teams, quality at the source, and reduced levels of inventory.
- Develop a manufacturing presence in all served markets.

BUSINESS UNIT FUNCTIONS

Manufacturing Planning

The manufacturing planning department works directly with the product development, purchasing, and marketing organizations in the development of new forklift truck designs. Manufacturing planning also helps develop manufacturing and quality systems to improve manufacturability. The department has ongoing projects with product development, purchasing, and marketing that utilize value analysis and value engineering procedures for the design, development, and production of new forklift trucks over the next three to five years.

As part of the new product development process, engineers in the manufacturing planning department work as a team with research and development engineers, purchasing managers, and marketing professionals to determine customers' future requirements. The team will survey dealers and customers and bring them in-house to discuss current products offered in the marketplace, both by Clark and by the competition. These discussions will include purchasing agents, mechanics, drivers, and other representatives from customer organizations and focus on product features that will be required by specific industries in the future. From this input the team will develop new product specifications. The team will concurrently examine Clark and its competitor's product cost and value relationships for each design by function, such as engine, drive line, and hydraulics, using a value analysis and value engineering approach. Each component is then examined from a quality and cost perspective to determine worldwide sourcing opportunities. The results of the analysis are integrated into the initial design concept for new products.

The multifunctional global manufacturing planning board provides an effective means for integrating manufacturing and other operational issues into the initial stages of the product development process. The board is composed of senior managers from the manufacturing, purchasing, materials, logistics, engineering, and marketing functions in North America and Europe. The board develops objectives for manufacturing new and existing products, identifies future customer needs, and examines the effect of product development plans on current and future manufacturing capabilities, sourcing strategies, and sourcing qualifications and standards. The board defines manufacturing strategies based on customer and market requirements, and strategically assesses sourcing issues worldwide.

Manufacturing planning supports the organization by assessing the type and level of technology required to improve product quality, reduce direct and indirect cost and manufacturing lead times, and enhance overall customer satisfaction. The department examines such issues as the appropriateness of applying robotics, the degree of vertical integration, and the type of manufacturing technology that can improve operations. Manufacturing planning also competitively benchmarks not only from the perspective of current products, but also from a manufacturing and purchasing perspective. Representatives visit competitors, company business units, and organizations in unrelated businesses to examine manufacturing procedures, material handling capabilities, facility layouts, types of equipment used, order entry, and purchasing systems. This allows Clark Material Handling to continually recalibrate existing targets for achieving best-in-the-world capabilities in all facets of the business.

The vice president of manufacturing planning believes that quality, delivery, and product and process innovation are critical to the long-term viability of Clark Material Handling. Key performance measures monitored monthly by manufacturing planning are as follows:

- *Warranty cost per model.* Warranty cost by major truck system (engine, drive line, hydraulics, and so forth) is tracked by reliability engineers from dealers and end users for each forklift truck model. Data are used to relate warranty cost and field failure frequencies to customer dissatisfaction levels. This information is shared with the manufacturing, engineering, and purchasing organizations and corrective action teams.

- *Truck preparation time.* This is a measurement of the amount of dealer touch-up time needed before a truck is sent to the final customer. The type and frequency of preparations, such as torque adjustments, paint, and shipping damage, are also identified and recorded. The service group collects and shares the data with the manufacturing, engineering, and purchasing organizations.

- *Order lead time.* This is a measure of the time between order receipt and customer delivery. The figures are presented as a percentage breakdown of the number of trucks shipped within 60, 90, and beyond 90 days by product group.

- *Delivery performance.* This measure is computed as the percentage of forklift trucks shipped on time, based on the initial customer promise date.

- *Number of trucks produced per employee.* The department measures the ratio of forklift truck production to total number of direct employees for each manufacturing operation.

Product Engineering

The product engineering department is responsible for developing new products and reengineering current products. The product development process begins with cross-functional teams' evaluation of Clark's and competitors' products, using value engineering. In the initial stage of the project, the product design project product manager leads the development effort, soliciting inputs from purchasing, marketing, and manufacturing team members on product development criteria and standards. As the project progresses, the lead role switches to manufacturing because this is where most of the activity will shift to.

New products are preprototyped using existing production tooling to give team members some idea of how the product will look before they actually build prototypes. Preprototyping also eliminates many design and manufacturing problems early in the product development cycle, and helps the organization purchase the correct tooling for producing prototypes. The prototypes are actually built in the engineering laboratory.

Once all engineering endurance and functional tests are completed on the prototypes, product engineering releases the new product to manufacturing. There are three phases that the new product must successfully complete before it is made in volume production: preproduction, pilot production, and production run. Product engineers continue to support the product during these phases, as well as in volume production.

The planning board is the mechanism for a cross-functional approach to the assessment of product needs. The board is responsible for defining the direction of products, deciding how to utilize the firm's engineering resources in North America and Europe, discovering opportunities for value analysis and value engineering, and determining the best approach to developing uniformly design world trucks (trucks containing standardized components and designs with the flexibility for change to satisfy a specific market). The product planning board consists of North American and European senior managers, representing the engineering, manufacturing, purchasing and marketing functions. Work committees implement the plans developed by the product planning board.

Design engineers on the manufacturing floor perform what are known as fit, form, and function activities. Requests for product design changes are evaluated by these design engineers from the standpoint of fit, form, and function. The design engineer evaluates these requests and implements them upon acceptance. In addition, the purchasing department gives product engineering product design change requests for product cost and warrenty reductions. Product engineers meet with marketing managers to prioritize changes and to assess the changes' reduction of cost and enhancement of customer satisfaction.

The vice president of product engineering cites quality, reliability, cost, speed to market, and product and process flexibility as critical to developing competitive advantages in the marketplace. Performance measures used in the product engineering department are divided into three categories: new product development measures, warranty and field failure measures, and design engineering measures. Following are product engineering performance measures:

New product development:

- *Project cost.* The department tracks weekly projected versus actual project cost in project review meetings held by project team members.

- *Product cost.* The department tracks weekly projected versus actual product cost based on preprototyping and prototyping. Figures are monitored weekly in project review meetings held by project team members.

- *Project schedule performance.* Project teams break down each project activity; they measure and compare on a weekly basis actual project activity time to an established engineering standard during the project review meetings. They share information with the product engineering staff.

Warranty and field failure:

- *Hourly cost of truck operation.* The service organization periodically collects information from dealers and end users on the hourly cost of operating Clark's forklift truck. It is used to establish product design criteria and value engineering targets.

- *Mean time between failures (MTBF).* Information on MTBF by major truck system is collected (engine, drive line, hydraulics, and so on) from dealers and end users; the results are reviewed periodically with the product planning board and are distributed to engineering and other relevant functional areas.

Design engineering:

- *CAD system response time.* Production engineering tracks weekly the average response time of the mainframe CAD system to the CAD workstations, using a computer program that automatically collects response time statistics. The information is used to assess the effect of CAD systems on product development cycles.

Quality Assurance and Reliability

The quality assurance and reliability function guides quality and reliability activities on new and current products and provides engineering services. Clark Material Handling has employed a decentralized approach to quality management, whereby responsibility for quality is integrated into various functional areas. For example, the purchasing function has its own quality engineer. Thus, the purchasing manager has direct responsibility for the quality of purchased materials. Plant directors have quality managers who report directly to them. Quality management is also integrated into the product design process using reliability engineers who verify product designs through product qualification tests.

The director of quality and reliability provides overall guidance to the management of companywide quality systems. He often plays the role of an internal quality advisor, counselor, and consultant. A critical aspect of his role is to support companywide TQM development without inheriting implementation and ownership responsibilities. It is important that the responsibility for quality resides in the users, not the quality control staff. Clark Material Handling has adopted a quality approach consistent with criteria established in the Baldrige Award guidelines—the focus is on assessing the needs of internal and external customers, measuring current product attributes against those needs, and developing quality systems that allow for continual improvement.

The quality planning board makes strategic quality plans for the business unit. The president of Clark Material Handling chairs the board. The firm believes that direct leadership by the top official in the organization is necessary to TQM's effectiveness. The quality planning board consists of a cross-functional group of North American and European senior managers representing the engineering, manufacturing, marketing, sales, materials, and purchasing organizations. A major focus of the quality planning board is improvement of customer satisfaction through enhanced product quality. Quality improvement teams have been established at the plant level. These teams are also multifunctional, and they explore quality improvement opportunities throughout the plant. Clark Material Handling believes that cross-functional approaches are necessary at all levels of the firm to effectively work on quality issues.

The director of quality and reliability believes that quality, product and process innovation, and cost hold the keys to Clark's success. Performance measures are monitored monthly for the quality, reliability, and engineering activities in the department. The performance measures are as follows:

Quality and reliability:
- *MTBF for new products.* MTBF laboratory data are collected on new products and compared to predicted MTBF standards by failure class. These results are generally reported after 1,000 hours of testing but may vary. Results are discussed in project review meetings.
- *MTBF for current products.* Forklift trucks are tracked in the field using the dealer network. Records are maintained by dealers and some customers. Reliability engineers periodically collect the data and determine the MTBF on each major truck system by product group.
- *Number of project problems corrected.* The department uses a process called FRACAS (failure reporting and corrective action system) to detect and correct project problems in new product development. This measure is monitored and presented monthly in product review meetings, in addition to the number of identified project problems that have been corrected.

- *Test driver utilization.* This measure is defined as the number of test hours divided by the total number of clock hours available. It is a monthly measurement of the utilization of test drivers and is used for product reliability studies.

- *Lost test time hours.* This is a measurement of time lost as a result of not having someone available to conduct laboratory tests. It is monitored to assess its effect on product development cycle time and is measured monthly, project by project.

Engineering services:

- *CAD system response time.* The department tracks weekly the average response time of the mainframe CAD system to the CAD workstations using a computer program that automatically collects response time statistics. The information is used to assess the effect of CAD systems on product development cycles.

- *CAD system utilization.* The quality department tracks weekly the percentage of CAD system utilization by individual workstation using a computer program that automatically collects utilization statistics. Figures are used to define hardware needs.

- *ECN throughput.* The department tracks weekly the number of engineering change notices processed by the engineering services area, segmented by product group.

Business Development and Program Management

The business development and program management process begins when cross-functional teams determine the critical attributes necessary for a new product. A project specification is developed that outlines the project scope, strategies and objectives, product specifications, cost targets, volume forecasts for each market, and a competitive analysis and comparison. Strategies, objectives, and volume forecasts focus on several key markets: North America, EURAME (Europe, Africa, and the Middle East), Latin America, and the Pacific Rim. The planning boards at Clark Material Handling establish quality, reliability, market share, financial, and other goals for the project, from which strategies and objectives are refined.

The planning board must then approve the project specification before proceeding to the next step, the development of the engineering scope. Approved projects are monitored through project review milestone meetings. Each meeting gives management authorization to proceed to the next phase of the project. Funding for the projects is also determined at the review meetings, which are attended by the general planning board as well as product and manufacturing planning board members.

The manager of IC (internal combustion) programs cite quality, cost, and product and process flexibility as key areas of strategic importance for Clark Material

Handling. Performance measures are the same as those used by product engineering to assess new product development, are as follows:

- *Project cost.* Projected versus actual project cost is monitored weekly in project review meetings.

- *Product cost.* Projected versus actual product cost based on preprototyping and prototyping activities is monitored weekly and reported in project review meetings.

- *Project schedule performance.* Project teams conduct a work content breakdown on each project activity and measure and compare actual activity time to an established engineering standard. Figures are monitored on a weekly basis in review meetings and shared with the product engineering staff.

Accounting

Clark Material Handling utilizes a standard, full-absorption accounting system and processes all accounting work for its North American operations in Lexington. The accounting information is reported by product group (light internal combustion, electric, PowrWorker, narrow aisle and heavy truck), and at the end of the month a separate P/L statement is reported for each product. Each line of business (product group) has a financial manager responsible for developing budgets, conducting financial analyses, reviewing capital investment requests, and constructing annual financial plans for the product group. Plant controllers develop departmental budgets. The accounting function also helps develop five-year operational plans for each line of business. On a monthly basis, financial managers measure actual results against objectives. A monthly balance of the year forecast is also conducted for each product group and compared against actual results. These mechanisms are used to track organizational performance against the profit plan monthly.

Accounting standards are established annually, and all product managers are given the current year's estimate by truck type. A summary of product cost by truck type is supplied quarterly to marketing and sales personnel to alert them to actual cost. However, product pricing is not directly related to product cost. Competitive pricing pressures rather than costs, determine what the forklift truck can be sold for. Clark Material Handling thus uses market-driven versus cost-driven pricing to establish price ranges.

The director of finance considers quality, delivery, and lead time as the keys to achieving sustainable advantages in the marketplace. Performance measures collected and distributed by the accounting function are presented here:

- *P/L statements.* Monthly profit and loss statements by product group display actual versus planned results, along with a comparison against the balance of the year forecast. Corporate staff, the business unit president and staff, financial directors, and product managers receive the report.

- *Budget variances.* Each department manager receives a monthly budget variance report comparing planned to actual spending.

- *Key financial measures.* Consolidated quarterly financial measures are presented to all Clark Material Handling employees in meetings conducted by the president. The following information is discussed: net sales income, inventory investment, cash flow, and return on net assets (RONA). Planned versus actual quarterly results are also presented.

Purchasing

The purchasing function has three primary areas of responsibility: manufacturing material support, new product development support, and supplier relationships. Purchasing must furnish the manufacturing units with the production and supply materials required to keep the facility operating. A quality engineer, who is a member of the purchasing organizations, works at the Lexington plant and supports the facility when issues arise concerning purchased materials, such as defective parts, wrong components, and incorrect specifications. Production buyers in the plants support manufacturing by determining purchasing lead time, supplier quality, and vendors for the procurement of new parts.

The purchasing department supports the firm's new product development efforts by participating in value analysis and value engineering. Five employees in purchasing help product engineering with value engineering projects and help determine world cost levels for specific materials, identify sources for material purchases, and qualify those sources to meet product quality and cost requirements.

Production buyers and the quality engineer qualify potential suppliers. The production buyer performs a preliminary analysis on new suppliers concerning their price competitiveness, financial stability, and material quality. If the candidate appears promising, the buyer and the quality engineer conduct a full quality audit of the potential supplier's facility. The findings are compared to standards outlined in the business unit's supplier quality manual. The purchasing organization then decides as to the acceptability of the potential supplier.

There are 264 suppliers who provide materials for the Lexington plant. Currently, 244 are certified suppliers. To become certified, a supplier must maintain a 99.9 percent fitness-for-use level (that is, one defect per 1,000 parts) for three consecutive months. Fitness for use is defined as the material's ability to physically perform its intended function. The 99.9 percent fitness-for-use level must be maintained on a monthly basis for a supplier to remain certified. The 20 suppliers who are currently not certified will be given time to meet the certification standard. The purchasing department will assist them by defining what is required for improvement. If the suppliers are not able to achieve the standard, they will be dropped.

A key element of Clark Material Handling's procurement strategy has been to streamline the supplier base. In 1985, materials were purchased from over 700 suppliers, compared to the current number of 264. At one time, the firm had over 115 fastener suppliers. Today, only 20 firms supply the company with fasteners. The supplier reduction process has resulted in improved and more consistent incoming material quality, more cooperative supplier relationships, higher levels of supplier commitment, and long-term procurement contracts instead of annual agreements. The purchasing department plans to continually refine its supply base and is moving toward sole sourcing where feasible.

The director of purchasing believes that quality, delivery, and product and process innovation are essential to global competitiveness in the material handling industry. Following are performance measures monitored within purchasing:

- *Cost improvement targets.* Production buyers and the purchasing manager establish annual cost reduction targets for each commodity. Performance against the targets is measured and reported monthly and a monthly cost improvement report is distributed to the vice president of operations and his staff.

- *Material price variance targets.* Annual material price variance targets are established for production buyers on each commodity; these targets incorporate projected cost reductions and forecasted inflation levels to assess the effect on the bottom line. Variance is displayed as a line item on the monthly P/L statements. Material price variances are forecasted on a monthly basis and compared to actual results.

- *Number of certified suppliers.* A list of all certified and noncertified suppliers is published monthly. The list is posted near the building entrance and distributed to purchasing and operations staff.

PLANT FUNCTIONS

Lexington Operation

The Lexington plant is a nonunion facility that opened in 1987. The plant manufactures 2,000- to 10,000-pound lift capacity electric forklifts. The plant also modifies gas-powered products shipped from Korea. Dedicated conversion and modification lines for electric forklift trucks are also ordered. Conversion consists of adding components to assembled forklift trucks (for instance, counterweights, uprights, and different tires). Some trucks also go through the modification line to add specific embellishments requested by customers. Three production processes are conducted

FIGURE 11–3
Organizational Structure of the Lexington Plant

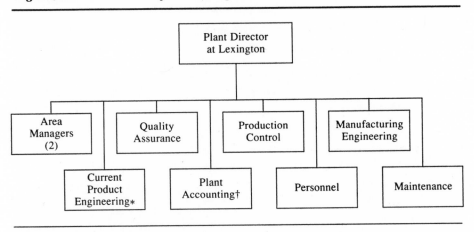

*Reports to director of current product engineering.
†Reports to vice president of operations.

at the Lexington plant: welding, assembly, and painting. The plant organization is flat and functionally structured. A diagram of the Lexington plant's organizational structure is presented in Figure 11–3.

The manufacturing process begins with the welding operation. From welding, material flows onto the assembly lines. After assembly is completed, the trucks go directly to the painting operation. The plant is integrating elements of JIT into management of the operation. In the Battle Creek and Georgetown plants, every model is built monthly. In the Lexington facility, every model is built weekly, thus moving the plant toward mixed-model production. The operation receives deliveries weekly from suppliers and utilizes point-of-use inventory stocking for all production materials. Production workers are responsible for the materials used in the manufacturing operation. They receive materials from the shipping area, store them at their point of use, and conduct daily inventory cycle counts. There is no receiving inspection on incoming materials in the Lexington plant. One of the advantages of weekly material deliveries has been that the plant's quality problems have decreased significantly, owing to the low quantities of on-hand materials. New parts purchased from noncertified suppliers are inspected by quality assurance, based on a sampling plan, until the supplier is either certified or dropped. Other elements of the JIT philosophy employed at the Lexington facility are as follows:

- The use of self-managed work teams, whereby the role of production management is to advise and support.

- An all-salaried work force that has direct access to everyone in the organization, including the plant director.
- No tracking of individual labor productivity.
- A participative management environment in which decisions are made at the lowest possible level of the organization.

The plant director cites quality, cost, and lead time as critical areas of competitiveness for Clark Material Handling. Performance measures monitored by the plant director are listed here:

- *Hours worked per unit.* This measure is defined as the number of hours worked by production employees divided by the number of units shipped during the same period; it is monitored and reported weekly.
- *Overtime hours per unit.* This measure is defined as the number of overtime hours worked by production employees divided by the number of units shipped during the same period; it is monitored and reported weekly.
- *Inventory turns.* Raw and WIP inventory turns are monitored and reported monthly. The objective is 25 turns per year.
- *Daily production targets.* The monthly production objective is divided into daily production standards for each area of the operation. Figures are monitored and reported daily.
- *First-pass ratio percentages for block test.* This measure is defined as the number of trucks from the assembly line that pass the functional block test with zero defects on the first attempt divided by the number of trucks built; the current standard is 75 percent zero defect trucks. The ratio is monitored and reported daily and referred to as "zero defect trucks—first time through block test."
- *First-pass ratio percentages for final inspection.* This measure is defined as the number of trucks that pass final inspection with zero defects on the first attempt divided by the number of trucks shipped; the current standard is 95 percent zero defect trucks. The ratio is monitored and reported daily and referred to as "zero defect trucks—first time through final inspection."
- *Order lead time.* The amount of time between receiving an order and actual customer delivery is measured monthly and presented as a percentage breakdown of the number of trucks shipped within 60, 90, and beyond 90 days by product group.
- *Delivery performance.* The percentage of forklift trucks shipped on time, based on the initial customer promise date, is measured monthly.
- *Number of trucks produced per employee.* This is a measure of the ratio of forklift truck production to total number of direct employees for each manufacturing operation.

- *Warranty cost per model.* Monthly warranty cost information by major truck system (engine, drive line, hydraulics, and so forth) is collected by reliability engineers from dealers and end users for each model. The data are used to relate warranty cost and field failure frequencies to customer dissatisfaction. Warranty cost information is shared with the manufacturing, engineering, and purchasing organizations and corrective action teams.
- *Plant absenteeism.* Figures are monitored and reported monthly; the standard is no more than 1.0 percent absenteeism annually.

Area Management

PowrWorker product group.   The PowrWorker product is a pallet truck designed for a wide range of material handling applications. PowrWorkers come in walkie and rider configurations. In the walkie configuration, the forklift is operated electrically; the user walks as he controls vehicle. When using the rider machines, the operator rides standing on a platform. The product is currently produced on a one-shift basis and includes welding, assembly, and painting operations. Workers are directly responsible for the quality of their work. Welders put an identification mark near completed frame welds so that during block testing (which is a functional check of the assembled truck whereby the unit is required to lift its rated capacity of weight and is inspected for hydraulic and oil leaks, fork elevation speed, and fork drift), and final inspection, work can be traced. Each work team considers the next operation as "the customer." Thus, each work team member wants to provide customer satisfaction through quality workmanship. If the workmanship is deficient, workers want immediate "customer feedback" so that deficiencies can be corrected.

Workers are cross-trained within and in some cases between work teams. For instance, welders can do assembly work when required. Work team members are responsible for their own point-of-use inventory. The plant uses an inventory tagging system to regulate material releases from point-of-use inventory racks. When jobs are released to the floor, material control furnishes workers with tags describing the material location and required amount for completing the order. The work team members then get the necessary quantity of material from the racks. Thus, only the amount of material needed for completing the order is removed from the storage areas. Daily cycle counts are also conducted by the work teams. Each worker is given cycle-counting responsibility for an assigned group of part numbers. Material control is notified of the results of the count and keeps a daily running total of the amount of material available in the storage racks.

A high level of employee involvement exists in every aspect of the Lexington plant. Work team members are involved in the hiring of new employees, product redesigns, supplier interactions, and presentations to various levels of Clark management. For example, workers once gave a presentation to the corporate board of directors. Work team members also gave representatives from Hershey Foods a presentation on self-managed work teams. Each work team conducts peer evaluations, which determine annual pay raises. The team members evaluate each other in the following areas:

- Quality of work.
- Job knowledge.
- Work performance.
- Adaptability and flexibility.
- Customer relations (with internal customers).
- Safety and housekeeping.
- Dependability and reliability.
- Initiative.
- Stewardship.
- Interpersonal relations and teamwork.

Work teams also receive annual bonuses based on Clark Material Handling earning a return on net assets (RONA) that is greater than the cost of capital. The president reports progress against RONA objectives to all plant employees during quarterly state-of-the-business addresses.

The Powrworker area manager believes that quality, cost, and delivery hold the keys to the continued success of Clark Material Handling. Performance measures monitored by the area manager are as follows:

- *Daily production targets.* The monthly production objective is divided into daily production standards for each area of the operation and is monitored and reported daily.

- *Hours worked per unit.* The number of hours worked by production employees is divided by the number of units shipped during the same period; figures are monitored and reported weekly.

- *Overtime hours per unit.* The number of overtime hours worked by production employees is divided by the number of units shipped during the same period; figures are monitored and reported weekly.

- *First-pass ratio percentages for block test.* The number of trucks from the assembly line that pass the functional block test with zero defects on the first attempt is divided by the number of trucks built. The current target is 75 percent zero defect trucks. Figures are monitored and reported daily.

- *First-pass ratio percentages for final inspection.* The number of trucks that pass final inspection with zero defects on the first attempt is divided by the number of trucks shipped; the current target is 95 percent zero defect trucks. Figures are monitored and reported daily.

- *Defects per unit.* The number of defects per unit by product group for the functional testing and final inspection areas is measured daily and reported weekly.

Current Product Engineering

The current product engineering department is responsible for ensuring that, from a manufacturing standpoint, any design problems in assembly are documented and design changes are made to eliminate the problems. The department is also responsible for resolving field and customer service issues discovered by the marketing and field services organizations. Design engineers correct such problems through product redesign if appropriate. The final responsibility of current product engineering is to use applications engineering to support customer requests (referred to as CERs—custom engineering requests). The department consists of the current product engineering manager, seven design engineers, and two data coordinators. Three of the design engineers work in the plant, and four at business unit headquarters. Two of the plant engineers work primarily on solving daily plant problems, and the third functions as an applications engineer. The four engineers at headquarters handle field issues and have some CER responsibility.

Data coordinators audit all incoming sales orders to ensure that they contain the proper engineering information. If an error exists, they determine what must be done to correct the order. Using a computer program, data coordinators also verify the forklift load capacity rating stamped on each truck nameplate before shipment.

The current product engineering manager cites quality, cost, and field service as critical to maintaining competitive advantage. Performance measures used by current product engineering, categorized by responsibility, are listed here.

Application engineering: customer request response time.   Application engineers must respond to customer requests and complete related designs on time. Customer requests are entered into a database by the data coordinators and forwarded to the engineer. A required delivery date is also entered into the database. Engineers have standard lead times for each type of request, from which a completion date is determined, and they receive a sheet from data coordinators displaying the latest date a design can be completed without affecting the required delivery date (that is, the "freeze date," which is reported and measured weekly). The standard requires the freeze date to be met.

Manufacturing support: engineering change request (ECN) backlog. The number of engineering change requests is measured monthly. Requests are entered into a database by data coordinators and the current product engineering manager and staff receive a monthly status report on the backlog.

Field service engineering: customer responsiveness. This is a nonquantitative measure used to monitor dealer and end user feedback on whether the engineers are solving field problems in a timely and effective manner.

Data coordinators: sales order throughput. This figure is monitored daily. The standard requires that no sales order reside in the data coordinator area for more than 24 hours.

Quality Assurance

Personnel in the quality assurance area at the Lexington plant serve as technical quality advisors to both internal and external customers. Quality assurance technicians interact daily with work team members and suppliers to determine how to improve product and material quality. Because the facility does not conduct receiving inspections on incoming material, the quality assurance department works closely with work team members to identify material quality problems and with suppliers to immediately correct defects.

The department also conducts daily audits on assembled trucks. The audit consists of selecting a unit, checking it against specifications, driving the vehicle for two hours, and documenting the results. When defects are discovered, immediate feedback is given to the responsible team and in weekly cross-functional quality improvement team meetings, a plan to eliminate future occurrences is developed. All completed forklift trucks undergo a final inspection by quality assurance. However, plans are to shift the final inspection responsibility to the work teams.

Every truck is driven through the warehouse for a minimum of 10 minutes to ensure that the product meets customer expectations. Before final inspection, the units are measured for the number of defects using on-line inspections in the assembly, painting, and block testing areas. From the inspections, the number of defects per unit is recorded daily by product group and graphically displayed throughout the manufacturing area.

SPC is used on selected operations in the plant, and control charts are displayed in the work areas. Multilevel SPC courses are conducted for all Lexington plant employees. The coverage ranges from basic SPC concepts to more advanced topics, such as experimental design. The quality assurance manager believes that continual quality improvement can occur only by continually educating employees, suppliers, dealers, and customers on the principles of TQM.

The quality assurance manager believes that quality, product and process innovation, and cost are the essential elements of global competition in the material handling business. Performance measures monitored and distributed by quality assurance are listed here:

- *Truck shipment accuracy rate.* This measurement is defined as the percentage of trucks shipped correctly (based on customer order specifications) to the dealer. Weekly percentages for the current month and the past 12 months are displayed in a bar graph, along with a trend line; the standard is 100 percent accuracy.

- *Accessory shipment accuracy rate.* This measurement is defined as the percentage of correct accessory shipments (based on customer order specifications) from the plant directly to the customer. Weekly percentages for the current month and the past 12 months are displayed, along with a trend line; the standard is 100 percent accuracy.

- *Defects per unit in on-line inspections.* The number of defects per unit is measured daily, and weekly percentages for the current month and the past 12 months are displayed, along with a trend line, for the following categories: Electric product line block test on high- and low-volume assembly lines, electric product line block test on high-volume assembly lines, electric product line block test on low-volume assembly lines, on-line inspection of TM trucks (three-wheel counterbalance electric riders with lift capacities of 2,500 to 5,000 pounds), on-line inspection of ECS trucks (electric riders designed for very narrow aisle applications), paint inspection, and PowrWorker inspection.

- *Defects per unit for an outgoing audit.* The monthly number of defects per unit detected during the outgoing product audit categorized by product group is displayed in a bar graph for the past four months. The graph also includes a composite trend line for all trucks.

- *Defects per unit for a frame weld audit.* The weekly number of defects per unit detected during the frame weld audit is displayed in a line graph for the current month and the past 12 months, along with a trend line.

- *First-pass ratios (zero defect trucks).*
  First time through the block test for the high-volume line. This is defined as the ratio of the number of trucks passed through block testing on the first attempt divided by the number of trucks built during the same period. Information is displayed in a line graph for the current month and previous 12 months with separate lines for each product group (ECS and TM). A composite percentage and the current standard are also displayed; the current standard is 75 percent.

  First time through final inspection for all electric and IC trucks. This measure is defined as the ratio of the number of trucks passed through final inspection on the first attempt divided by the number of trucks passed into shipping during the same period. Information is displayed in a line graph for the current month and previous 12 months with separate lines for electric and IC trucks. A composite percentage and the current standard are also displayed; the current standard is 95 percent.

- *Final inspection return responsibility.* The number of trucks that failed inspection because of a specific responsibility area is divided by the number of trucks passed into shipping during the same period. Figures are shown in a bar graph of the percentage of forklift trucks that failed final inspection owing to quality problems related to one of the following areas: electric truck modification, electric truck assembly, internal combustion combined (modification and conversion line), and order entry or material planning. The graph includes weekly ratios for the current month and the past 12 months for each category; a composite line of all responsibility areas is also displayed.

- *Outgoing audit summary by area responsibility as a percentage of total defects.* This information is presented in a bar graph of monthly defects attributed to a responsibility area as a percentage of total monthly defects. It displays monthly percentages for the following areas: assembly, modification repair, vendor, and other, and shows results of the past four months.

Plant Accounting

The objectives of plant accounting at the Lexington plant are to provide timely financial information to the organization to support managerial decision making and to supply managers with an accurate interpretation of financial data. Plant accounting is not just a collector of historical financial information. The department is actively involved in helping functional managers understand what the numbers really mean. The plant accounting staff educates them on how to use the financial data to more effectively run their portion of the business.

The plant utilizes a traditional full-absorption accounting system, with special adaptations tailored to fit Clark's needs. However, the system does not capture detailed labor statistics. The accounting department plays only a minor role in plant cycle counting activities. In the past, the department has participated in periodic inventory audits to verify cycle counting accuracy. However, in 1990, the physical inventory requirements were waived by Price Waterhouse, owing to the accuracy of the perpetual inventory system, which is above 99 percent. The advent of weekly supplier deliveries has resulted in reduced levels of material tracking, inventory investment, surplus and obsolescence, required storage space, and material documentation requirements.

The plant accounting department is no longer involved in traditional financial accounting activities, such as bookkeeping and monthly closings. Those activities are now conducted at business unit headquarters. The department is heavily involved in management accounting studies requiring the extraction, analysis, and interpretation of meaningful financial data from financial accounting records. The plant controller is viewed as the purveyor of financial information necessary to support plant operations.

The plant controller views quality, cost, and lead time as essential to Clark's success. Following are performance measures collected and distributed by plant accounting:

- *Budget variances.* Each department manager receives a monthly budget comparing planned to actual spending.

- *Inventory forecast performance.* This figure monitors daily forecasted versus actual inventory expenditures for each commodity and is reported monthly.

- *Daily production commitment performance.* This daily report includes the following items: first-pass ratio percentages, defects per unit, monthly production schedule, production commitment for the next day, firm production commitment for today, actual production for the past day, accumulated production totals, accumulated variance, number of missing parts for each assembly line, and shipping schedules by product group.

PERFORMANCE MEASUREMENT SYSTEMS

The performance measurement systems used at the plant level are maintained by each department. The measures are collected functionally and consolidated in periodic reports published by the quality assurance manager, the plant controller, and the plant director.

Quality performance measures are displayed throughout the plant in tables, charts, and graphs. Weekly quality assurance update reports provide a detailed summary of plant quality performance. The plant controller and plant director provide monthly performance summaries to business unit and plant staffs. The reported information is used to monitor performance trends and to discover improvement opportunities.

The business unit's performance measurement system is based on both financial and nonfinancial information received from manufacturing operations, dealerships, and customers. Business unit management evaluates manufacturing operations on the same criteria, measures, and standards as those used by plant management. The major differences between these systems are the level of detail and the reporting frequencies for each measure. The plant performance measurement system provides greater detail on each of its measures than does the business unit system. Furthermore, the performance measurement reporting frequency is higher in the plant system than the business unit system. Some measures are used in both systems. Summaries of the performance measurement systems used at the plant and business unit levels are presented in Tables 11–1 and 11–2, respectively.

PERFORMANCE MEASUREMENT SYSTEM LINKAGES

The primary vehicles for performance measurement linkages between Clark Equipment and Clark Material Handling are periodic P/L reports supplied by the business unit to corporate staff, performance presentations by the president of Clark Material Handling to corporate executives, and formal meetings between the general planning board and functional planning board members. An important feature of Clark's performance measurement linkages is the development of formalized, cross-functional relationships at every organizational level. Multifunctional global planning boards integrate performance measurement information collected from various functions and levels into the strategic planning process.

Cross-functional work committees that implement planning committee proposals also provide performance reports to the boards. In the area of product development, the use of multifunctional project teams link performance across organizational levels and functions in the initial stages of the product development cycle. Quality improvement teams, facilitated by the director of quality, use cross-functional interactions at the plant level. In summary, the use of formal multifunctional interactions helps Clark Material Handling link performance system measurement across department areas and between organizational levels.

The president of Clark Material Handling holds quarterly state-of-the-business meetings with all employees to facilitate performance measurement system linkages. The president discusses performance issues directly with employees and receives immediate feedback on the presented performance results. The meetings provide a direct communication link on performance issues between the highest and lowest organizational levels. In the other direction, periodic performance meetings conducted by production workers with plant staff, business unit management, and the board of directors also provide performance measurement linkages across the entire corporation. A detailed description of the methods that Clark uses to ensure performance measurement linkages is provided here:

- *Daily morning meetings.* The plant meets with manufacturing and production control personnel to discuss daily production targets, and with personnel, engineering, and materials managers to discuss current issues.

TABLE 11–1
Plant Performance Measurement System at Clark Material Handling

Department	Performance Criterion	Performance Measures	Performance Standards
Plant staff	Manufacturing performance	Daily production commitment	Daily production target
		Weekly defects per unit	Zero defects
		Weekly first-pass ratios	Block test—75% Final inspection—95%
		Weekly truck shipment accuracy	100% accuracy
		Weekly accessory shipment accuracy	100% accuracy
		Monthly shipping schedule	Monthly shipping target
		Monthly hours worked per unit	Improving trend
		Monthly overtime hours per unit	Improving trend
		Monthly raw and WIP inventory turns	25 turns per year
		Monthly warranty cost	Financial plan
	Cost	Monthly budget variances	No variances
		Monthly inventory forecast variances	No variances
	Personnel performance	Monthly absenteeism	<1.0% annually
		Weekly lost time accidents	Improving trend
Current product engineering	Applications engineering performance	Weekly customer request response time	Design release freeze date
	Plant support	Monthly number of ECNs completed	Improving trend
		Monthly ECN backlog	Improving trend
	Field service engineering	Customer responsiveness	Positive feedback from dealers and users
	Data coordinator effectiveness	Daily sales order throughput	No orders in area more than 24 hours

TABLE 11–2

Performance Measurement System for Clark Material Handling's Business Unit

Department	Performance Criterion	Performance Measures	Performance Standards
Business unit staff	Profitability	Monthly P/Ls	Financial plan
	Cost	Monthly budget variances	No variances
	Manufacturing performance	Monthly warranty cost	Financial plan
		Monthly order lead time	Improving trend
		Monthly on-time delivery percentage	Improving trend
		Monthly number of trucks produced per employee	Improving trend
	Supplier performance	Number of certified suppliers	All suppliers certified
	Product development	Project cost (weekly)	Projected cost target
		Project schedule (weekly)	Project timetables
		Product cost (weekly)	Projected cost targets
		Monthly number of project problems corrected	All identified problems corrected
		Forklift operation cost per hour	Improving trend
Engineering and manufacturing staffs	Quality and reliability	Mean time between failures	Design targets
Engineering staff	Product development	Weekly CAD system response time	Acceptable response time
		Weekly CAD system utilization	High utilization
		Weekly ECN throughput	Improving trend
		Monthly lost test time hours	Improving trend
		Monthly test driver utilization	Improving trend
Operations staff	Cost	Monthly commodity cost reductions	Cost reduction targets
		Monthly material price variances	Material price variance targets

- *Daily production commitment performance.* Information is provided in a daily report that includes the following items: first-pass ratio percentages, defects per unit, monthly production schedule, production commitment for the next day, firm production commitment for today, actual production for the past day, accumulated production totals, accumulated variance, number of missing parts for each assembly line, and shipping schedules by product group. It is discussed daily in morning meeting with the plant director and distributed daily to plant staff and work teams.

- *Weekly sales order status report.* Marketing gives this report to the manufacturing staff. The report makes incoming orders requiring design work more visible and provides the plant with an order delivery date. It is also used by current product engineering to plan labor requirements. The report is distributed to product engineering, material control, inventory control, and order entry personnel in the plant.

- *Weekly quality assurance update report.* This report contains the truck shipment accuracy rate, truck accessory shipment rate, defects per unit, first-pass ratios, final inspection return responsibilities, and area responsibilities as a percentage of total defects. Information is displayed in the form of bar and line graphs with 12-month trend lines and performance standards. The weekly charts are also displayed in the production area, and the report is distributed to the plant management and key support personnel.

- *Weekly quality improvement team meetings.* Attendees develop plantwide quality improvement projects. The meetings are facilitated by the director of quality and reliability and the teams are cross-functional.

- *Monthly plant operations report.* The plant director publishes a monthly plant performance report summarizing all manufacturing measures, which is distributed to all plant department managers, the vice president of operations and his staff, and the business unit president.

- *Monthly plant staff meeting.* The meeting is attended by plant management staff, who discuss monthly plant performance, assess progress against established goals, and develop action plans for plant improvements.

- *Monthly ECN activity report.* The report displays the following ECN activity information: number of ECN requests received, number of ECN requests completed, ECN backlog, and types of ECNs received. It is distributed to current product engineering staff and the vice president of operations and his staff, and shows operations staffs ECN throughput and volume activity.

- *Monthly planning board meetings.* Global multifunctional planning boards, composed of North American and European vice presidents and directors, meet to formulate strategies in the following areas: manufacturing, quality, administration, product development, and distribution. Planning boards report to the general planning board, which meets annually to establish corporate policy.

- *Quarterly state-of-the-business meetings.* Clark's president meets with all employees to present planned versus actual quarterly financial performance in the areas of net sales, inventory, return on assets, and cash flow. He also discusses nonfinancial issues such as quality.

The methods that Clark Material Handling employs to link performance measurement systems will help it achieve its objective of supplying unparalleled customer satisfaction in all markets served.

LESSONS LEARNED

This case illustrates how performance measurement of systems and functions can be linked to support strategic objectives.

Customer and Resource Linkage

A key interaction exists between the manufacturing planning and marketing organizations that facilitates the customer-resource link. Manufacturing planning works directly with marketing in developing new products and improving product manufacturability. As part of the product development process, engineers in the manufacturing planning function work as a team with marketing to determine customer requirements. The team conducts customer surveys and brings customers on-site to discuss current products offered by Clark and its competition. New product specifications are developed from customer inputs. The teams also conduct value analyses on competing products via reverse engineering to examine cost and value relationships for each system category comprising the product.

The interaction between current product engineering and the plant functions also faciliates the linkage between customers and resources. Current product engineering is responsible for ensuring that, from a manufacturing standpoint, design problems identified in assembly are eliminated. The department is also responsible for resolving field and customer service issues discovered by the marketing and field service organizations. In addition, current product engineering supports applications engineering to fulfill engineering change requests (ECRs) that often accompany incoming sales orders. The department works directly with various plant functions to help direct organizational resources toward improved customer satisfaction.

Finance and Resource Linkage

The Clark Material Handling business unit uses a traditional full-absorption accounting system that tracks many of the traditional measures. However, the firm has incorporated several metrics that allow for the bottom-line assessment of resources deployed to a particular aspect of the business. For example, in the area of new product development, projected versus actual product cost based on preprototyping and prototyping activities guides the actions of product development teams. These teams focus resources to eliminate problems revealed by the cost measures. For existing products, the cost per hour to operate trucks is collected from dealers and end users. Also measured is warranty cost per model. These metrics are used to focus corrective action teams on problems that inhibit profitability and customer satisfaction. Other metrics linking resources and finance are commodity cost improvement targets and material price variance targets. This case shows how firms can implement customer-resource and resource-finance linkages to achieve strategic objectives.

Chapter Twelve

The Trane Corporation Self-Contained Systems Business Unit

This chapter again illustrates how linkages between the three performance measurement systems and primary functions can be accomplished: finance and customers, customer and resource, and finance and resource. The firm has the strategic objectives of cost and quality, which are monitored by the performance measurement system.

COMPANY BACKGROUND

The Trane Corporation is a worldwide manufacturer of air-conditioning products with headquarters in Lacrosse, Wisconsin. The corporation is the largest commercial air-conditioning manufacturer in the United States and is recognized as the industry leader. The Trane Corporation is divided into 10 autonomous strategic business units (SBUs). The Self-Contained Systems SBU is part of the Commercial Systems Group and began operations in April 1988. Sales in 1989 totaled $28.5 million. The firm's customer base is 90 percent make-to-order and 10 percent engineer-to-order. Although Self-Contained Systems's products are produced in low volumes (five units per day) and can be ordered in 40,000 different configurations (not including sales order specials), the manufacturing process is repetitive. The SBU headquarters and manufacturing facility are both located in Macon, Georgia, and are housed in the same building. Total SBU employment is 180, which includes 126 production and 54 office workers. All employees are salaried. Self-Contained Systems utilizes planning bills of materials composed of five levels and has 1,200 active part numbers in the inventory system. The SBU employs elements of MRP, JIT, and TOC to plan, monitor, and control production processes as well as the overall business. Interviews were conducted with the following individuals:

FIGURE 12-1
Organizational Structure of Self-Contained Systems SBU

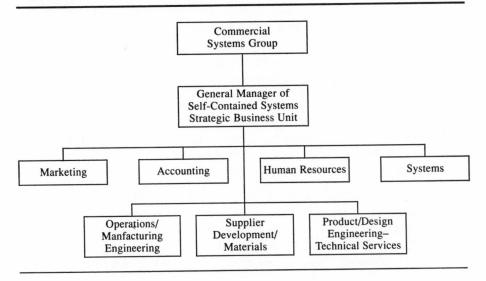

- Vice president and general manager, self-contained systems.
- Marketing manager.
- Operations manager.
- Cell manager.
- Supplier development/materials manager.
- Product/design engineering manager.
- Accounting manager.
- Human resources manager.

SBU ORGANIZATION

The SBU is functionally structured and includes the accounting, human resources, systems, marketing, supplier development/materials, operations/manufacturing engineering, and product/design engineering-technical field service organizations. Sales is located in a separate organization and sells all products produced by Trane. The functional managers report directly to the general manager. The SBU organizational structure is presented in Figure 12-1.

STRATEGIC OBJECTIVES

The Trane Company has a corporate objective of developing world-class manufacturing capabilities within all SBUs and uses a common set of performance measures across business units. Self-Contained Systems created a document called the "Macon Team Charter," which outlines the SBU mission, strategy, and tactics for maintaining world-class manufacturing performance. These elements of the charter are presented here:

1. *Mission:* Maximize the on-going value of shareholder equity by passionately and efficiently satisfying customer needs based on the following success criteria:

   • Make money now and in the future.

   • Serve "all" customers with a passion, both internal and external.

   • Utilize throughput (T), net assets (NA), and operating expense (OE) measures to bridge the gap between effective operational and profitability and return on investment measures.

2. *Strategy:* Global market leadership with a sustainable competitive advantage through

   • High quality via total quality control (TQC).

   • Low total cost (that is, total business cost).

   • Quick/flexible response via rapid execution in all functional areas (that is, time-based competition).

3. *Tactics:* Develop a highly variable cost structure and low breakeven point for the business by focusing on:

   • *World-class manufacturing processes:* modular bills of materials drum-buffer-rope scheduling; visible buffer management by self-directed work teams; cross-trained work teams; quality at the source; mixed model production for very short ship cycles.

   • *Outsource/single source partnerships:* will develop only those processes that add significant value and/or competitive advantage; when these criteria are not satisfied, will outsource to single source vendors and leverage these partnerships for quantum reductions in lead time, cost/quality improvement, inventory reductions, and stable schedules.

   • *Reduce lead time:* material lead time has the biggest impact on total business cost and the ability for quick response; also presents an opportunity to leverage short manufacturing cycles for competitive advantage; will focus resources on developing vendor plans to significantly reduce lead times by modifying manufacturing processes, reducing parts count, improving forecasting and scheduling techniques, and evaluating specification changes.

- *Lead without supervisors/unions:* develop competent self-directed work teams; develop participative management environment where quality of work life and organizational values/goals are shared.
- Develop human resources: develop skills to challenge old habits; build sound team work; implement effective problem solving; and cross train competent generalists who clearly understand organizational goals.

In developing operational performance measures based on the concepts of throughput (T), net assets (NA), and operating expenses (OE), the following definitions and relationships are used for these terms by Self-Contained Systems:

- *Throughput (T):* The rate at which the business generates money through sales. Throughput is measured as net revenue less commission and material cost. Therefore, throughput is maximized by optimizing both market price and share and by minimizing material cost without offsetting increases in NA or OE.
- *Net assets (NA):* All the money the business invests to purchase and produce things the system intends to sell. Net assets are measured as plant/equipment plus inventory plus receivables minus payables.
- *Operating expenses (OE):* All the money the business spends in turning net assets into throughput. Operating expense is measured as selling, general, and administrative expenses (SG&A) plus factory spending plus interest charges.

These definitions are modifications of the original T, I (inventory), and OE measures developed by Dr. Eli Goldratt.[1]

SBU FUNCTIONS

General Management

The general manager believes that speed is at the core of whether Self-Contained Systems is going to be successful strategically. A critical element of organizational speed is people empowerment: individuals developing ownership through delegating responsibility and accountability to the source, creating a "thinking work force" willing to challenge existing assumptions, and energizing autonomies, which all results in massive involvement versus mere participation. The empowerment of people allows individuals to act on their own and permits the organization to respond in a faster and more flexible manner. However, a prerequisite to people empowerment is education. Thus, the SBU management team, which consists of the general manager and the functional department managers, developed educational materials

TABLE 12-1
Macon Way Education Modules for Self-Contained Systems SBU

Employee Stock Option Plan—details	Stock Option Plan process
T-OE-NA	MRP/JIT/TQC—WCM
TOC—managing priorities	Financial statements
Planning BOM strategies	Quality Improvement
MPS policy	Process
Teamwork	Rings of defense
Trane overview	Basic refrigeration
Participative management/people empowerment	Shop math/reading prints
Supplier development philosophy	Basic Self-Contained
Visual floor management	Systems product training
Interview skills	Increased Customer Service
Counseling/terminations	for field offices
Interview tell sessions	Acoustics for field offices
Employee orientation tell sessions	Modular bill concept
Material point certification/inventory quality	
Labor economics	
Self-Contained Systems markets/customers/strategy	
Product/BOM change process	
Operations report/MBO process	
T-OE-NA ECN justification process	

called the "Macon Way Modules," designed to educate all employees on various aspects of the business. A listing of the modules is presented in Table 12-1. The management team is also responsible for conducting the educational sessions. All education modules were incorporated into an employee education/orientation package known as the "Why Book," which also contains the Macon Team Charter materials.

The general manager views the ability of the organization to avoid the local optimization of functional areas as critical to the success of the SBU. The general manager is a certified Jonah (extensive two-week education program on the TOC philosophy developed by Dr. Goldratt) and believes that each functional discipline must support the global objectives of the business. Thus, the focus is on global optimization of the entire business unit versus local optimization of departments.

To achieve global optimization of the business unit, the general manager states that functional strategies must be linked to overall business unit strategy, along with interrelationships existing between the functions. Additionally, each functional area must develop success criteria and performance measures based on its supporting strategy. Finally, education is again required to help the organization "internalize" strategic objectives and understand how the business will be conducted.

FIGURE 12–2
Global Optimization Concept Scheme for Self-Contained Systems SBU

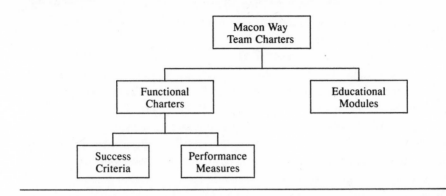

To accomplish this, departmental managers developed "functional charters" that outlined functional strategies for supporting overall business objectives, success criteria their to those objectives, and performance measures used to monitor success criteria. Each charter was individually presented to the management team for review and suggested improvements. This ensured integration across all functional areas. A diagram illustrating the global optimization concept used by Self-Contained Systems is presented in Figure 12–2.

The general manager identified quality as the most important strategic area for the SBU. Cost and delivery were cited as the next most critical areas, followed by product and process flexibility. He believes that an effective performance measurement system should assist in simplifying the operation so that it can be "managed by sight." A key part of managing by sight is the use of very simple and easy-to-read performance measures that are visually displayed for viewing by the entire organization. The general manager believes that if the right criteria are measured, the SBU should be able to quickly prioritize those areas requiring additional efforts. He also states that employees must be empowered to measure themselves and must then develop the means to accomplish their objectives without unnecessary management intervention.

The tracking of daily performance trends is believed to be fundamental to the effective use of a performance measurement system. The general manager equates waiting every 30 days to assess performance to driving a car by looking into the rear-view mirror. However, the general manager also notes that analyzing performance data over substantial periods of time (weekly, monthly, quarterly) is necessary to discover the root cause of a problem and develop the appropriate corrective actions for its elimination.

Marketing

Two primary areas comprise the marketing organization. One area focuses on booking the order, while the other area is concerned with internal order processing. The marketing engineers are responsible for doing what is necessary to book the order. Their first objective is to help the sales engineers (600 salespeople in 125 cities) sell the product. The Trane Corporation has one of the most technically trained sales forces in the industry. Every salesperson is a degreed engineer. Sales support by marketing engineers includes providing selling tools on products, technical support, assistance in customer visits to the Macon facility, and making direct customer contacts. External customers include owners, contractors, and engineers, although most of the time equipment is sold to a contractor. In many cases, contractors need assistance in developing specifications; thus, marketing engineers can also play a role in the specification process.

Once a specification is written, it is submitted to the various vendors, and they begin to develop bids. The marketing function is also involved in the bidding process through the establishment of prices via control price sheets and by authorizing a price range for a given configuration within which the sales force must stay. Once the price is agreed upon, the order is generated by sales and received in marketing via mail, fax, or telephone. Upon receipt of the order, marketing engineers review it and run a performance selection model, which compares what the specified equipment will do compared with the order requirements. After the marketing engineers have reviewed the order and are satisfied that it is correct, the order is then given to marketing personnel responsible for order entry. A BOM is configured for the order by product engineering and is added to the MRP system.

Self-Contained Systems currently uses two separate order entry systems. The advanced order entry system (AOS) is a Trane Corporation system that is linked to all the business units as well as the field offices (1,125 field offices in total). However, the business unit wanted a system that was more specialized for their needs; they installed an MRP system developed by CINCOM. Until an interface is developed between the two systems, orders continue to be entered on both systems.

After the order is entered, it is added to the master production schedule (MPS) by marketing, and a scheduled ship day is matched to the customer request date. Generally, marketing establishes a ship date sooner than the customer has requested. This "time buffer" is generally about one week. Because of the strong customer orientation instilled in the SBU, the organization is willing to hold a unit at their expense if it is completed before the customer wants it. In reality, most customers are not disappointed with an early completion and will usually take the unit immediately. Upon completion of the order, marketing also works with the delivery carriers and the customer to determine the best means of transporting the unit to the job site. Thus, marketing is responsible for coordinating the traffic function.

Upon delivery of the unit, the customer service area in the marketing department handles any questions pertaining to the order. The customer service area is also involved in processing customer change orders and informing the customer about shipment delays or other problems. This is done in an effort to minimize the impact of problems on the customer. The order processing procedure used by Self-Contained Systems is illustrated in Figure 12–3.

The marketing manager views the function as being the interface between the SBU and the customer. He also believes that customer involvement by the marketing function is essential. An important aspect of serving external customers in the marketing department is ensuring that the organization is capable of accommodating customer specifications. Before an order is accepted by marketing, marketing engineers coordinate with each functional area to make sure all specifications or requests are achievable. This is extremely important regarding sales order specials, which are orders for configurations or specifications that are not offered, and special requests, such as a unique type of paint. In these cases, the order is reviewed by an order review board, which consists of managers from the affected areas (usually product engineering, operations, accounting, and supplier development/materials), and a decision is made about whether the order request can be met. Thus, the capability of the organization to satisfy customer needs is assessed and planned as a team when special orders are received by marketing.

The marketing manager cites cost competitiveness as the key strategic area for Self-Contained Systems. He believes that the SBU does not have to be the lowest cost producer in the marketplace, but it must be cost competitive. Quality is considered the next most important area. The marketing manager views quality in the general sense and includes meeting customer requirements relative to delivery, product reliability, field support, and overall expectations. Finally, product and process flexibility is considered critical to the success of the business because of its impact on the organization's ability to effectively serve the customer.

The marketing manager believes in using as few performance measures as possible, with the key being establishing measures that are meaningful. Departmental performance measures are collected by the individuals responsible for the actions related to the measurement, and they display those measures prominently around their work area. Key performance measures that are tracked daily in marketing are customer hours, daily order performance (order pace), daily order price, MPS performance, and the closure rate on large projects (projects worth $100,000 or more). Customer hours is defined as the number of contact hours spent with customers in the field. The objective for marketing engineers is to visit at least four customer

FIGURE 12–3
Order Processing Procedure for Self-Contained Systems SBU

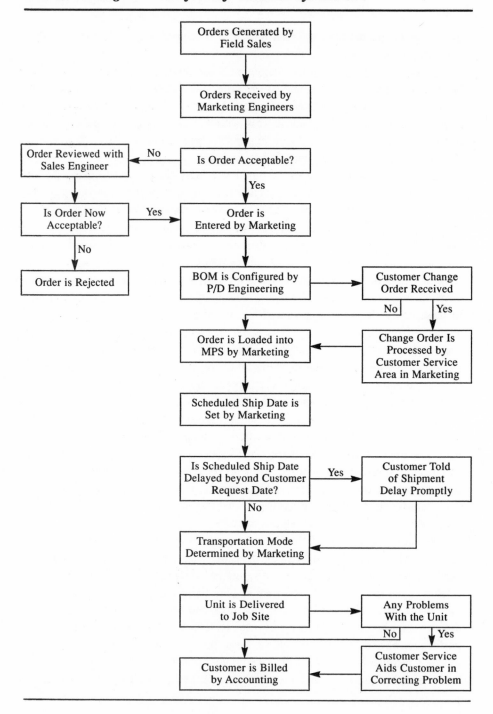

locations per month. The order pace is simply the number of daily incoming orders received by the department.

The order price is the actual unit price negotiated by field sales with the customer for a given configuration. This information is recorded daily on a flip chart called the "order board" which is displayed in the marketing department. The order board graphically shows the order pace trend relative to the forecast and the order price as it relates to the financial plan. Anyone in the SBU can readily see and assess the order performance for the day, week, or entire month. The accounting department developed a financial model that estimates product costs for any of the 40,000 configurations offered. Thus, the order price is compared with the estimated cost used in financial planning for the specified configuration.

MPS performance relates to the SBU's ability to meet schedule commitments within an accepted tolerance band (within $\pm$ 7 percent of MPS weekly; within $\pm$ 5 percent monthly). Since marketing is responsible for master scheduling, MPS performance is monitored, graphed, and displayed daily by marketing as well as other functional areas. MPS changes are also monitored in a similar way. Self-Contained Systems has established time fences within the MPS that allow for only a certain type and percentage of changes to occur. The MPS is planned in weekly buckets, with the horizon divided into the following three zones:

Zone	Time Frame	MPS Status
A	0–4 weeks	Frozen
B	5–6 weeks	Firm
C	> 6 weeks	Slush (7–10 weeks)
		Water (> 10 weeks)

The following types and percentage of MPS changes allowed within the zones, along with the required approvals, are presented below:

Zone	Type Changes	Percentage	Required Approvals
A	Emergency	<2%	Operations manager
			Engineering manager
			Supplier development manager
			General manager
B	Field or customer orders	<5%	Operations manager
			Engineering manager
			Supplier development manager
C	Any	Slush—20%	Master scheduler
		Water—100%	Engineering manager (if a sales order special)

Master schedule changes are monitored daily and formally discussed in weekly master scheduling meetings. The meetings are attended by the master scheduler, operations manager, supplier development/materials manager, an engineering representative, a materials coordinator, an order services administrator, and the systems manager.

The final critical performance measure tracked in the marketing area is the closure rate on major projects valued at $100,000 or more. In many cases, field sales will solicit the assistance of the SBU to help win the order. Information, such as total jobs won and projects dropped or lost due to either price, ship cycle, or product features, is graphically displayed on the order board and updated daily.

Operations

The manufacturing area consists of 10 "feeder cells" managed by self-directed work teams that supply the main assembly line with subassemblies. One- to two-day material buffers containing completed subassemblies have been created for several "nonconstraint" cells to protect the main assembly line from disruptions due to a problem encountered in a given work area (i.e., machine breakdowns, quality problems, material outages, labor shortages). This tactic allows the manufacturing operation to process units in a flowlike manner. The units are manually pushed down the assembly line. Point-of-use storage is employed for all raw materials, eliminating the need for material stores or the tracking of material-move transactions. The production area layout is given in Figure 12-4.

A production control build board containing build sheets for in-process units is located at the front of the line. The build sheets are sequenced by the cell manager in the order in which coils are to be fabricated. The coil processing work center is the gating operation of the production process that triggers the release of materials by the other cells upon the start of coil fabrication. After a coil is completed, a green dot is placed on the build sheet, which signals the base work center to place the base on the assembly line. The placement of the base on the line represents the "launching" of the order. The build sheet follows the unit down the line and is the only document work teams have for building the order. A sample build sheet is given in Table 12-2.

Two days are required for the completion of a coil, while three days are required to manufacture the entire unit after the base is placed on the assembly line. A two-day buffer of coils is maintained by the coil fabrication and coil finishing work teams, thus allowing for a total manufacturing lead time (or floor cycle) of three days. Upon the completion of the coil and launching the base on the assembly line, the unit is assembled as it "flows" down the line. After one work team completes its tasks, the unit is passed on to the next work team. Feeder cell material flows are controlled via some method of kanban (racks, bins, or cards), which signals the start of either

FIGURE 12–4
Production Area Layout for the Self-Contained Systems SBU

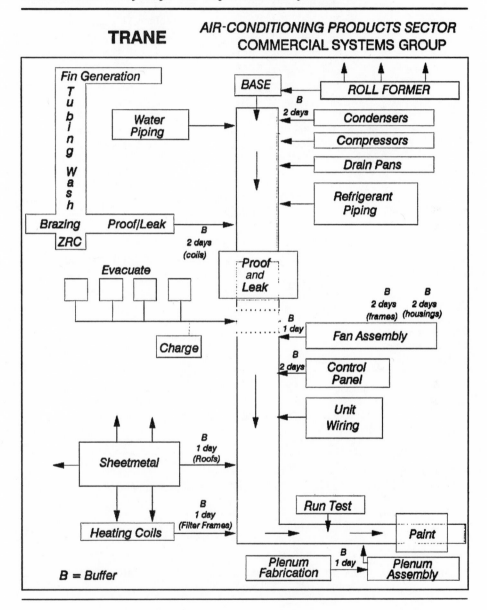

TRANE   *AIR-CONDITIONING PRODUCTS SECTOR*
                COMMERCIAL SYSTEMS GROUP

TABLE 12-2
SBU Sample Build Sheet

Sales Order Number _____   MO Number _____
   Job Name _____   Build Comp. Date _____
   Unit Tagging _____ Scheduled Build Date _____ Build Order _____

Tonnage			Volume 208 ___
	20 ___	42 ___	230 ___
	22 ___	46 ___	460 ___
	25 ___	52 ___	575 ___
	29 ___	58 ___	Other ___
	32 ___	65 ___	
	35 ___	72 ___	
	38 ___	80 ___	

Economizer Coils	4 row cleanable	___	Values	Energy saving	___
	2 row cleanable	___		Standard	___
	4 row noncleanable	___		Head press ctrl.	___
	None	___		Spring loaded	___
				No spring load	___
				None	___

Water Flow Switch _____

Fan Motor	___ hp	Electric heat	___	
Fan Type	___ HED	Hot water coil	1 coil ___	
	___ ODP		2 coil ___	
	___ TEFC	Steam coil	1 coil ___	
Fan rpm	___		2 coil ___	
Inlet guide vanes	___	Airside econo	___	
Variable volume	___	SEI's applicable	_____	
Constant volume	___	(special)		
Inverter ready	___			

Control Options	Generic interface	___	Unit disconnect	___
	Tracer interface	___	Dirty filter switch	___
	Night heat/morning warmup	___	Mixed air temperature	___
	Time clock	___	Sensor	___
	AAM control module	___	Without system controls	___

Unit Ship with		Number of sets		
Throwaway filters	___	Remote space sensor	___	
Farr 30/30 filters	___	Extended rpm	___	
Cleanable filters	___	Spring isolators	___	X10350041-10
None	___		___	X10350041-09
			___	X10350041-08
			___	X10350041-07

Discharge plenum	Standard height	___	Extra height	___	Field cut holes	___
	Low height	___	None	___		

Agency UL ___   CSA ___   None ___

an internal operation within the cell or an operation in another work cell that will supply them with material. Work teams were allowed to develop their own kanban systems. The roll former and sheet metal cells are the only two workcenters in the plant that supply material to each of the other cell workcenters.

The production area uses elements of MRP, JIT, and TOC to manage the manufacturing process. MRP is viewed as a planning tool used to support the procurement and release of materials in a JIT manner. The MRP system is not used to create shop floor orders or to schedule the production floor. It is strictly used for its raw material planning capabilities.

Once an order moves from the planning to the execution phase, kanbans are used for shop floor control. Initially, the SBU managed the production floor via kanban exclusively. However, it was discovered that the kanban system worked well and required very little inventory on the floor until a problem occurred in a feeder cell. If a machine broke down or a quality problem occurred in a cell, material shortages would occur, resulting in the shutdown of the assembly line. The organization then decided to employ the concepts of TOC to protect the flow of the line against "statistical fluctuations" within the cells and the "dependency" relationship between the assembly line and the feeder cells. Material buffers composed of completed subassemblies were installed at critical control points in the process. The result was a smoother manufacturing flow on the assembly line.

After the buffers were in place and manufacturing flow improved, the concept of drum-buffer-rope (DBR), another element of TOC, was adopted to synchronize all production processes. The coil fabrication process is the plant's gating operation and is used to regulate material flow. The coil production rate is the "drum" that synchronizes the production processes. Coil fabrication lead time is two days per coil. The "buffer" is a two-day supply of coils, which protects the line from disruptions due to problems in the coil area. The gating operation is capable of producing between 7 to 10 coils per day, depending on the coil type. The "rope" is the release of materials based on the start of coil fabrication and the launching of orders at coil completion.

Daily schedules are stressed in the plant, and buffer management guidelines are established to assist the work teams in making overtime and other manpower decisions. The colors green, yellow, and red are used to communicate current buffer size and trigger various actions by work team members. For instance, the coil area is considered green when the buffer contains 15 to 20 coils. A green condition means that the work team is on schedule. If the buffer contains between 8 to 14 coils, a yellow condition exists. A yellow condition suggests that overtime and/or a manpower shift may be in order. Once the buffer drops below 8 coils, the work team has reached a red condition. Mandatory overtime is recommended until the work area is back to the green condition. Along with DBR, the kanban system is still used to regulate the flow of materials within and between feeder cells.

Work team members are referred to as production technicians, and they report directly to the operations manager. Production technicians are cross-trained on all production tasks within the work cell. Many are capable of working in any of the 10 work cells and on the assembly line. Each work team has a team coordinator and a material point person who have additional responsibilities besides production. The team coordinator monitors how well the work team is doing relative to the daily production schedule. Team coordinators meet daily with the operations manager to inform him of any schedule deviations. They also make manpower shifts between cells, determine overtime requirements, coordinate with support areas (maintenance, engineering, materials) for assistance, and generally help maintain the production flow. Team coordinators are selected by the operations and cell managers and the position is rotated within work teams.

Material point people handle the materials control responsibilities in the plant. They:

- Receive incoming materials.
- Stock inventory materials at their point of use.
- Initiate inventory transactions for the multiple-point milestone backflushing system used to relieve consumed materials from inventory (material usage is "backflushed" at milestone points in the manufacturing process as opposed to single-point backflushing at total unit completion).
- Complete paperwork on scrap materials.
- Ensure inventory accuracy for each work team.

The material point people are trained by the cell manager, who was initially in charge of managing the daily activities of the team coordinators. Currently, the cell manager is the manager and educator of the material point people (that is, the material point coordinator) but still supports the work teams when necessary.

The operations manager now works directly with each team coordinator regarding daily production issues. A critical responsibility of the material point people is to support the daily cycle-counting activities conducted by production technicians. An accurate count is essential in a backflush environment. To stress the importance of accurate inventory counts, the organization has instituted a program called adopt-a-part. If the production worker's count is 100 percent accurate, he receives a green dot. If he miscounts, he receives a red dot. The dots are visually displayed on the performance recognition board outside the cafeteria. If a work team has nine consecutive weeks of 100 percent accuracy, they are taken to lunch.

All production workers are salaried, and their time is recorded daily on a flip chart in the work team area. Time cards are collected bi-weekly. The SBU has budgeted two hours per day for each worker to participate in "nonproduction" activities. This nonproduction time is incorporated in the production standard (112 hours per air-conditioning unit, which includes 25 percent nonproductive time). The nonproduction activities include education sessions, problem solving, preventive maintenance, and participation in joint worker-manager committees. There is no quality function within Self-Contained Systems. Each production technician is responsible for quality at the source. Customer-supplier relationships have been stressed to both the internal and external work teams. Internal customers are defined as the preceding work centers, while internal suppliers are the proceeding work centers. External customers are defined as the receivers of the finished units (i.e., contractors, builders) with the work teams serving as the external suppliers to the customers. Because of the plant layout, production workers often serve as their own internal customers and suppliers. Thus, feedback on quality is very quick. The work team that is responsible for the error is required to correct the mistake, determine the root cause of the problem, and develop corrective actions to eliminate reoccurrence.

Production workers also have a strong link to external customers. The name of the building is put on each production build sheet as opposed to a sales order number. This helps the worker relate what they are producing to an actual high-rise structure under construction. Often, an artist's rendition of the building that the unit is being built for is posted on a wall outside of the cafeteria to give workers a direct link between the job and the customer. Production workers have actually followed the units to the job site, interacted with the customers, and seen the units installed. The workers conduct plant tours for customers who make site visits to the plant. Customers are impressed when production technicians ask them about previous jobs and the buildings in which the units were installed.

Production workers also do some of their own purchasing. In the sheet metal area, workers tell the supplier development/materials department when to buy more material. The workers are controlling two different gauges of material with one sheet size by monitoring the height of the stacks. The workers also have direct responsibility control over several spending accounts: small tools, gauges, scrap, and spoilage. Production workers have input on cell layouts, equipment purchases, hiring decisions, counseling sessions, and employee terminations. They are even allowed to attend trade shows. In summary, production workers are given the autonomy necessary to be fully involved in the decision-making processes of the organization.

Each work team conducts a daily production meeting (a "get-started" meeting) to set priorities for the day. The operations manager has a weekly meeting with all production technicians to determine what areas should be improved. The weekly meetings may include managers and support staff from other functional areas. Work teams also meet at least twice a week without management to discuss any internal problems within the cell. Production workers serve with managers and support staff on committees that range from safety to employee compensation. The financial performance of the SBU is shared with workers on a monthly basis through state-of-the-business meetings conducted by the general manager.

The operations manager cites quality, delivery, cost, and process and product innovation as the most important strategic areas for the business. The cell manager also views quality as the most important area, followed by lead time, cost, and process and product flexibility. The performance measurements used to manage the manufacturing operation are displayed graphically, either on individual performance boards stationed in each work cell or on the performance recognition board located outside of the cafeteria. The measures include:

- Monthly inventory turns on raw material and raw-in-process (RIP).
- Daily, weekly, and monthly MPS performance ($\pm$ 7 percent weekly and $\pm$ 5 percent monthly).
- Inventory accuracy (adopt-a-part program).
- Monthly hours paid per unit (plant efficiency measure; standard is 112 hours per unit).
- Weekly spoilage and scrap dollars by work team.
- Weekly plant spoilage and scrap dollars.
- Monthly small tool and gauge spending by work team.
- Daily number of units shipped.
- Daily number of units completed by each work team.
- Monthly machine downtime on critical equipment.
- Weekly absenteeism (goal is less than 2 percent).
- Weekly overtime.

The operations manager intends to develop a performance measure for housekeeping whereby nonmanufacturing personnel would grade the operation. He believes that good housekeeping sends a quality message to visiting customers and promotes safety. The operations and cell managers believe that performance measures must be simple to understand, visible, and maintained by the individuals responsible for the work. They have found that when work teams are made aware of their performance in a timely manner, the teams generally develop ways to improve without outside intervention. Also, the operations manager is able to quickly assess the status of production processes by "wandering around" the production floor (i.e., management by sight).

Supplier Development/Materials

The supplier development/materials function is involved in planning and procuring materials to support production requirements. Materials are scheduled in weekly buckets by the CINCOM MRP system. It is a net-change regenerative system that is run nightly. Normally, there are approximately 1,000 purchased parts numbers and between 400 to 500 sales orders in the MRP system. The net-change routine takes approximately three hours of CPU time. Material planners and buyers use the MRP output to purchase materials necessary to support the MPS. Materials for an order are expected to be available when the coil fabrication for the unit begins. Planning BOMs are used to drive material requirements. Configured sales orders cannot be used effectively to drive all the requirements of the operation because of material purchases driven by vendor kanbans and forecasted requirements.

A major role of the supplier development/materials department is to cultivate cooperative, long-term relationships with sole-source vendors (98 percent of vendors are sole-sourced). The department actively works with vendors to reduce procurement lead times. One method for accomplishing material lead time reductions used by supplier development is the establishment of equivalent lead times. For example, the SBU has a vendor that supplies a component purchased in 77 different variations. However, only four raw material variations are needed to support the various component options. The procurement lead time for the component was 10 weeks, although it only took 4 weeks for actual fabrication; the other 6 weeks constituted the vendor's procurement lead time. The management team and the vendor devised a plan whereby supplier development would make a commitment to the quantity of the vendor's raw material required in weeks 5 through 10 of the planning horizon and convert it into a firm order for components in week 4. Thus, supplier development ended up with an "equivalent lead time" of four weeks.

Kanban is used with several local vendors. Kanban racks are stationed on the production floor that signal material replenishment to the vendor when empty. JIT vendors have access to the SBU's MPS and are given reports that show future requirements. The vendor then executes to those requirements by delivering the materials in kanban quantities. Information from the packing slips is entered directly into the MRP system without the use of purchase orders. If for some reason a kanban rack of material is used before the next scheduled JIT delivery, production technicians will often call the vendor directly for replenishment. The supplier development/ materials function is constantly searching for ways to eliminate non-value-added procurement activities from the organization.

Supplier development is also involved in several important functional interactions that occur both formally and informally. Planners and buyers spend approximately 50 percent of their time on the production floor learning about the materials used in the process. The supplier development manager believes that it is important for planners and buyers to know what the materials look like, where they are used, and why. This interaction provides material personnel with product knowledge and helps them to better serve internal customer needs. An MPS meeting is held every Friday morning. It is attended by the master scheduler, operations manager, supplier development/materials manager, a product engineering representative, a material coordinator, an order services administrator, the systems manager, and, occasionally, the general manager. The meeting members examine the following areas:

- Weekly performance against the MPS.
- Anticipated future MPS performances.
- The impact of material and machine breakdown problems on the MPS.
- Sales order specials requirements.
- Necessary actions to support the MPS.

Weekly change control meetings are also held on Fridays to review proposed engineering change notices (ECNs) with the change control team. The team consists of the product engineering manager, operations manager, supplier development/ materials manager, and others, as required. The team decides whether proposed ECNs will be approved.

The supplier development/materials manager believes that quality is the key criteria for business unit success. She also views cost, delivery, and lead time as elements of total business costs and ranks them second in strategic importance. Next comes process and product innovation, followed by process and product flexibility. Performance measures used by the supplier development/materials function are monitored daily and visually displayed graphically in the department by the individuals that are being measured. A key measure is material outage days. Material outage days are classified into five categories:

1. *Vendor late delivery:* outage occurring as a result of a late delivery by the vendor. This category is further divided into two additional classifications: with follow-up and without follow-up.
2. *MPS changes:* outage occurring as a result of changes in the master schedule.
3. *Vendor quality:* outage occurring as a result of poor vendor quality.
4. *BOM and inventory accuracy:* outage occurring as a result of BOM and/or inventory accuracy errors.
5. *Material planning:* outage occurring as a result of a lack of execution by supplier development/materials personnel.

The material outage classification scheme helps to focus the efforts of the department on root causes. The daily number of MPS messages is collected and tracked by each planner and buyer. The messages are ranked by severity and then graphed and examined for unfavorable trends. The goal for each planner or buyer is to have no MRP messages. The number of days a received defective material is in the return or review area is measured daily by the department. Supplier development/materials is responsible for returning any defective or unnecessary material received by the SBU. Measures used by supplier development/materials that are external customer oriented and that are tracked daily are the number of service orders received, the number of service parts ordered, and service parts order processing time. The supplier development manager believes that the department must be driven by the needs of both internal and external customers.

Product/Design Engineering

Product/design (P/D) engineering is responsible for product design, engineering support work (which includes support work for manufacturing), and field technical service (a consulting service to the field). The organization is composed of engineers, design technicians, and draftsmen. Design technicians are a cross between draftsmen and engineers. These individuals are a major benefit to the department because of their ability to handle responsibility levels that are beyond drafting and because they possess great flexibility. P/D engineering also supports plant quality needs, particularly as related to design.

The products of Self-Contained Systems have been redesigned, and approximately 60 percent of the part requirements have been eliminated from the product family. An example of such product innovation is the reduction in the number of cabinet sizes needed to support the 40,000 product configurations offered by the SBU. Initially, 14 cabinet sizes were required. Today, the 40,000 product configurations require only two cabinet sizes.

An innovation that greatly helped the manufacturing organization was the creation of "visual aid" drawings. Prior to this development, the organization maintained manufacturing drawings used by production, engineering drawings used by P/D personnel, and service drawings used by service parts personnel. At that point, approximately170 drawings were utilized by the three areas. P/D engineering was able to consolidate the necessary information from the three sources into 40 visual aid drawings, which are now used by all three groups. The visual aids are also located on the production floor and are under engineering change control. When product design changes occur, P/D engineers literally walk onto the floor, explain the nature of the change to the affected work teams, and replace the old drawing.

P/D engineering is also responsible for the numeric control (NC) tapes used in manufacturing. The department has CAD/CAM capabilities that allow for the direct downloading of NC programs from engineering to production equipment. The engineering function is also involved in lead time reduction efforts through parts standardization. P/D engineering conscientiously tries to standardize parts wherever possible and will make design changes on existing products to accomplish lead time reductions through part standardization.

The P/D engineering manager has instilled a strong internal and external customer orientation within the department. He expects interaction by engineering personnel with internal customers, especially work team members. The function is actively involved in helping the SBU achieve its MPS objectives by supporting the production floor. Frequent contacts between engineering and marketing occur in design improvements, new options, sales order specials, and on whatever is needed to meet marketplace requirements. The P/D engineering manager also sends engineers to talk to external customers to gain a better understanding of their requirements. The P/D engineering manager cites quality as the top strategic area for the SBU. Cost is next in importance, if viewed as the total cost of doing business. Delivery is considered the third most important strategic criteria, followed by lead time. Performance measurement information collected within the engineering department is visible and accessible to everyone in the business unit. Flip charts are located throughout the P/D engineering area. The measures are monitored on a daily basis and include the following:

- *Sales order specials throughput:* rate at which sales order specials are processed by the organization.

- *Engineering change notices (ECNs):* (*a*) backlog—the number of ECNs yet to be completed and (*b*) throughput—rate at which ECNs are processed by the organization.

- *Warranty (service) claims:* rate at which service claims are processed by the organization.

- *Bill of material accuracy:* the percentage of error-free BOMs is determined by P/D engineering via daily audits; BOM accuracy is critical in a backflush environment because of its impact on inventory accuracy and, ultimately, on customer delivery.

- *Warranty (service) expense dollars:* acts as an indicator of product quality and customer satisfaction.

The P/D engineering manager uses performance measurement information for decisions pertaining to the allocation of departmental resources. He focuses on daily performance trends to anticipate functional as well as total business needs.

Accounting

The accounting function supports its internal customers in budget development, forecasting, and cost control. After a sales order is loaded into the MRP system and material requirements are generated, accounting personnel generate the material cost for the order. Once the unit is built and all materials used are completely backflushed, material costs are then run against the backflush requirements to determine the actual material cost for the order. The SBU utilizes a simplified cost accounting system that has eliminated detailed labor reporting requirements from the manufacturing operation. Currently, labor represents only 4 percent of total product cost. Material is 77 percent of the cost of producing a unit, while overhead depicts 19 percent of product cost. Since only one product is produced in the facility, overhead allocation methods are not necessary. The accounting department has a financial model that can estimate product costs for any of the 40,000 configurations offered. This model is used by the marketing department for the development of unit price ranges for sales engineers.

The accounting manager believes that cost, lead time, and process and product flexibility are essential to competitive success. Performance measures are visibly displayed in the work area in the form of charts and graphs. Daily performance is measured in the following areas:

- *Hours paid per unit:* defined as the number of paid production hours required to complete an air-conditioning unit. The current target is 155 hours per unit; the actual engineering standard is 112 hours per unit, which includes a 25 percent allowance for other employee activities (actual standard without the allowance is 84 hours per unit). In April 1988 (start-up) 1,089 hours per unit were required; 374 hours per unit was the average in 1988.

- *Productivity:* measured as the ratio of hours paid per unit to the total number of production employees; current goal is 1.24.

- *Voucher processing:* monitors the rate at which expense vouchers are processed by the organization.

- *Invoice discounts:* monitors the frequency at which the department takes advantage of invoice cash discounts offered by vendors.

- *Expense report processing:* monitors the weekly rate at which expense reports are closed.

- *Direct base billing outstanding:* measurement of the daily dollar amount of receivables outstanding.

On a monthly basis, the accounting department develops an operations report that includes all measurements used to assess total business performance for the month, last 30 days, and year to date. Figures for the previous year are also included. Trend lines and bar charts displaying quarterly values are incorporated into the report. The report is distributed to the management team and formally discussed in the monthly sales and operations planning meeting. The performance measurement data are used by the team to make decisions about the future direction of the business. The management team looks over a 12-month horizon and discusses issues pertaining to won and lost orders and to what is seen on the business horizon. The accounting manager sees the role of the accounting function as providing the other functional areas with such tools as simplified accounting and easy-to-understand reporting. He believes that these tools will enable SBU personnel to make decisions faster and more effectively, along with providing organizational flexibility.

Human Resources

The human resources manager sees his role as a developer of interpersonal skills. He wants to spread human resources management skills throughout Self-Contained Systems. This becomes critical in an organization that employs an "open environment" (production workers are involved in the hiring process, in counseling and termination of employees, and in educating and training of new employees, and they have full access to all financial statements) and utilizes all-salaried self-directed work teams to produce products. The human resources manager is a firm believer in the empowerment of people and states that it is extremely important in an organization as "flat" as Self-Contained Systems (two levels between the production technicians and the group vice president; one level between the workers and the general manager). Unlike many traditional organizations, the human resources manager is involved in the day-to-day operations of the business beyond the typical human resources management duties. His inputs are solicited in areas from product design to production scheduling.

The human resources manager believes that quality is the most important strategic business area for the SBU. Second is process and product flexibility, followed by cost. Performance measures tracked by his function and displayed on the performance recognition board near the cafeteria are:

- *Absenteeism:* weekly and monthly percentages (that is, the ratio of the number of employees absent to the total number of employees) are displayed graphically; the standard is less than 2 percent.

- *Safety measures:*
  a. Lost-time accidents—weekly lost-time accident rate is exhibited graphically.
  b. Industry safety ranking—current objective is to be number 1.

- *Performance appraisal timeliness:* human resources manager has created a board showing the on-time percentage for performance appraisals given by management team members. Managers are required to pay $20.00 to the human resources department for all late appraisals; the "pot" is split at the end of the year by those managers who achieve 100 percent performance. If there are no 100 percent achievers, the monies are carried forward to the next year.

The human resources manager is a strong advocate of the "management by walking around" (MBWA) philosophy proposed by Peters and Waterman in their book entitled *In Search of Excellence*. He states that initially the product/design engineering manager used an MBWA measure that was the number of trips into the plant by the P/D engineers. The measure was dropped after it was found that it was no longer needed. The human resources function will continue to assist in evolving SBU's high employee involvement environment in the direction of excellence.

PERFORMANCE MEASUREMENT SYSTEMS

The performance measurement systems used at Self-Contained Systems are visual, easy to understand, focused on daily trends, and are helping the organization in achieving world-class capabilities. The systems can be classified into two categories:

1. *Functional area performance measurement systems.* Those systems used to communicate departmental performance in key areas to other business areas, allocate resources to support functional objectives, and maintain internal customer-oriented relationships between functional areas.

2. *Total business performance measurement system.* This system focuses on key performance criteria, measures, and standards used to monitor the SBU's progress toward organizational excellence; measures are shared across functional boundaries and multiple functions are responsible for the achievement of established performance standards.

The measures classified as part of the total business performance measurement system are published monthly in the operations report and are discussed each month by the management team in the sales and operations planning meeting. An illustration of the functional and total business performance measurement systems used by Self-Contained Systems are presented in Tables 12–3 and 12–4, respectively.

PERFORMANCE MEASUREMENT SYSTEM LINKAGES

A key feature of how performance measurement system linkages are accomplished within the SBU is the visual display of measures within the work area by each

TABLE 12–3
Functional Area Performance Measurement System for Self-Contained Systems

Function	Performance Criteria	Performance Measure	Performance Standard
Operations	Cycle counting	Percentage of accuracy	100% accuracy
	Spoilage/scrap	Daily spoilage and scrap dollars by work team	Improving trend
	Small tools/gauges	Daily small tool and gauge account dollars by work team	Improving trend
	Housekeeping (future)	Housekeeping grading scale	Highest grade
Supplier development/ materials	Material outages	Total daily number and percent due to vendor late delivery, vendor quality, BOM/inventory accuracy, and material planning	No outages
	MRP exception messages	Daily ranking of number of MRP messages by planner	No messages
	Defective material	Number of days defective materials are held in return or review area	Improving trend
	Service orders	Daily number of service orders received	Improving trend (less service orders)
	Service order parts	Daily number of service order parts shipped	Improving trend
	Service order processing time	Number of days to process a service order	Improving trend
Marketing	Customer hours	Number of hours spent with customers by marketing engineers	4 customer locations per month spending the number of hours necessary
	Order pace	Daily number of incoming orders	Order forecast
	Price	Daily price of booked orders	Budgeted price
P/D engineering	Sales order specials	Number of days to process	Improving trend
	Warranty claims	Number of days to process	5 days

TABLE 12–3
Concluded

Function	Performance Criteria	Performance Measure	Performance Standard
Accounting	Expense vouchers	Number of days to process	Improving trend
	Invoice discounts	Frequency of using available cash discounts	100% usage
	Expense reports	Number of days to process	Improving trend
	Direct base billing outstanding	Daily dollar value of receivables	Improving trend
Human resources	Performance appraisal timeliness	Percentage of on-time performance of appraisals by management team	100% on time

functional area. The measures are simple and accessible to all employees. The display of performance measures allows for management by sight and helps other departments develop ways to support functional as well as total business unit objectives. The development of functional charters that support business unit strategy and tactics is also critical to achieving linkages between functional and business unit systems. Success criteria development is driven by the functional objectives supporting overall SBU performance.

The charter development process, which includes a critique of all charters by the management team, ensures linkages across functional performance measurement systems. The educational modules will improve overall organizational understanding of the business and will indirectly assist in establishing performance measurement system linkages. Formal interfunctional meetings play an important role in performance measurement system linkages. The weekly MPS meeting provides a mechanism for linkages between the functional systems used in marketing, operations, supplier development/materials, and engineering. Meeting attendees understand how measures, such as T, OE, and NA, used in functional areas relate to global measures. This understanding is essential for the avoidance of departmental suboptimization situations. Weekly engineering change control meetings to review proposed ECNs provide the same benefits to the engineering, supplier development/materials, and operations functions with regard to the product.

TABLE 12–4
Total Business Performance Measurement System for Self-Contained Systems

Performance Criteria	Performance Measures	Performance Standards
Manufacturing performance	Units per day	5.6 units per day
	Man hours paid per unit	155 hours per unit
	Man hours paid per unit per production worker (productivity ratio)	1.24
	Floor cycle	3 days
Inventory management	Turns	Finished: 20 per year
		RIP: 10 per year
		Total: 10 per year
	Inventory accuracy	98%
	Percentage of material outage days due to late delivery, vendor quality, or other reasons	No outages
	Percentage of permanent homes for point-of-use inventory on plant floor (i.e., permanent locations)	100%
	Machine downtime hours due to material outages	0 downtime hours
Shipping performance	Percentage of on-time delivery	98%
	Average days late	0 days
	Weekly promise cycle versus customer request date	Promise cycle = customer request date
	MPS changes	Weeks 1–2: <2%
		Weeks 2–6: <5%
	Ship cycle	7 weeks
MPS performance	Weekly MPS deviations	±7%
	Monthly MPS deviations	±5%
P/D engineering performance	Number of ECNs completed monthly	Improving trend (increase monthly number completed)
	Average ECN backlog	<25
	ECN throughput rate	30 days per ECN
	Percentage of new products/options introduced in last 2 years	5% of total sales

TABLE 12–4
Concluded

Performance Criteria	Performance Measures	Performance Standards
Marketing performance	Closure rate on major jobs (>$100,000):*	
	Total jobs won	Improving trend
	Projects dropped	Improving trend
	Projects lost:	
	Price	Improving trend
	Ship cycle	Improving trend
	Features	Improving trend
	Percentage of international units sold	5% of total sales
	Percentage of market share	50%
Business performance	Operating income dollars before interest and taxes	Financial plan
	Cash flow before interest and taxes	Financial plan
	Order dollars (actual bookings)	Financial plan
	Sales dollars (actual billings)	Financial plan
	Operating expenses	Financial plan
	Return on sales	Financial plan
	Return on net assets	Financial plan
	Sales dollars per person	Non production: $517,000 Production: $284,000
	Scrap/spoilage	0.8% of total sales
	Service expense	1.8% of total sales
Accounting performance	Sales expense disposition	20 days
Vendor performance	Percentage of on-time delivery	95%
	Percentage of defect free	98%
	Lead time:	
	Percentage of less than 8 weeks	85%
	Percentage of less than 3 weeks	35%
Customer contact	Customer days:	
	Average days per month customer in Macon SBU personnel in field	5 30 days per month for the combination
Personnel/safety performance	Absenteeism rate	<2.0% annuall
	Lost-time accidents	<2.5 days annually

*Expressed in total units, total dollars, and as a percentage of sales.

Perhaps the most important formal interface between functional areas that provides performance measurement system linkages is the monthly sales and operations planning meeting. The monthly operations report provides the management team with all of the total business measures and is the basis on which business unit strategy and tactics can be evaluated and altered in the meeting. The following list provides a detailed description of the methods used by Self-Contained Systems to ensure performance measurement linkages.

- *Visual measurement displays:* These displays provide a visual assessment of daily performance measures and weekly performance trends on key indicators and allow for management by sight. They assist in the development of horizontal and vertical linkages by focusing daily management efforts on those areas of the business warranting immediate attention and act as a daily performance control tool.

- *Weekly MPS meeting:* These meetings provide the means for evaluating planned versus actual master production scheduling performance (± 7 percent weekly; ± 5 percent monthly) in an interfunctional manner (marketing, operations, supplier development/materials, P/D engineering, systems and general manager).

Performance measurement linkages are created and reviewed via action plan development, with shared responsibilities in the following areas:

- Accurate inventory records (98%+).
- Accurate BOM (98%+).
- Daily execution of all planner and buyer expedite messages.
- Vendor quality execution.
- Daily backflushing/reconciliation/adjustments/order closing.
- Daily cycle counting and variation reconciliation.
- Daily work team coordinator meetings/actions.
- Contingency planning.
- Regular preventive maintenance.
- Daily updates of visible work team performance measures.
- High-quality floor documentation/clearly written work requirements.

- *Weekly engineering change control meeting:* This meeting allows for the interfunctional review (P/D engineering, operations, supplier development/materials, and others as required) of proposed engineering change notices (ECNs) and required management action steps regarding the following items:

- ECN backlog.
- ECN throughput.
- Warranty expense dollars and processing rate.
- BOM accuracy issues.
- Sales order specials throughput.

- *Monthly sales and operations planning meeting:* This meeting is used by the management team to assess total business performance. The management team focuses on monthly trends concerning total business performance measures used to evaluate business unit strategy and then alters tactics over the next 12 months. Daily and weekly performance measurement information is consolidated in graphs and charts for the monthly operations report distributed to the management team prior to the meeting.
- *Quarterly operations report:* This report focuses on specific plans for the current quarter and operating performance for the previous quarter; contains performance highlights regarding production rates, productivity, shipments, ECN throughput, inventory accuracy, BOM accuracy, and financial performance. It also includes:

- Performance disappointments.
- Financial statements comparing budgeted and actual performance for the period, quarter, and year.
- Detailed plans for improving current quarter business performance.
- Results on key performance criteria for the previous and current years in table form.
- A three-year projection on the key performance criteria.
- A report distributed to Macon employees and Commercial Systems Group management.

- Specific business performance measures used in the SBU presented in the report are illustrated in Table 12–5.

- *Annual operating plan:* This plan does not contain retrospective commentary; it focuses on operating plans for overall business improvement in the current year. The document contains the following information:

- A plan review.
- Financial objectives.

TABLE 12-5
Total Business Measures Forwarded to the Commercial Systems Group from Self-Contained Systems SBU

Performance Measurement	Unit of Measure
Operating earnings before interest and taxes (OEBIT)	Dollars
Cash flow before interest and taxes	Dollars
Return on sales	Percent of OEBIT
Return on net assets	Percent of OEBIT
Sales	Dollars and number of units
Market share	Percent
Orders	Dollars
Sales dollars per head count ratios	Dollars
Production and nonproduction employees	
Hours paid per unit	Dollars
Production employees	
Customer days	Average number of days per month
Scrap/spoilage	Percent of sales
Inventory turns	Finished, raw-in-process, total
ECN throughput	Days
Floor cycle	Days
Monthly MPS performance	Percent
On-time shipments	Percent
Vendor performance	Percent of on-time; percent of quality defects
Vendor lead time	Percent <8 weeks; percent <3 weeks
International units	Percent of sales
New products/options	Percent of sales
> $100,000 closures	Percent
Absenteeism	Percent
Lost-time accident rate	Days; rank
Special order designs	Percent of sales
Inventory accuracy	Percent
BOM accuracy	Percent

- Priority assessments.
- Operating objectives.
- Risks, concerns, and opportunities.
- Exhibits summarizing departmental and field sales operating plans, TOC priorities, and a key procedure checklist.

A three-year projection on the business performance measures illustrated in Table 12–8 is also included. The plan is distributed to the management team and commercial systems group management.

The methods employed by Self-Contained Systems to achieve performance measurement system linkages help the organization to approach a global optimum in the markets they serve.

LESSONS LEARNED

This case provides several lessons on the development of performance measurement linkages between systems and functions on strategic objectives:

Finance and Customer Linkage

Marketing engineers assist customers in developing product specifications, and they determine a price range for the product configuration. Thus, Self-Contained Systems directly translated customers' needs into financial terms based on the resources needed to fulfill those needs. This translation is made possible by a financial model furnished by the accounting department that estimated product costs for the 40,000 configurations offered by Self-Contained Systems. With such information supplied by marketing engineers, sales engineers can negotiate a reasonable price associated with a given product configuration to customers based on the financial impact on organizational resources. The firm can also directly determine the profit impact of a specific customer order.

Customer and Resource Linkage

The marketing function provides order requirements directly to product engineering for the configuration of a BOM for the air-conditioning unit. After the creation of the BOM, the unit is added to the master schedule by the marketing function. This activity provides a direct link between the customer-resource systems and functions. Marketing is also responsible for ensuring that the organization is capable of accommodating customer specifications with its current resources. Before an order is accepted, marketing engineers coordinate with each functional area to make sure all specifications and requests are achievable with available organizational resources. In situations where a configuration or specification generally not offered is requested, a review board consisting of managers from the affected areas examines the order and decides whether to accept it.

MPS performance is used to assess the organization's ability to meet schedule commitments driven by customers' needs. The MPS performance metric is shared across functional areas to monitor and control the effective use of organizational resources in supporting customers' delivery expectations. It is also used to focus cross-functional resources on continual improvement efforts in specific departmental areas for improved customer responsiveness.

Finance and Resource Linkage

Since direct labor costs represent only 4 percent of total product cost, Self-Contained Systems uses a simplified cost accounting system that has eliminated detailed labor reporting requirements from the manufacturing function. After a sales order is loaded into the MRP system and material requirements are generated, the accounting function generates the material costs for the order. Once the unit is built and all materials used are completely backflushed, material costs are then run against the backflush requirements to determine the actual material cost for the order. The firm uses a multiple-point milestone backflushing system to relieve consumed material from inventory. Thus, Self-Contained Systems can trace the financial impact of consumed material resources as products move through the manufacturing processes.

The Self-Contained Systems SBU case shows how firms can begin to develop linkages between all of its performance measurement systems and functions to become a successful global competitor and an industry leader.

Chapter Thirteen

The Colgate-Palmolive Company Hill's® Pet Products Division

This chapter is our last example of how firms can develop customer-resource and finance-resource linkages between performance measurement systems and functions. Hill's® Pet Products Division has a performance measurement system that monitors the strategic objectives of quality, delivery, and flexibility.

COMPANY BACKGROUND

The Colgate-Palmolive Company is a worldwide manufacturer of oral health care products, headquartered in New York City. The Hill's® Pet Product Division of Colgate (located in Topeka, Kansas) is the industry leader in the production of specialized, veterinary-grade pet food products for the treatment of nutrition and dietary deficiencies in animals. The product is manufactured in two forms. Hill's® Pet Product's dry-side operations produce a pelletized product composed of various grains, dry poultry meals, vitamins, and minerals. Dry finished product is packaged in 10-, 20-, and 40-pound bags. The firm's can-side operation produces a wet product composed of meat by-products, grain, vitamins, and minerals. It is packaged in 6- and 15.5-ounce cans. There are two product types:

1. A science diet® that provides life-cycle nutrition for dogs and cats from puppies and kittens to mature animals. The firm also produces science diets that are considered "lite products," which are designed for weight control and reduction in dogs and cats. Science diets are sold through veterinarians and pet shops.

2. The other product type is a prescription diet.® Prescription diets are not medicated but are nutritionally balanced to help sick and diseased animals. The firm

TABLE 13–1
Product Line Offerings of Hill's® Pet Products

Canine Product Formulations

d/d®	Food allergies
g/d®	Special nutritional needs of older dogs
h/d®	Heart disease
i/d®	Intestinal disease
k/d®	Kidney disease
p/d®	Growing puppies, pregnant dogs
r/d®	Obesity
s/d®	Bladder stones
v/d®	Advanced kidney disease

Feline Product Formulations

c/d®	Bladder disease
h/d®	Heart disease
k/d®	Kidney disease
p/d®	Growing kittens, pregnant cats
r/d®	Obesity

---

sells prescription diets® that aid in curing kidney, bladder, heart, and other ailments in dogs and cats. (For a full listing of Hill's® product offerings, see Table 13–1.) Prescription diets® are sold only by veterinarians.

Hill's® customer base is 100 percent make-to-stock. The manufacturing processes are 100 percent continuous (high volume flow). There are three manufacturing facilities currently producing specialized pet food products: Los Angeles, California; Bowling Green, Kentucky; and Topeka, Kansas. A new facility located in Richmond, Indiana, began operations in 1991. The Topeka plant has a total employment of 307, which includes 235 hourly and 72 salaried employees. Of the 235 hourly workers, 90 are classified as direct and 145 as indirect employees. The plant is a three-shift, eight-hour operation and produces 45 pet food formulations. There are 1,500 active part numbers in the inventory system and approximately three levels in the typical bill of materials (BOM) for each product. Hill's® Pet Products is currently involved in implementing MRP and total quality management (referred to as "total quality excellence," or TQE) divisionwide, along with JIT and focused factory concepts for selected facilities, to effectively plan, monitor, and control its manufacturing processes. Interviews were conducted with the following individuals:

- Vice-president of operations.
- Division cost accounting manager—Topeka plant.
- Dry department manager—Topeka plant.
- Can department manager—Topeka plant.
- Plant engineering manager.
- Plant accounting manager.

DIVISION ORGANIZATION

The division is functionally structured and consists of distribution, research and development (R&D), operations/information systems, human resources, financial, and new business development departments. The functional executive vice presidents report directly to the president of Hill's® Pet Products. Each executive vice president has a staff of vice presidents who are directly responsible for specific subfunctional areas. Under the vice presidents are directors who manage specific elements of the subfunctional areas. Plant managers report to the director of manufacturing. A facility director presently oversees the Richmond operation. He has two direct reports: a plant manager for the can operation and a plant manager for the dry operation. The Richmond organizational structure is temporary but was considered necessary by division management to ensure a smooth startup. The division organizational structure is presented in Figure 13–1.

STRATEGIC OBJECTIVES

Corporate Objectives

The Colgate-Palmolive Company has a corporate objective of overall sales and profitability growth through the 1990s, with Hill's® playing a major role. Throughout the 1980s, Hill's® Pet Products has represented approximately 10 percent of Colgate's sales volume but has contributed 25 percent of the corporate profits, along with substantial cash flow. Thus, Colgate's strategic objectives relative to Hill's® is to enhance the business so that revenue and profit growth can be sustained through the 1990s and beyond. A key to Colgate's growth objectives for Hill's® is the achievement of TQE (that is, total quality excellence) in all of its facilities. To support this corporate initiative, Colgate has recognized Hill's® as a primary strategic

FIGURE 13-1
Organizational Structure of Hill's® Pet Products

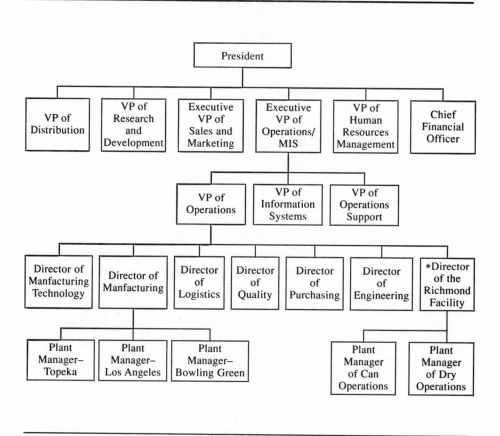

*Temporary organizational structure.

Note: Not all functional vice presidents and directors are shown.

business unit in its portfolio, is investing capital in a new facility and process control instrumentation/equipment for existing facilities, and is encouraging Hill's® to develop business and manufacturing strategies that are consistent with corporate objectives.

Business Level Objectives

Hill's® Pet Products has a mission of continuing to be the preeminent supplier of small animal dietary management products in the world. Recent changes in the market have caused the firm to reassess its current strategy. The veterinary distribution channel has been the mainstay of Hill's® since its inception as a result of the support of veterinarians. However, the pet store distribution channel has grown quickly in recent years, with the advent of pet marts and super pet stores. Each market segment requires different types of marketing and pricing structures. Also, customers' expectations are different in each segment. Thus, a key business-level strategic issue faced by Hill's® is how to compete in the industry.

- Should Hill's® continue to service both the veterinary and pet store distribution channels using their current structure?

- Should Hill's® create two separate businesses to supply the veterinary and pet store channels?

These options are under consideration by the firm's management team.

Hill's® Pet Products has developed business initiatives in three areas: people, technology, and facility. Each manufacturing operation has developed a charter outlining strategies and tactics for supporting the initiatives. Functional directors have also developed charters displaying specific actions necessary to support the business initiatives and plant charters. The firm has defined five strategic objectives necessary to support overall corporate and business level strategies:

1. Quality.

2. Dependability (in servicing customer orders and equipment operation).

3. Flexibility (product and process).

4. Cost.

5. Product development (that is, product innovation).

Each plant has a manufacturing strategy that focuses on various combinations of the five strategic objectives. Thus, each facility is measured on its performance based on its manufacturing objectives as described in the plant charter. In this way, direct competition among the manufacturing facilities is avoided via performance measurement since each plant will have different standards for the same measures based on the strategic focus of the facility.

Hill's® Pet Products has also established specific objectives that apply to all manufacturing facilities. These objectives are listed below:

- *Superior product quality:* continue to produce the highest quality pet food on the market; key elements to achieving this objective are:

- Remove as much variation from the process as possible to ensure product consistency.

- Use certified vendors to ensure that the highest quality raw materials are used in the product.

- Train employees on the importance of quality and in the techniques of TQE.

- *Maximize asset effectiveness:* utilize *all* resources to their maximum effectiveness; assets must be managed to allow the operation to support the capacity demands of the market.

The relationship between Hill's® business initiatives, strategic objectives, functional charters, and plant charters is illustrated in Figure 13–2.

Manufacturing Objectives

Hill's® Pet Products has developed strategic objectives in five areas for creating competitive advantages in the marketplace. Each manufacturing facility will make a unique contribution to the strategic success of the firm based on specific objectives established for the facility. Listed below are the manufacturing objectives for the four plants:

- *Richmond:* The primary focus is on *flexibility;* the facility is designed to be a flexible plant and operates under the JIT philosophy. The plant also focuses on the development of the most appropriate leading-edge technology for the business. Sociotechnical concepts will also be explored in Richmond (i.e., development of the most effective work designs, training programs, and continuous improvement efforts for the firm, given its technology).

- *Los Angeles:* The primary focus is on *dependability.* The Los Angeles plant is the epitome of a focused factory; it is small and landlocked and produces a limited variety of finished product.

- *Bowling Green:* The focus is on *dependability* and *cost.* The Bowling Green plant produces a simplified product mix at high volumes.

- *Topeka:* The focus is *flexibility, dependability,* and *product development.* The dry side of the operation focuses on flexibility; it is currently running 18 different diet formulations. The can side focuses on dependability. The Topeka plant currently produces all can products; after the Richmond startup, the can side began long production runs with minimal changeovers. The Topeka operation is developing part of the plant into a pilot facility to support product development activities.

All four facilities emphasize the production of high-quality products and effective asset utilization as part of their manufacturing objectives.

FIGURE 13–2

Relationship Between Business Initiatives, Strategic Objectives, Functional Charters, and Plant Charters

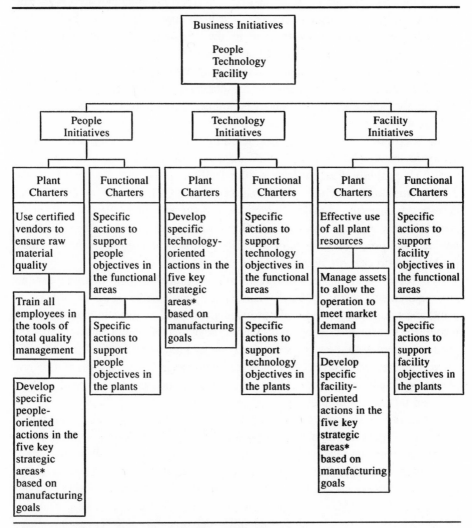

*Quality, dependability, flexibility, cost, and product development.

DIVISION FUNCTIONS

Operations

The Topeka plant is the oldest facility (original phase was built over 40 years ago) and contains both can and dry operations. Both science and prescription diets® are produced in the Topeka facility. The can operation produces only the large cans (15.5 ounces). The product was packaged in small cans (6 ounces) by contract packers until the Richmond plant became operational. Large cans represent 85 to 90 percent of the firm's can volume (that is, number of cans), although there is more growth now in the small-can market because of the convenient size. Approximately 12 percent of Hill's® Pet Products's dry volume is manufactured at the Topeka plant. The facility has approximately 300 employees and is the only unionized facility in the company. Topeka has been chosen as the primary facility for new product development because of its current capability and expertise in efficiently manufacturing short production runs and its proximity to the R&D staff. The plant is considered the "scale-up" facility because of its ability to manufacture the more difficult diet formulations.

Hill's® currently does not have a pilot facility. In the past, the firm has gone directly from R&D bench-top to full-scale production. This method of new product development has caused major disruptions to plant operations. Part of the Topeka plant is to be converted into a pilot facility for the development and testing of new products and processes. The pilot operation will also be used to reverse-engineer product and process problems encountered at the other plants.

The Topeka operation is focusing on providing flexibility in satisfying product mix requirements demanded by the marketplace (particularly on the dry side of the plant) and equipment flexibility for producing new product formulations. Topeka is recognized by Hill's® as being on the leading edge of TQE within the company. The plant is beginning to transfer its acquired quality know-how to other facilities. Finally, an increased emphasis on employee involvement has begun, promoting employee participation and training activities. Plant management personnel are also involved in assisting employees in better understanding the business.

The Los Angeles plant is approximately 12 years old. It is the smallest plant within Hill's® Pet Products. The plant only produces dry products. The production mix is limited to seven formulations (feline and canine science diets®, with feline c/d® to utilize excess capacity). The Los Angeles plant is essentially landlocked, with limited opportunity for expansion. Division management is developing a plan to redesign the material flow within the facility to more effectively utilize space. The plant has become a focused factory, with dependability (delivery and equipment uptime) being the hallmark of its manufacturing competence.

The Bowling Green facility was built approximately seven years ago to manufacture dry science and prescription diet® products. Total employment is approximately 200. Hill's® is in the process of upgrading the technology used in the operation, along with the capabilities of its personnel. The plant will utilize focused factory concepts by producing a simplified product mix of five or six formulations in high volumes. The emphasis in Bowling Green will be cost and dependability. The plant will continue to produce only dry products.

The Richmond, Indiana, plant began operations in 1991. The facility has been developed to produce can and dry products. The can side of the plant produces both large and small can products. The dry side of the facility is capable of producing all dry product formulations (both science and prescription diets®). This facility provides the vehicle for Hill's® to freely utilize JIT concepts for the first time. Richmond will operate under the JIT philosophy of reduced inventory levels (both raw materials and finished goods), high quality, and employee involvement. The plant is capable of holding only one and a half days' worth of finished product. Richmond provides Hill's® with increased flexibility and leading-edge technology and sociotechnical concepts for use in other plants. The plant employed a focused factory startup, utilizing a plant manager for each process (i.e., dry-side and can-side plant managers). The Topeka plant was actively involved in the Richmond startup. The plant assisted in equipment selection and facility layout and supplied managerial and supervisory staff.

The vice president of operations cites quality, product and process flexibility, and product and process innovation as being critical to the strategic success of Hill's® Pet Products. He believes that by developing unique manufacturing competencies at each plant, based on strategic business objectives, the firm will successfully execute its growth strategy. The vice president of operations examines key manufacturing performance measures in quality, dependability, flexibility, cost, and safety through monthly reports supplied by the plant managers. The measures are formally shared with the division manufacturing staff via monthly meetings and informally with division sales and marketing organizations. The director of manufacturing technology is developing an executive reporting system that will allow division management ready access to plant performance information.

The vice president of operations has begun to monitor a new measure used by Hill's®, called total asset utilization. This measure displays the difference between planned available asset utilization and actual utilization for various categories to assess long-term asset effectiveness in the facilities. For example, one category focuses on scheduled versus unscheduled downtime. Division management will focus on downtime trends for targeting continuous improvement activities for each plant, based on its manufacturing focus, to enhance asset utilization. Division management believes that total asset utilization is a good measure when facilities are at or near full capacity. The vice president of operations also believes that effective utilization of assets should lead directly to increased sales and profits, thus supporting corporate growth objectives.

Accounting

Division accounting utilizes a standard full-absorption accounting system designed to track price, material, labor, and manufacturing-related variances. Each plant uses the same accounting system. Hill's® has consolidated databases at the division level for the development and control of standards. All plant accounting information is entered into the division mainframe and coded by a numbering system to identify each plant. The plants are no longer required to report individual employee labor hours against standards. Each plant establishes a total labor pool of dollars based on the actual payroll for the month. An analysis is then conducted on total planned versus actual labor expenditures. Since direct labor represents only 2 to 6 percent of manufacturing cost for all plants, division accounting devotes minimal time to labor variance analysis. The division accounting system is not linked to Colgate's corporate system. Currently, Colgate receives a quarterly report on the financial results of Hill's® Pet Products.

Price analyses are conducted by division accounting. An average manufacturing cost is determined for each product because the products can be produced at several facilities, with each plant having a different cost structure. Margins are then added to the average cost to establish pricing levels. However, product pricing has been recently based on competitive market pressures versus internal cost constraints. Product profitability studies are also conducted by division accounting to determine company profitability. Division accounting was also involved in the installation of the accounting system, as well as an MRP installation at the Richmond facility. Richmond is implementing a PRISM™ MRP system designed specifically for process manufacturing environments. An effort is being made to tie the accounting and MRP systems together to avoid duplications.

The division accounting manager believes that quality, product and process innovation, and delivery hold the keys to success for Hill's® Pet Products. Historically, the measure of cost per pound (i.e., manufacturing cost per pound) has been used to assess the manufacturing performance of the plants. However, the measure was not utilized properly. Instead of reducing cost per pound through investing in plant quality improvements, plant spending was reduced. This short-term mentality created a never-ending loop such that, as spending was decreased, quality began to deteriorate, leading to incremental cost increases. The cost increases were addressed by additional decreases in spending. The division management team now realizes that quality measures, along with other performance indicators, are required to effectively monitor and control manufacturing cost. Key measures have been developed for quality, dependability, flexibility, cost, and safety. The following measures are supplied by the manufacturing organizations monthly to division management and distributed throughout the division manufacturing and accounting organizations:

Quality

- *AIB inspection score:* Plants are checked quarterly for cleanliness and sanitation by the American Institute of Bakers (AIB).

- *Customer complaints:* The number of customer complaints per 100,000 units shipped is recorded monthly for can and dry products.

- *Process quality:* The combination of yield and scrap losses measured in pounds, plus any pounds of packaged product that are discarded, is subtracted from the total pounds of combined raw material (CRM) used in a given month and divided by the raw material pounds to compute a process quality (PQ) percentage.

  PQ = [CRM pounds − (Yield pounds lost + Scrap pounds lost + Packaged product discarded pounds) / Raw material pounds × 100%]

Dependability

- *Case fill rate:* This is defined as the monthly percentage of customer orders filled; it is an indicator of dependability to the customer.

- *Unscheduled downtime:* A percentage of monthly unscheduled downtime is reported; unscheduled downtime is an indicator of equipment dependability.

Flexibility

- *Average changeover time:* Monthly average changeover time for each department is reported.

Cost measure

- *Total manufacturing cost improvement:* This is defined as the monthly total manufacturing cost divided by the monthly total standard cost multiplied by 100 percent; it allows for the examination of cost-improvement efforts in the plants.

Safety measures

- *Lost-work-day frequency:* The monthly total number of lost work days is multiplied by 200,000 and divided by the total number of manhours worked during the month.

- *Serious injury rate:* The monthly total number of OSHA recordable injuries is multiplied by 200,000 and divided by the total number of manhours worked during the month.

- *Total incident rate:* The monthly total number of all plant injuries is multiplied by 200,000 and divided by the total number of manhours worked during the month.

The lost-work-day frequency, serious injury, and total incidents rates are calculated per OSHA requirements, in which the measures are based on the exposure of 100 full-time workers, using 200,000 employee hours as the equivalent (i.e., 100 employees working 40 hours per week for 50 weeks per year).

PLANT FUNCTIONS

Topeka Operation

The Topeka plant manufactures both science and prescription diets for dogs and cats. Unlike commercial pet foods, all products are nutritionally based and are never "least-cost" formulated. The Topeka facility uses a set formulation for all products regardless of commodity price fluctuations, whereas commercial pet food manufacturers "flex" their formulas based on the price of soy beans, corn, rice, and so on. The products are considered expensive and are targeted toward a customer base described as "upscale." The Topeka plant is the largest producer of prescription diets® within Hill's®. A tremendous sense of pride exists among workers in the facility, which is due to their involvement in creating products that literally prolong the lives of cherished pets. Zoo food is also produced at the facility. Diets for primates and large felines (e.g., lions and tigers) are manufactured. However, the majority of Topeka's production is the science and prescription diets® for cats and dogs.

The plant organizational structure is currently composed of three managerial levels: a department management level, a superintendent level, and a shop-floor supervision level. The plant has plans to eliminate the superintendent level. A diagram of the Topeka plant organizational structure is given in Figure 13-3.

There are three distinct manufacturing processes within the Topeka facility. The dry operation (or the dry side) produces pelletized products (referred to as kibbles), which are packaged in bags. The can operation (or the wet side) grinds ground mixed grains and frozen meats together and packages it in cans. A material handling operation that premixes the grains, vitamins, and minerals feeds both sides of the plant. The meats used are not for human consumption and are primarily beef and pork by-products (hearts, liver, spleens). Grains used in the products consists of soy, corn, and rice, along with grain by-products, such as hulls, to provide a fiber source. The dry products are pelletized through a coating process. The kibbles are coated with various materials (referred to as topicals) to improve its taste. The topicals may

FIGURE 13–3
Organizational Structure of the Topeka Plant

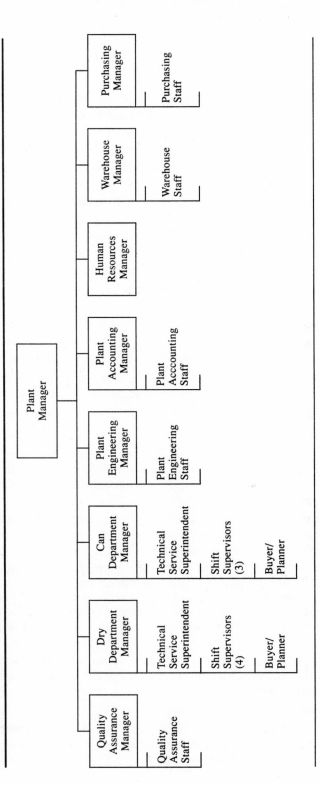

be certified yeast, eggs, or lard. The manufacturing process is currently not in a straight-line flow. Products tend to crisscross through the facility. However, the plant does have a natural "spine," which allows for the creation of a focused facility: a dry side and a wet side with raw material flowing in one end of the plant and finished product shipped out of the other end. Plans are under way to reconfigure the facility in this manner.

The Topeka plant does not have an MRP system. Topeka has developed an in-house scheduling program that classifies each product into four categories: A, B, C, and D. The A and B items tend to be produced continuously due to market requirements. Thus, plant management allocates 24 to 48 hours of production capacity weekly to these products to satisfy demand. The C and D items are produced based on sales forecast tonnage projections. The plant is scheduled on a five-week cycle.

The plant manager cites quality, delivery, and product and process flexibility as the key strategic objectives for Hill's® Pet Products. Key performance measures are informally monitored daily (via daily morning recap meeting with department managers) and formally assessed weekly (via weekly performance reports and weekly management staff performance meeting) by the plant manager, and his direct reports are as follows:

Quality measures

- *Scrap and rework cost:* Scrap and rework information is collected hourly by quality assurance (QA) and reported daily for each shift; data is compiled into a summary report by plant accounting and is distributed weekly to the plant management staff.

- *Process yields:* A weekly yield report is generated by plant accounting, displaying daily yields by product class and department; it is distributed weekly to the plant management staff.

- *Process quality:* Process yield data are used to compute process quality by subtracting the pounds of rejected finished product from the raw material yield poundage and then ratioing the value to the total amount of material used to obtain a process quality percentage; process quality percentages are monitored weekly and are formally reported in the monthly performance report.

- *Sanitation:* Quarterly AIB inspection scores are closely monitored, and the facility holds internal inspections periodically to improve overall plant sanitation efforts.

Dependability/flexibility measures

- *Plant up-time:* Total theoretical plant runtime is divided into four major categories: actual runtime, average changeover time, policy (scheduled) downtime, and unscheduled downtime. Unscheduled downtime is further divided into process-related and maintenance-related downtime. Both downtime and changeover information are collected daily and formally reported for the four categories in a weekly downtime and average changeover time report; performance data is used to assess utilization effectiveness.

- *Case fill rate:* This rate measures the percentage of customer orders filled in a given month; it is reported formally in the monthly performance report.

Cost improvement measure

- *Total manufacturing cost improvement:* the actual cost of producing products for the month is divided by the standard cost; this measure is used to monitor those variances associated with manufacturing finished products and is formally reported in the monthly performance report.

Safety measures

- *Lost workday frequency:* The total number of lost work days for the month is divided by the total number of manhours worked during the month; it is reported formally in the monthly performance report.

- *Serious injury rate:* The total number of OSHA recordable injuries for the month is divided by the total number of manhours worked during the month; it is reported formally in the monthly performance report.

- *Total incident rate:* The total number of all plant injuries for the month is divided by the total number of manhours worked during the month; it is reported formally in the monthly performance report.

All incident rates reported are based on the exposure of 100 full-time workers, using 200,000 employee-hours as the equivalent (100 employees working 40 hours per week for 50 weeks per year), per OSHA standards.

Quality Assurance

Three elements of quality assurance are used in the Topeka plant to monitor and control process and product quality:

1. The plant quality assurance department.
2. Theracon.
3. The plant operators.

The plant QA department conducts tests on all incoming ingredients, assists operators in monitoring process quality, and conducts all analytical tests on finished products. Theracon is an independent quality laboratory used to evaluate Hill's® finished products. This organization serves as the final judge for product releases. Plant operators collect process control information on specific process parameters and are responsible for building quality into the product during its manufacture.

The plant QA department consists of 21 QA technicians, three QA supervisors, a QA superintendent, and a QA manager. The department focuses approximately one-third of its efforts toward ingredient testing, one-half toward process evaluation, and one-sixth toward the analytical testing of finished product. The plant QA function provides the Topeka organization with quality information that goes beyond that collected by the operators on the production floor. A key role of the QA technicians is to provide operators with immediate feedback on the quality results of each production run. The technicians also assist production workers in monitoring process quality on each manufacturing operation.

Theracon was created by the founder of Hill's® Pet Products to supply an external check on product quality attributes. The product is examined for appearance and consistency for each production run. The laboratory makes the final determination of whether the product is fit for shipment. Irregularities discovered by Theracon in product appearance and/or consistency result in the destruction of the product, even if the analytical results are acceptable. Finished products that are determined unacceptable are never reworked or "blended off." Dry product is held at the plants until all plant analytical tests plus Theracon's evaluation are completed. Generally, three to five days are required before final disposition on dry product can be made.

Can product must be stored for an extended period of time (feline: 3 to 5 days; canine: 14 to 30 days) before evaluation by Theracon. Storage of can finished product is necessary to allow the grains in the mixture to hydrate and gain texture. Theracon evaluation results are forwarded to the plant QA department. Along with finished product quality results, Theracon provides the plants with overall process control information. By examining product consistency from shift to shift, the plants are able to assess whether overall plant operations are stable or "drifting" from established averages. Thus, inconsistencies in the process can be identified and corrected.

The operators running the equipment control the quality of the finished product. The Topeka plant is integrating a philosophy of TQE into the organization, whereby every operator is an "evaluator" (as opposed to inspector) of the product while it is being produced. The operators are trained in various process control techniques (such as X-bar and R charts, run charts, and so on) used to monitor specific process parameters for their operator. The operators are also trained to evaluate incoming product on attributes other than those they directly influence. Thus, the Topeka organization has adopted the attitude of total quality responsibility for all product attributes to all operators, regardless of where those attributes were created.

The three elements of quality assurance utilized in the Topeka facility illustrate the organization's commitment to superior product quality. The organization believes that it not only has a quality obligation to the purchaser of the product but also to the animal itself. Thus, the facility will discard product displaying nonconformities in smell, color, and texture. Performance measures collected and distributed by the plant QA department include:

1. *Raw material testing:* The quality of incoming ingredients is tracked daily by vendor. Results are reported weekly to the purchasing manager, and long-term vendor quality trends are evaluated by plant management staff.

2. *Analytical test results:* The quality assurance lab composites a sample at the end of each shift; tests are conducted to determine moisture, ash, fat, and mineral contents. Tests help determine whether product is released, and results are reported to shift supervisors. Long-term quality trends are evaluated by plant management staff.

3. *Daily finished product produced:* The daily number of pounds of products packaged by the dry and can operations on each shift is tracked and reported daily to the shift supervisor.

4. *Finished product disposition results:* Finished products are dispositioned daily by the QA department for each shift into the following four categories:

   • T1: Product is considered having perfect quality with no deviations on process parameters during the run.

   • T2: This is an average production run; it may have at least one process parameter that drifted outside of control limits during the run. Product is considered acceptable for shipment.

   • T3: Product is considered suspect; it is held for further analysis.

   • T4: Product is rejected and destroyed.

Dry Department

The dry department (or dry side) manufactures science and prescription diet products that are extruded to form "kibbles," coated with flavor enhancers and packaged into 10-, 20- and 40-pound bags. Production rates vary by product, ranging from 7,500 to 15,000 pounds per hour. The department produces 13 different product formulations. Product is manufactured on three shifts, each composed of a supervisor and nine production workers. The first shift actually has 2 supervisors and 13 production workers since they have the additional responsibility of producing product samples used in sales and promotion campaigns.

The dry department operation begins by receiving grain from the grain room (that is, the material handling operation) containing premixed vitamins and minerals according to product formulation specifications. The material is pneumatically transferred from the grain room to bins located above the extruder. The mixture is metered into the extruder by augers to monitor feed rates. Water, steam, and white grease (if specified in the formulation) are also injected into the extruder. The extruder operates as a pressure cooker. The ingredients are compressed between screws and an outside liner within the apparatus at a constant pressure and temperature. When the compressed material hits the face of the die, the pressure is relieved and the material expands, popping out in the form of a pellet (called a kibble). The kibble is pulled away from the extruder with an airlift and is transported to an oven. The oven reduces the moisture content of the kibble from 23 percent to approximately 7 to 10 percent.

Various topicals are then applied to the product. Topicals are flavor enhancers that make the product more palatable for animals. Dogs enjoy the taste of eggs, so an egg coating is often applied to canine products. Cats tend to like food that is tart; thus, an acidified yeast topical is added to many feline diets. Topicals are controlled via instrumentation displaying micromotion readouts, and checks are made every two hours to ensure that the rate at which the coating is added meets formula specifications. The quality assurance lab takes a composite sample of the product every 30 minutes after the topicals have been applied. The sample is inspected for size and uniformity, along with moisture content. A visual examination of the topical is also conducted.

The finished product is then conveyed through an auger system to packaging, where it is stored in four bins. From the bins, the product is transferred to the packaging machines (there are currently two) for bagging. An explanation for the large amount of bin space in the operation is that the extruder is capable of running at a faster rate than the packaging equipment. Thus, the dry department manager attempts to schedule a "fast" product followed by a "slow" product to allow the packaging operation to catch up. The dry operation is in the process of eliminating the bins and is installing equipment for on-line packaging. Bins are creating contamination situations that are no longer acceptable. Also, the storage of finished product in bins increases overall product variability as operating conditions on the extruder change. For example, temperature changes on the extruder heads from variations in cooling water temperature have a direct impact on kibble length, a critical product parameter.

The dry department manager cites quality, product and process flexibility, and lead time as key success criteria for Hill's® Pet Products. Performance measurement information collected and monitored daily by the department includes:

• *Yield results:* Yield results are determined by measuring the daily number of pounds extruded per shift and the daily number of pounds packaged per shift along with the amount of waste created at various stages of the process. Average yield for the dry department is currently 83 percent. Yield results are formally reported to the dry department manager via a daily department operations report prepared by supervisory personnel.

- *Extruder amperage:* A run chart is maintained on the extruder, which records the number of amps the extruder is using in 15-minute intervals; it is used as a record of extruder downtime. The cause of any downtime is written on the chart, which also provides information on the uniformity of the run—at faster rates, the extruder uses more amps, which increases output but also increases variability in kibble length; at lower rates, the extruder uses less amps, which decreases output but decreases kibble length variability. The variance seen in the extrusion process directly relates to product variability.

- *Machine downtime:* This is the daily running total of machine downtime by product area, piece of equipment, and by date for extrusion and packaging areas. The unscheduled downtime target is 11 percent. Machine downtime is formally reported in a weekly downtime and changeover report prepared by plant accounting.

- *Average changeover time:* Changeover times are monitored and collected daily by plant personnel. The target is 74 minutes per changeover; other Hill's® plants take up to 16 hours to changeover on the same products. It is formally reported in the weekly downtime and changeover report.

- *Number of changeovers:* The number of changeovers for the dry department is budgeted monthly. Changeover frequency is driven by product demand and monitored daily, and it is formally reported in the weekly downtime and changeover report.

- *Kibble length:* X-bar and R charts are used to monitor kibble length of extruded product. The operator measures the length of 10 kibbles periodically and plots the average and the range. If the average exceeds control limits, the operator adjusts the extruder; if average is grossly out of limits, the run is aborted; if the range exceeds the control limits, the run is aborted. The length of the kibble is a measure of the consistency of the extrusion process; inconsistencies in the extruder translate to nonperforming diets.

- *Kibble width:* The periodic measurement of kibble width (not plotted) indicates when extruder dies are worn; as the die wears, the product is allowed to expand more, thus signaling that the dies are worn.

- *Analytical test results:* The QA lab composites a sample at the end of each shift; tests are conducted to determine moisture, ash, fat, and mineral contents. Tests help determine whether product is released; results are reported to shift supervisors. Long-term quality trends are evaluated by plant management staff.

The dry department manager stressed the fact that under no circumstances will product failing to pass analytical testing be shipped to the customer. If the product is not 100 percent acceptable, it is thrown away. The Topeka plant will not sacrifice product quality for short-term output increases.

Can Department

The can department (or wet side) produces science and prescription diet® products through a process of blending and grinding raw grains and meat materials. The operation involves hydration, heat activation, and sterilization technologies. The finished product is packaged in 15.5-ounce cans. Production rates in the can department can reach 750,000 cans per day. Currently, all wet products sold by Hill's® are produced by the Topeka can operation. Product is manufactured on a three-shift basis. There are 80 production workers and 3 shift supervisors.

The can operation starts by receiving ground mixed grains and frozen meats from the grain room and meat storage areas, respectively. The department then proceeds to grind and blend the ingredients in specified percentages, as outlined in the product formulation. Metal containers are then filled with the mixture by weight and seamed. The cans containing the product are then sterilized, cooled down, labeled, encased, and warehoused.

The can department manager is an advocate of TQE and expects each production worker to consider the person in the next operation as the customer. He believes that this concept will help employees understand the influence they have on the next step in the process and help focus their attention on the key items that must be done perfectly to ensure a high-quality product. To ensure high product quality in the can department, quality must be monitored and controlled, from raw materials to packaging. Raw materials are graded as they are received into the facility. The plant has developed predictive computer models that allow employees to preselect the ingredients required for a specified formulation and determine how the interactions between raw material specifications affect the finished product.

Instrumentation and process control procedures have been installed to provide control during manufacturing. For example, the process has computer-aided equipment, with feedback loops for the automatic adjustment of valves that regulate product flow. Statistical process control (SPC) is used on key process parameters in the canning area. Seaming is a critical dimension for canning operations since this protects the finished product from contamination (a seam is a metal strip with a thickness of 2 to 3 thousandths of an inch). The department is purchasing a piece of equipment that automatically collects and stores on-line data on seamed cans in a microprocessor and allows for real-time analysis of seam quality.

The can department manager believes that quality, product/process flexibility, and delivery are the most important strategic objectives for Hill's® Pet Products.

Performance measures collected and monitored daily within the can department include:

- *Yield results:* Yield results are determined by measuring the daily number of pounds processed per shift and the daily number of pounds canned per shift, along with the amount of waste created at various stages of the process. Average yield for the can department is currently 97 percent and it is formally reported to the can department manager via a daily department operations report prepared by supervisory personnel.

- *Machine downtime:* A daily running total is kept of machine downtime by product area, piece of equipment, and by date for the can processing and packaging areas. The unscheduled downtime target is 16.5 percent. Downtime is formally reported in a weekly downtime and changeover report prepared by plant accounting.

- *Average changeover time:* Changeover times are monitored and collected daily by plant personnel. The target is 76.5 minutes per changeover. Changeover times are formally reported in the weekly downtime and changeover report.

- *Number of changeovers:* The number of changeovers for the can department is budgeted monthly. Changeover frequency is driven by product demand and monitored daily. Changeovers are formally reported in the weekly downtime and changeover report.

Plant Engineering

The plant engineering department functions as a support group for all manufacturing activities in the facility. The department is involved in maintaining existing equipment, developing capital requests for the purchase and installation of new equipment, and upgrading the physical plant. Plant engineering also has some process engineering responsibilities in the Topeka operation, although the division engineering staff supplies process engineering support.

The plant engineering manager is an advocate of employee involvement and promotes training activities within the department. For example, the plant is installing a new wastewater treatment system. Currently, plant wastewater is being treated by the city sewage treatment facility for a monthly fee. Although the responsibility for the new system has not been finalized between production and plant engineering, the plant engineering manager requires his personnel to be trained on the equipment. Another area requiring training is sanitation. Plant management is concerned about maintaining high sanitary conditions and good manufacturing practices, necessary for a food-grade operation. Equipment must be sanitized daily. Only food-grade lubricants can be used in much of the machinery in the plant. Thus, it is essential that all plant engineering personnel understand the sanitation requirements of the Topeka plant.

The plant engineering manager cites quality, delivery, and product and process flexibility as critical areas for the company. He utilizes performance measures that have a direct reflection on plant engineering's ability to service the production floor. The plant engineering manager ties departmental measures to the targets and goals developed by the manufacturing departments. Performance measures used in the plant engineering department include:

• *Downtime:* Downtime is captured in 15-minute intervals on all equipment by maintenance personnel; the cause of downtime is also recorded. Any downtime less than 15 minutes is not captured. It is estimated that only 1 hour of total downtime per 24-hour period is not accounted for.

• *Sanitation:* The facility is rated on a quarterly basis by the American Institute of Baking (AIB), and visits are unannounced. The plant is rated on a 200-point scale for each of the following categories:

• Pest control.
• Employee practices.
• Maintenance for sanitation.
• Cleaning practices.
• Overall plant sanitation effort.
• The total maximum score is 1,000; the plant standard is 855.

• *Work order completions:* The daily number of work orders completed per shift are measured against the number scheduled for completion. The root cause of any variance is determined, and corrective action is then taken to eliminate backlog.

• *Preventive manitenance:* The number of preventive maintenance jobs completed per shift is measured daily against the number scheduled for completion. The root cause of any variance is determined, and corrective action is then taken to eliminate backlog.

• *Maintenance, repair, and operating (MRO) supply stockouts:* Stockroom employees keep a daily log of all MRO stockouts; the log also contains the type of item stocked out (i.e., mechanical, electrical, plumbing, safety-related). The log is submitted daily to the MRO buyer in the plant engineering department and is submitted weekly to the plant engineering manager.

• *Departmental expenditures:* Spending levels in the department are tracked daily. The plant engineering manager sets an annual spending target for major maintenance dollars (that is, money for major expenditures above the day-to-day operating budget). The departmental objective is developed for the amount of major maintenance dollars to be saved for the year. Weekly spending targets are developed, which do not include the targeted savings amount, and invoices are then tracked daily against spending targets.

Plant Accounting

The Topeka plant utilizes a traditional standard full-absorption accounting system, which, until recently, focused on direct material, direct labor, and manufacturing overhead variances. All overhead is allocated based on direct labor, although it only accounts for 2 to 3 percent of Topeka's total manufacturing cost. Currently, the cost accounting department is focusing its efforts on tracking the activities that drive the business. The primary emphasis has shifted from a "cost focus" to an "activity focus" on measures that directly affect quality, dependability, and flexibility. The plant accounting department is addressing the overhead allocation issue by defining various "drivers" in each portion of the facility to be used as the basis for overhead allocation decisions. For example, the pre-mix area supplies raw material to both the dry and can sides. An allocation method, based on pounds of material produced for each side, is under consideration. Warehouse cost allocations based on square footage are also being explored. Finally, machine runtime as an allocation basis is being examined for use in some areas of the plant.

The plant accounting manager realizes that the accounting information provided in the past has not supported proactive decision making and the continuous improvement objectives of the business. The information historically has been after the fact. Thus, the plant accounting department has adopted measures that monitor business effectiveness. Also, the department has shifted its emphasis from external to internal reporting. Plant accounting now focuses on providing information to plant management personnel that is timely, and it allows for proactive initiatives. The department is also more involved in problem solving. Plant accounting personnel are now using their skills to help drive the continuous improvement efforts within the operation. In summary, the plant accounting department at the Topeka plant is constantly finding ways to become more useful to management on a daily basis.

The plant accounting manager suggests that quality, delivery, and product and process flexibility hold the keys to long-term success for Hill's® Pet Products. The department provides weekly, monthly, and quarterly performance reports and summaries on key measurement areas for use by production workers, plant management and staff personnel, and division management. The following performance information is consolidated and distributed by plant accounting:

1. *Weekly yield report:* This report shows daily yields by product, standard yields for the product, pounds of raw material used, pounds of finished goods produced,

scrap and rework totals (in pounds and percentages), pounds of unaccounted for material (difference between pounds of raw material used and pounds produced), and the dollar opportunity for each product based on the pounds of unaccounted for material. It also includes packing yields. A separate report is generated for can and dry operations. The report is then distributed to plant management staff.

2. *Weekly downtime and average changeover report:* This report displays a daily total of runtime hours available, hours produced, changeover hours, other scheduled (planned) downtime, unaccountable time, and the daily number of changeovers. It includes month-to-date unscheduled downtime percentage (actual versus target) and month-to-date average changeover time (in minutes: actual versus target). Month-to-date and year-to-date machine running efficiency, changeover time, other scheduled and unscheduled downtime percentages are also included. A separate report for the can and dry operations is generated. The report is distributed to plant management staff.

3. *Monthly performance report:* Performance information is provided for AIB inspection scores, customer complaints per 100,000 units (for can and dry departments, also total), process quality percentages (for can and dry departments, also total), case fill rate, unscheduled downtime for can and dry departments, average changeover times for can and dry departments, total manufacturing cost improvement percentages, lost workday frequency, serious injury rate, and total incident rate. The report shows baseline, 12-month running average, plus quarterly and annual targets for each measure. It also shows monthly performance for the entire year, and it contains graphs of the following performance information:

• *Volume:* A line graph of the monthly planned versus actual pounds and cases of product produced (in millions) for the can and dry operations is produced, along with a bar graph showing volume performance for the previous two years.

• *Case fill rate:* A line graph of monthly planned versus actual case fill rate (percentage of orders filled) is produced along with a bar graph showing baseline, previous year, and year-to-date percentages.

• *Yield:* A line graph of monthly actual versus standard yield percentages for the can and dry operations is produced, along with a bar graph of year-to-date yields for the can and dry operations.

• *Process quality:* Again, a line graph of monthly actual versus targeted process quality percentages for the can and dry operations is produced along with a bar graph of baseline and year-to-date percentages for the can and dry operations.

• *Unscheduled downtime:* A line graph of monthly actual versus targeted unscheduled downtime percentages for the can and dry operations is produced, along with a bar graph of baseline and year-to-date percentages for can and dry operations.

• *Changeover time:* A line graph of monthly actual versus targeted average changeover times (in minutes) for the can and dry operations is produced, along with a bar graph of baseline and year-to-date average changeover minutes for can and dry operations.

- *Safety:* A line graph of monthly actual versus targeted total incident rate, OSHA recordable rates, and lost workday frequency is produced, along with a bar graph of baseline and year-to-date values. The report is distributed to plant and division management.

4. *Quarterly performance summary:* Measurement results of the performance information provided in the monthly performance reports are summarized quarterly in charts and graphs. The summary is posted in the plant for all employees to review.

PERFORMANCE MEASUREMENT SYSTEMS

The performance measurement systems used at the plant level are maintained by each department. The measures are collected functionally and consolidated by the plant accounting department. The plant accounting function provides plant and division management with periodic performance summary reports in the form of tables, charts, and graphs. The summary reports are used to monitor trends and to develop improvement strategies. The division performance measurement system is based on financial and nonfinancial information received from the manufacturing facilities. Division management evaluates the manufacturing operations on the same criteria, measures, and standards used by plant management. The primary differences between these systems are the level of detail and reporting frequency associated with each measure. The plant performance measurement system provides greater detail on each measure than the division system. Also, the performance measure reporting frequency is higher in the plant system than in the division level system. Finally, the division system uses different performance standards on the same measure for each facility based on its manufacturing objectives and focus. A summary of the performance measurement systems employed at the plant and division levels is presented in Tables 13–2 and 13–3, respectively.

PERFORMANCE MEASUREMENT SYSTEM LINKAGES

Performance measurement system linkages between Colgate-Palmolive and Hill's® Pet Products are primarily accomplished via periodic financial reports. Hill's® is currently measured by Colgate corporate management against its profit plan and volume growth objectives. The division is using asset utilization measures as a link to the profitability and

TABLE 13–2
Plant Performance Measurement System for Hill's® Pet Products

Department(s)	Performance Criteria	Performance Measures	Performance Standards
Plant staff/ accounting	Quality	Monthly scrap cost	Financial plan
		Monthly rework cost	Financial plan
		Weekly process yield percentage	Dry—84% Can—97%
		Monthly process quality percentage	Dry—83% Can—95%
		Quarterly AIB score	Score ≥ 855
	Dependability	Monthly unscheduled downtime percentage	Dry—11% Can—16.5%
		Monthly case fill rate percentage	95%
	Flexibility	Monthly average changeover time	Dry—74 minutes Can—76.5 minutes
	Cost	Monthly total manufacturing cost improvement percentage	100% (no variances between actual and standard manufacturing cost)
	Safety	Monthly lost-time frequency	3.7
		Monthly serious injury rate	10.1
		Monthly total incident rate	20.0
Quality assurance	Quality/ volume	Daily raw material testing results	All results within specification
		Daily lab results for each shift	All results within specifications
		Daily pounds of finished product produced	Daily target
		Daily finished product disposition	No T4 material
		Daily finished product released	Daily target
Dry operation	Quality/ volume	Daily pounds extruded per shift	Daily target
		Daily pounds packaged per shift	Daily target
		Daily process yield per shift	84%
		Daily lab results for each shift	All results within specifications
		Daily extruder amp usage pattern	Minimal variation

TABLE 13–2
Concluded

Department(s)	Performance Criteria	Performance Measures	Performance Standards
		Daily kibble length by shift	Within control limits
		Daily kibble width by shift	Within control limits
	Dependability/ flexibility	Daily machine dowtime	11%— unscheduled downtime
		Daily average changeover time	74 minutes per changeover
		Daily number of changeovers	Monthly budget
		Daily extruder amp usage (down when no amps are used)	Down during scheduled time only
Can operation	Quality/ volume	Daily pounds processed per shift	Daily target
		Daily pounds canned per shift	Daily target
		Daily process yield per shift	97%
	Dependability/ flexibility	Daily machine downtime	16.5%— unscheduled downtime
		Daily average changeover time	76.5 minutes per changeover
		Daily number of changeovers	Monthly budget
Plant engineering	Quality	AIB score	Score ≥ 855
	Dependability	Daily machine downtime	Dry—11% Can—16.5%
		Daily work order completions by shift	Daily shift target
		Daily preventive maintenance jobs completed by shift	Daily shift target
		Daily MRO supply stockouts	No stockouts
	Cost	Daily spending levels	Achieve weekly spending targets

TABLE 13–3
Division Performance Measurement System for Hill's® Pet Products

Performance Criteria	Performance Measures	Performance Standards
Asset utilization	Monthly scheduled downtime percentage	Division target for each plant
	Monthly unscheduled downtime percentage	Division target for each plant
	Monthly scheduled maintenance percentage	Division target for each plant
	Monthly unscheduled maintenance	Division target for each plant
	Monthly machine utilization	Division target for each plant
	Monthly plant run time percentage	Division target for each plant
Quality	Monthly scrap cost	Financial plan
	Monthly rework cost	Financial plan
	Monthly process yield percentage	Division target for each plant
	Monthly process quality percentage	Division target for each plant
	Quarterly AIB score	Division target for each plant
Dependability	Monthly case fill rate percentage	Division target for each plant
Flexibility	Monthly average changeover time	Division target for each plant
Cost	Monthly total manufacturing cost improvement percentage	100% (no variances between actual and standard manufacturing cost)
	Monthly production cost per pound	Division targets for each plant
	Monthly production cost per pound	Division target for each plant
Volume	Monthly production quantities (pounds and cases)	Division target for each plant
Safety	Monthly lost-time frequency	Division target for each plant
	Monthly serious injury rate	Division target for each plant
	Monthly total incident rate	Division target for each plant

volume measures assessed by corporate staff. Hill's® Pet Products division management believes that effective asset utilization has a direct impact on corporate profitability and growth objectives, thus providing linkages to corporate measures. The objectives will be accomplished through enhanced asset effectiveness via improved plant run times, plant yield improvements, reductions in plant unscheduled downtime, more effective preventive maintenance, and so forth. Hill's® division management shares asset effectiveness results with the corporate staff. Division management informs Colgate management on asset utilization improvements in this manner.

Performance measurement system linkages between division management and the plants are accomplished primarily through individual monthly performance reports that present performance results in the following areas:

- Quality.
- Dependability.
- Flexibility.
- Cost.
- Safety.

The information is displayed in tabular and graphical form. The reports are sent from the plant managers to the director of manufacturing. The director of manufacturing distributes the reports throughout the division manufacturing function. Currently, the plant performance results are shared informally with other division functions. Plans are underway to develop formal mechanisms for sharing manufacturing performance results with all division functions.

The director of manufacturing technology was developing an executive reporting system at the time of this writing that would further enhance performance measurement system linkages between division and plant management. Division and plant level performance measurement linkages are also accomplished through quarterly performance presentations made to functional vice presidents by plant management personnel. The presentations focus on current plant performance and action plans for future improvement.

Several vehicles are used within the plants to link departmental performance measurement systems to overall plant performance. Mechanisms utilized for plant-wide performance measurement linkages include:

- *Daily department operations reports:* These reports are generated by can and dry department supervisory staffs daily and indicate the number of pounds extruded and processed and the number of pounds packed per shift. They also provide daily totals and a running monthly total, used to monitor departmental performance against commitments. The reports are distributed to the can and dry department managers.

- *Daily morning recap meeting:* This is an 8:00 A.M. plant management staff meeting to discuss plant activities that have taken place in the preceding 24 hours. Targets for the current day and important events scheduled for the next two to three days are also discussed.
- *Weekly yield report:* This report contains yield performance information for the can and dry operations and is distributed to plant management staff.
- *Weekly downtime and average changeover time report:* This report contains downtime and changeover information for can and dry operations and is distributed to plant management staff.
- *Weekly work order recap report:* It describes work order completions by department and is distributed to the division engineering group and plant management staff.
- *Weekly department meetings:* Each department has internal meetings to assess its effectiveness in supporting plant objectives and to develop action steps for improvement.
- *Weekly plant staff meetings:* Plant performance for the week is examined, key performance measures in each category (quality, dependability, flexibility, etc.) are analyzed, and action plans to enhance performance are developed.
- *Monthly performance report:* Plant performance in the areas of quality, dependability, flexibility, cost, and safety is highlighted. The report is distributed to plant management staff and the director of manufacturing.
- *Quarterly performance summary:* Key performance results in the above-mentioned categories are summarized in graphs, tables, and charts. The summary is posted in the manufacturing area and provides feedback on plant performance to production workers.

In addition, the plants have a "Quality Pays" bonus system based on the number of customer complaints per quarter and on AIB scores. A bonus is paid quarterly to all employees according to the results of these measures. AIB scores are announced plantwide each quarter via the intercom system. Thus, monetary incentives have been installed to support plant quality efforts. The techniques used by Hill's® Pet Products to achieve performance measurement system linkages between organizational levels and departments congruent with corporate, business-level, and manufacturing objectives have been designed to help the firm to maintain its leadership position in the specialized pet food industry.

LESSONS LEARNED

This case reveals several lessons on the development of performance measurement linkages between systems and functions on strategic objectives.

Customer and Resource Linkage

Hill's® defines dependability in servicing customer orders as a strategic objective. Therefore, the firm actively manages its organizational resources in a manner that maximizes asset effectiveness. Assets are managed to allow Hill's® operations to support the capacity demands of its markets. Key dependability metrics used by the firm are case fill rate, defined as the monthly percentage of customer orders filled (an indicator of dependability to the customer), and the percentage of unscheduled downtime (an indicator of equipment dependability). These metrics are used to focus organizational resources on improvement efforts leading to better support of customer delivery expectations.

The use of an independent quality lab to evaluate finished products also provides a link between customers and resources. The independent lab provides Hill's® with customer performance measurement information used to guide the use of organizational resources toward quality improvement activities.

Finance and Resource Linkage

Hill's® uses a standard full-absorption accounting system designed to track cost, material, labor, and manufacturing-related variances. Direct labor costs represent between 2 and 6 percent of the total product cost. Each plant establishes a total labor pool of dollars based on the actual payroll for the month. An analysis is conducted on the total planned versus actual labor expenditures. The impact of improved resource usage on the firm's financial performance is monitored via the total manufacturing cost improvement index. This index is defined as the monthly total manufacturing cost divided by the monthly total standard cost, multiplied by 100 percent. The index allows Hill's® to examine the financial impact of plant improvement efforts (that is, improvements in resource deployment). The plants are also beginning to focus on tracking the activities that drive the use of organizational resources. Thus, the primary emphasis has shifted from a pure cost focus to an activity focus using measures that show the affect of resource usage on its finances and strategic objectives.

This case displays how linkages between the customer-resource and finance-resource performance measurement systems and functions can be used to establish manufacturing excellence.

Endnotes

CHAPTER ONE

1. I Magaziner and M Patinkin, *The Silent War* (New York, NY: Random House, 1989).

2. D H Freedman, "Is Management Still A Science?" *Harvard Business Review*, November–December 1992, pp 26–38.

3. S R Rosenthal, *Effective Product Design and Development* (Homewood, IL: Business One Irwin, 1992).

4. S C Gardiner, and J H Blackstone, "The 'Theory of Constraints' and the Make-or-Buy Decision," *International Journal of Purchasing and Materials Management*, Summer 1991, pp 38–43.

5. B H Maskell, *Performance Measurement for World Class Manufacturing* (Cambridge, MA: Productivity Press, 1991).

6. H Mather, *Competitive Manufacturing* (Englewood Cliffs, NJ: Prentice Hall, 1988).

7. J F Cox, and J H Blackstone, Jr, *Managing Operations: A Focus on Excellence* (Fort Worth, TX: Dryden Press, forthcoming 1994).

8. H Mather, "Optimize Your Product Variety," *Production and Inventory Management Journal*, Second Quarter, 1992, pp 38–42.

9. P Sellers, "The Dumbest Marketing Ploy," *Fortune*, October 5, 1992, pp 88–95.

10. T Fry, and J F Cox, "Manufacturing Performance: Local Versus Global Performance Measures," *Production and Inventory Management Control*, Second Quarter 1989, pp 28–44.

11. D Hull, "An Analysis of Field Service Inventory Management Practices of Selected Electronics Firms," Doctoral Thesis, University of Georgia (1992).

12. E M Goldratt, *Haystack Syndrome* (Croton-on-the-Hudson, NY: North River Press, 1990).

13. T A Stewart, "Why Budgets Are Bad for Business," *Fortune*, June 4, 1990, pp 115–119.

14. R Eccles, "The Performance Measurement Manifesto," *Harvard Business Review*, January–February 1991, pp 131–137.

15. P F Drucker, "The Emerging Theory of Manufacturing," *Harvard Business Review*, May–June 1990, pp 94–102.

16. E M Goldratt, and J Cox, *The Goal: A Process of Ongoing Improvement*, 2nd rev. ed. (Croton-on-the-Hudson, NY: North River Press, 1992).

17. H B Woolf (editor-in-chief), *Webster's New Collegiate Dictionary* (Springfield, MA: G. & C. Merriam Company, 1974).

18. E M Goldratt, and R Fox, *The Race* (Croton-on-the-Hudson, NY: North River Press, 1986).

19. E M Goldratt, *Theory of Constraints* (Croton-on-the-Hudson, NY: North River Press, 1990).

20. Ibid.

CHAPTER TWO

1. E M Goldratt and J Cox, *The Goal: A Process of Ongoing Improvement*, 2nd rev. ed. (Croton-on-the-Hudson, NY: North River Press, 1992).

2. C W Hofer, and D Schendel, *Strategy Formulation: Analytical Concepts* (St. Paul: West Publishing, 1978).

3. C R Christensen, K R Andrews, J L Bowers, R G Hammermesh, and M E Porter, *Business Policy*, 5th ed. (Homewood, IL: Richard D. Irwin, 1982).

4. Goldratt and Cox, *The Goal* (1992).

5. K M Crawford, J F Cox, and J H Blackstone, Jr, *Performance Measurement Systems and the JIT Philosophy: Principles and Cases* (Falls Church, VA: APICS, 1988).

6. C J McNair, W Mosconi, and T F Norris, *Beyond the Bottom Line: Measuring World Class Performance* (Homewood, IL: Dow Jones–Irwin, 1989).

7. T Hill, *Manufacturing Strategy: Text and Cases* (Boston, MA: Irwin, 1989).

8. E M Goldratt, *Theory of Constraints* (Croton-on-the-Hudson, NY: North River Press, 1990).

9. J F Cox, J H Blackstone, Jr., and M S Spencer (editors), *APICS Dictionary*, 7th ed. (Falls Church, VA: APICS, 1992).

10. E M Goldratt, *Theory of Constraints*.

11. R J Schonberger, *World Class Manufacturing: The Lesson of Simplicity Applied* (New York: The Free Press, 1986), p 2.

12. J F Cox, "An Analysis of the Failure of World Class Manufacturing and Other American Dreams," *APICS Educational and Research Foundation Newsletter* 5, First Quarter 1993), pp 3–4.

CHAPTER THREE

1. T E Vollmann, "Foreword," in *Managing Human Resources: Integrating People and Business Strategy* (Homewood, IL: Business One Irwin, 1992).

2. James F Cox, and John H Blackstone, Jr., *Managing Operations: A Focus on Excellence* (Fort Worth, TX: Dryden Press, Forthcoming, 1994).

3. E M Goldratt and J Cox, *The Goal*, rev. ed. (Croton-on-the-Hudson, NY: North River Press, 1987).

4. E M Goldratt, "Late Night Discussion: 6," *Industry Week*, December 2, 1991.

5. G Stalk, and T M Hout, *Competing Against Time* (New York, NY: The Free Press, 1990).

CHAPTER FOUR

1. H T Johnson and R S Kaplan, *Relevance Lost: The Rise and Fall of Management Accounting* (Boston, MA: Harvard Business School Press, 1987).

2. B J Finch and J F Cox, "Inventory: An Asset or Liability?" *Production and Inventory Management Journal*, Second Quarter 1989, pp 25–37.

3. R S Kaplan, "Measuring Manufacturing Performance: A New Challenge for Managerial Accounting Research," *The Accounting Review*, October 1983, pp 686–703.

4. J Miller, A J Nanni, and T E Vollmann, "What Shall We Account For?" *Research Report: Boston University Manufacturing Roundtable*, August 1986, pp 1–24.

5. E M Goldratt, and R E Fox, *The Race* (Croton-on-the-Hudson, NY: North River Press, 1986).

6. R A Howell, and S R Soucy, "The New Manufacturing Environment: Major Trends for Management Accounting," *Management Accounting*, July 1987, pp 21–27.

7. R A Howell and S R Soucy, "Cost Accounting in the New Manufacturing Environment," *Management Accounting*, August 1987, pp 42–48.

8. R A Howell and S R Soucy, "Capital Investment in the New Manufacturing Environment," *Management Accounting*, November 1987, pp 26–32.

9. Johnson and Kaplan, *Relevance Lost*.

10. G Foster, and C T Horngren, "JIT: Cost Accounting and Cost Management Issues," *Management Accounting*, June 1987, pp 19–25.

11. G W Plossl, "Manage by the Numbers—But Which Numbers?" in *American Production and Inventory Control Society 30th Annual Conference Proceedings* (Falls Church, VA: APICS, 1987) pp 499–503.

12. F S Worthy, "Accounting Bores You? Wake Up," *Fortune*, October 12, 1987, pp 43–48.

13. W J Burns, and R S Kaplan, *Accounting and Management: Field Study Perspectives* (Boston, MA: Harvard Business School Press, 1990).

14. B J Finch and J F Cox, "Inventory: An Asset or Liability?" *Production and Inventory Management Journal*, Second Quarter 1989, pp 25–37.

15. T Fry, and J F Cox, "Manufacturing Performance: Local Versus Global Performance Measures," *Production and Inventory Management Journal*, Second Quarter 1989, pp 28–44.

16. G W Plossl, "Cost Accounting in Manufacturing: Dawn of a New Era," *International Journal of Production Planning and Control* 1 (1990), pp 61–68.

17. B H Maskell, *Performance Measurement for World Class Manufacturing* (Cambridge, MA: Productivity Press, 1991).

18. J A Brimson, and C Berliner, *Cost Management for Today's Advanced Manufacturing: The CAM-I Conceptual Design* (Cambridge, MA: Harvard Business School Press, 1988).

19. R W Hall, H T Johnson, and P B B Turney, *Measuring Up: Charting Pathways to Manufacturing Excellence* (Homewood, IL: Business One Irwin, 1991).

20. R S Kaplan, "Measures for Manufacturing Excellence: A Summary," *Journal of Cost Management*, Fall 1990, pp 22–29.

21. R Cooper and R S Kaplan, "Profit Priorities from Activity-Based Costing," *Harvard Business Review* 69 (May/June 1991), pp 130–135.

22. H T Johnson, "It's Time to Stop Overselling Activity-Based Concepts," *Management Accounting*, September 1992, pp 26–35.

23. J T Low, "Is Activity-Based Costing a Better Way to Derive Product Costs?" *Business Advisory Services Conference*, May 5, 1992.

24. J Darlington, J Innes, F Mitchell, and J Woodward, "Throughput Accounting: The Garrett Automotive Experience," *Management Accounting*, April 1992, pp 32–38.

25. E M Goldratt, *Theory of Constraints* (Croton-on-the-Hudson, NY: North River Press, 1990).

26. Ibid.

CHAPTER FIVE

1. E M Goldratt, *The Haystack Syndrome* (Croton-on-the-Hudson, NY: North River Press, 1990).

2. E M Goldratt, "What Is the Theory of Constraints?" *APICS—The Performance Advantage*, June 1993, pp 18–20.

CHAPTER SIX

1. R J Schonberger, *World Class Manufacturing: The Lessons of Simplicity Applied* (New York, NY: The Free Press, 1986).

2. J E Ross, *Total Quality Management: Text, Cases and Readings* (Delray Beach, FL: St. Lucie Press, 1993).

3. E M Goldratt, and R E Fox, *The Race* (Croton-on-the-Hudson, NY: North River Press, 1987).

4. T A Stewart, "Reengineering: The Hot New Managing Tool," *Fortune*, August 23, 1993, pp 41–48.

5. M Hammer and J Champy, *Reengineering the Corporation: A Manifesto for Business Revolution* (New York, NY: Harper Business, 1993).

6. E M Goldratt, "What Is the Theory of Constraints?" *APICS—The Performance Advantage*, June 1993, pp 18–20.

7. A Lockamy III, and J F Cox, "Using V-A-T Analysis for Determining the Priority and Location of JIT Manufacturing Techniques," *International Journal of Production Research* 29, no. 8 (1991), pp 1661–1672.

8. A F Celley, W H Clegg, A W Smith, and M A Vonderembse, "Implementation of JIT in the United States," *Journal of Purchasing and Materials Management* 22 (Winter 1986), pp 9–15.

9. P W Hamilton, "Just-in-Time: It's Not Just Inventory Control," *D&B Reports*, July/August 1985, pp 25–29, 55.

10. R J Schonberger, *Japanese Manufacturing Techniques: Nine Hidden Lessons in Simplicity* (New York, NY: The Free Press, 1982).

11. L Perry, "Simplified Manufacturing: Less Is Best," *Industrial Management*, July/August 1986, pp 29–30.

12. Schnonberger, *Japanese Manufacturing Techniques*.

13. S M Lee and M Ebrahimpour, "Just-In-Time Production Systems: Some Requirements for Implementation," *International Journal of Operations and Production Management* 4 (1984), pp 3–15.

14. K M Crawford, J F Cox, and J H Blackstone, Jr, *Performance Measurement Systems and the JIT Philosophy: Principles and Cases* (Falls Church, VA: APICS, 1988).

15. Y Monden, *Toyota Production System* (Norcross, GA: Institute of Industrial Engineers, 1983).

16. Ibid.

17. Ross, *Total Quality Management*.

18. S Nakajima, *TPM Development Program* (Norwalk, CT: Productivity Press, 1989).

19. Ibid.

20. Monden, *Toyota Production System.*

21. Ibid.

22. K Suzaki, *The New Manufacturing Challenge* (New York, NY: The Free Press, 1987).

23. J W Clauch, and P D Stang, *Set-Up Reduction* (Palm Beach Gardens, FL: PT Publications, Inc., 1989).

24. R L Harmon, and L D Peterson, *Reinventing the Factory* (New York: The Free Press, 1990).

25. S Shingo, *Non-Stock Production: The Shingo System for Continuous Improvement* (Cambridge, MA: Productivity Press, 1988).

26. A Ansari, and B Modarress, *Just In Time Purchasing* (New York, NY: The Free Press, 1990).

27. Ibid.

28. R J Schonberger and E M Knod, *Operations Management: Improving Customer Service* (Homewood, IL: Irwin, 1991).

29. G D Robson, *Continuous Process Improvement: Simplifying Work Flow Systems* (New York, NY: The Free Press, 1991).

30. J D Blackburn, *Time-Based Competition: The Next Battle Ground in American Manufacturing* (Homewood, IL: Business One Irwin, 1991).

31. M Umble and M L Srikanth, *Synchronous Manufacturing: Principles for World Class Excellence* (Cincinnati, OH: South-Western Publishing, 1990).

32. A V Feigenbaum, "Total Quality Control," *Harvard Business Review* 34 (November/December 1956), pp 93–101.

33. Juran, J M, *Juran On Planning for Quality* (New York, NY: The Free Press, 1988).

34. Juran, J M and F M Gryna Jr, *Quality Planning and Analysis* 2nd ed (New York, NY: McGraw-Hill, 1980).

35. M Walton, *The Deming Management Method* (New York, NY: Putnam Publishing Company, 1986).

36. Ibid.

37. Crosby, P B, *Quality Is Free* (New York, NY: McGraw-Hill, 1979).

38. M Imai, *Kaizen: The Key to Japan's Competitive Success* (New York, NY: McGraw-Hill Publishing, 1986).

39. Ross, *Total Quality Management.*

40. Ibid.

41. "Quality Programs Show Shoddy Results," *The Wall Street Journal,* May 14, 1992.

42. J Mathews, and P Katel, "The Cost of Quality," *Newsweek,* September 7, 1992, pp 48–49.

43. Ibid.

44. E M Goldratt, "Late Night Discussion: 6," *Industry Week,* December 2, 1991.

45. J F Cox, J H Blackstone, Jr. and M S Spencer eds. *APICS Dictionary,* 7th ed. (Falls Church, VA: APICS, 1992).

46. Ibid.

47. Ibid.

48. Ibid.

49. A Lockamy III and J F Cox, "Using V-A-T Analysis for Determining the Priority and Location of JIT Manufacturing Techniques," *International Journal of Production Research* 29, no. 8 (1991), pp 1661–1672.

50. Goldratt and Fox; Umble and Srikanth, op. cit.

51. Goldratt, E M, "What Is the Theory of Constraints?" *APICS—The Performance Advantage,* June 1993, pp 18–20.

CHAPTER SEVEN

1. R J Schonberger, *World Class Manufacturing: The Lessons of Simplicity Applied* (New York, NY: The Free Press, 1986).

2. E M Goldratt, "Logistics and Commodities," *Jonah Course* (New Haven, CT: Avraham Y Goldratt Institute, 1988).

3. G Fuchsberg, " 'Total Quality' Is Termed Only Partial Success," *The Wall Street Journal,* October 1, 1992, pp B1, B7.

CHAPTER TWELVE

1. E M Goldratt and J Cox, *The Goal: A Process of Ongoing Improvement,* 2nd rev. ed. (Croton-on-the-Hudson, NY: North River Press, 1992).

Index

Thank you for choosing Irwin Professional Publishing (formerly Business One Irwin) for your business information needs. If you are part of a corporation, professional association, or government agency, consider our newest option: Custom Publishing. This service helps you create customized books, manuals, and other materials from your organization's resources, select chapters of our books, or both.

Irwin Professional Publishing Books are also excellent resources for training/educational programs, premiums, and incentives. For information on volume discounts or Custom Publishing, call 1-800-634-3966.

Other books of interest to you from Irwin Professional Publishing . . .

Global Quality
A Synthesis of the World's Best Management Methods

Richard Tabor Greene
(884 pages)
Co-published with ASQC Quality Press

Finally, a book that organizes the chaos of quality improvement techniques! Greene compiles 24 global quality systems, the 30 characteristics they share, plus eight new business systems into this convenient reference. Also reveals seven new quality improvement techniques being tested in Japan!
ISBN: 1-55623-915-7

MRP
Integrating Material Requirements Planning and Modern Business

Terry Lunn with Susan A Neff
(275 pages)
The Irwin Professional Publishing/APICS Series in Production Management

Shows how to use MRP to manage and maintain material flow, solve scheduling dilemmas, and integrate the various functions of your business. You'll find reliable techniques for determining the resources needed to satisfy the demands of your company and your customers.
ISBN: 1-55623-656-5

Frontline Teamwork
One Company's Story of Success

Louis W Joy III and Jo A Joy
(225 pages)
The Irwin Professional Publishing/APICS Series in Frontline Education

"*The Goal* with soul! Refreshing . . . the first user-friendly book on teamwork. Thought-provoking!"
—John Allen, Manager (former), Training & Development,
Toyota Motor Corporation, Georgetown, KY
Here is a lively, engaging story that traces a company's progression from traditional management to teamwork and total quality—highlighting typical challenges, rewards, and decisions employees must face along the way. Includes easy-to-implement guidelines for structuring project teams and self-directed work teams.
ISBN: 1-55623-955-6

The American Keiretsu
A Strategic Weapon for Global Competitiveness

David N Burt and Michael F Doyle
(215 pages)

How can you ensure that your suppliers will support your quality, cost, *and* time-to-market goals? *The American Keiretsu* explores each facet of strategic supply management and presents alternatives for solving this critical issue. Inside, you'll find out how you can apply the Japanese keiretsu strategy within an American business framework to reduce supplier risk and build competitive advantage.
ISBN: 1-55623-852-5

Available at libraries and bookstores everywhere.